CARL SANDBURG REMEMBERED

by

William A. Sutton

The Scarecrow Press, Inc.
Metuchen, N.J. & London
1979

PS
3537
A 618
Z 874

Library of Congress Cataloging in Publication Data

Sutton, William Alfred, 1915-
    Carl Sandburg remembered.

    Includes index.
    1. Sandburg, Carl, 1878-1967--Friends and associates
--Addresses, essays, lectures. 2. Authors, American--
20th century--Biography--Addresses, essays, lectures.
I. Title.
PS3537.A618Z874   811'.5'2 [B]   78-31298
ISBN 0-8108-1202-9

TABLE OF CONTENTS

iii

Table of Contents   v

FOREWORD

Ever the Winds of Chance was the title by which Carl Sandburg referred to the manuscript for his (so far unpublished) second autobiographical segment. It was just by chance that a host of people fell into the adventure of knowing Carl Sandburg. One of these, Lilla Perry (whose manuscript of four decades of Sandburg friendship provides important segments of this book), was attending an American Library Association Convention in 1919 with her husband when she met Sandburg. The writer himself went to the Sandburg home, Connemara, to meet with Margaret Sandburg, a daughter, concerning research on Sherwood Anderson. (The account of this meeting appears in this book, starting on page 256.)

As The People, Yes suggests, the people of this country were more important to Sandburg than its physical aspects, of which he was also quite aware. Thus he was a fisher of people. He often and readily formed associations with people he met, usually quite casually. This book records a sample of the vivid and exciting memories left in the minds of those who met him.

It happened that one of the memorable writers of the century was also a memorable person.

William A. Sutton
Ball State University
September 30, 1977

vii

PART I

Sandburg warming up, March 12, 1956. [Photo courtesy of
Dr. Harvey Jacobs, Editor, Indianapolis News. By permission.]

THE PERRY FRIENDSHIP

Introduction

A diarist since the age of twelve, Mrs. Lilla Perry, of Los Angeles, kept a careful record of her meetings with Carl Sandburg, many of which involved his being a guest in her home, once for a period of a month while he worked on Remembrance Rock. After her friend died in 1967, she prepared a manuscript of two hundred typed pages of her memories of the man she referred to as "My Friend, Carl." The first section of this book consists of excerpts from that manuscript, published by the permission of the executor of her literary estate, E. Caswell Perry, of Alhambra, California.

About Lilla Perry's Manuscript

[The following comment, in a letter, dated March 9, 1970, was received from Capt. Kenneth M. Dodson, author of Away All Boats (Boston: Little, Brown, 1954). The excerpt appears here by his permission.]

How did you track down Lilla Perry? She and her late husband knew the Sandburgs over many years. My wife and I have hoped that some good use might be made of her Sandburg manuscript which I've read, I believe in two different drafts. She tried so hard to get it published, but like so many others, found a subject so close to her heart, turned down. Regardless of any faults, that manuscript contains a lot of valuable and authentic information. It's easy to tell whether or not a writer really knew Carl Sandburg -- and also whether Sandburg liked him or not. He had a barrel full of cliches to toss out to reporters who irritated him. These have so repeatedly been printed as truths straight from the prophet's mouth, and when printed, gave him something to 'ho-ho" about.

EXCERPTS FROM THE PERRY MANUSCRIPT

Tirade Against Billy Sunday [p. 2]*

I have no idea what my introduction of myself may have been when I went forward on that hotel porch at the [American Library Association convention in July, 1919, at Saratoga, N. Y.] to meet him. We were soon seated there with seemingly endless things to talk about. I had just read his second book, Cornhuskers, and had known his Chicago Poems as well. I recalled to him with laughter the stir in New York City his "Lines to a Contemporary Bunkshooter" had made. The magazine in which it had first been printed had had to be withdrawn from the subway book-stalls--fine advertisement for an unknown free-verse poet! It was a tirade against Billy Sunday. "What do you know about Jesus?"

"And the publishers had made me tone that down a bit, " he said with a broad grin. "As originally written I had it, 'What in hell do you know about Jesus?'"

Looking Forward to Family and Friends [p. 9]

With his first West Coast visit in the offing, Everett and I discussed asking him to make his head-quarters with us. We both wanted him. "But when you invite him, " my husband suggested, "at least give him a picture of the kind of household he'll be getting into, with five oftentimes tumultuous children all over the place. There are people who couldn't take it, you know. "

In my invitation for him to stay with us I gave a facetious picture of our exuberant household, ending, "If you've got the courage to try it, we want you. "

---

*Page numbers refer to the original manuscript.

[Sandburg's reply, from the Editorial Rooms of the
Chicago Daily News, dated January 14, 1921, was that it
could be "homelike" to have healthy and noisy children about.
He was looking forward to meeting the family and friends of
the Perrys.]

Love Poems [p. 12]

At a larger gathering one afternoon during that first
visit [to Los Angeles in January, 1921] one daring spirit
among the women spoke up and complained, "But you never
write any love poems, Mr. Sandburg. I thought poets always wrote love poems. "

Sandburg looked at her meditatively for a moment.
"Perhaps I've written them, but maybe I've written them just
for myself, without any intention of publishing them.   There
is one entitled 'Troths' which I put in Chicago Poems that
you might call a love poem. "

[Sandburg then quoted five lines dealing with memories
of dust on bees' wings, lights in women's eyes, sunset sky-
coloring, averring that some of his memories would cheat
death.]

Visiting Sandburg's Outfit [pp. 14-16]

[When Mrs. Perry went on a visit to relatives in the
eastern part of the country in June, 1921, she stopped to
visit friends in Hinsdale, not far from the Sandburg home in
Elmhurst. She had written Carl to say she would be there.
She received...] a most welcoming phone call.   "If your
friends can't drive you over, I will bicycle over to see you.
But I'd really like you to see my outfit here, though, if you
can. "

My friends drove me over.   They were people of
whom Sandburg might well have known, having their own distinction.   Their thrill at having a chance to meet Carl Sandburg showed clearly the place and name he had made for
himself even at that time.

Sandburg met us at the gate on our arrival, excused
himself to my friends, and took me into the house to meet
Mrs. Sandburg.   She was ill in bed at the time, he told us.

My friends should have recognized this as a dismissal, but perhaps they were too eager to see something more of him. They left the car and seated themselves in the garden to await our return. Margaret, Sandburg's eleven-year-old daughter, played hostess to them. When she came to me at her mother's bedside to tell me that my friends were still there, she tactfully added that her father had some work to finish and would not be downstairs until later. I went back to the garden, repeated Margaret's explanations, and saw my friends on their way.

Margaret struck us at that time as a very precocious youngster. My friends as well as I were impressed with her grown-up manners and her conversational gifts. I mention this because, when I saw her several years later, she had had a nervous break-down, was very much an invalid, and completely changed in physical and seemingly in her mental make-up. Having seen and appreciated the unusual quality of the young girl before disaster struck her, I have always been aware of this tragedy in the Sandburgs' lives.

I find the following account of that first visit in my journal:

I went back to Mrs. Sandburg. She was having some sort of trouble requiring her to lie flat on her back. She told me what it was, but I have forgotten. She was no invalid, she declared, and would be glad if I would stay and talk with her. She was a slender, worn-looking little woman with most beautiful eyes. They were deep blue with long lashes. To myself I called them fringed-gentian eyes. Her grey hair lay in little ringlets around her face, a delicate, lovely face.

We were getting on famously when in a short time Sandburg himself reappeared. He asked what I thought of the stories he had sent Margaret to give me to look over. She hadn't given them to me. When questioned she said, "But how could I, Daddy? Mrs. Perry was visiting with Mother. She couldn't look at them then!"

Margaret was forgiven and the stories produced. That is what Sandburg was working on then, getting ready a volume of children's stories.

"Would adults care for them?" I asked.

"If they don't I shall consider the stories a failure. They must allure but baffle children."

"Read one of them to Mrs. Perry, Carl."

While he read, Mrs. Sandburg lifted herself on her pillow and watched him with smiling eyes. He kept glancing at me for approval at the good spots. Later, however, when he talked about San Francisco and his adventures there after leaving us in Los Angeles in the Spring, he looked at her as he spoke and they seemed to be talking things over together. Again and again, as my questions set up new trains of thought, he would turn to her and say, "Oh, I forgot to tell you--"

"But San Francisco! San Francisco!" He let himself go at the name and then followed a catalogue of its charms, of its physical features, rolled out in his rich, vibrant voice with a rhythm that made it seem like a bit of his own free verse. "About San Francisco there is the intangible, the ineffable, the something that Los Angeles will never have in a thousand years. Los Angeles is to San Francisco what Berlin is to Paris or (he turned with a smile of some special meaning to his wife), what Moscow is to Stockholm." [Sandburg had spent late 1918 and early 1919 on a journalistic assignment to Sweden and Norway, on the perimeter of the Russian Revolution, in which both Sandburgs, who probably still considered themselves Socialists in 1921, had an intense interest.]

Proletarian Poet in a Plutocratic Palanquin [p. 21]

[When Sandburg visited California in 1924, he had a series of engagements which had been made for him and was deeply engaged in collecting material for his American Songbag (1927).] A Mrs. Rickerby, wife of a former professor at Pomona College, had written him saying she would like to turn over to him her late husband's entire collection of folk songs. The Perrys had no car at this time to take him to Pomona, but one of our friends sent her chauffeur and limousine to take him there. It was a full day's effort, and, when he returned, I remember one of his comments on the day's adventure which brought a laugh at our dinner table.

"You know," he said, "sitting there in that luxurious

car with a chauffeur up in front I said to myself, 'How
come! A proletarian poet in a plutocratic palanquin!'"
[Sandburg had been an organizer for the Socialist party and
had ridden in the campaign train of the Socialist candidate
for president in 1908, Eugene V. Debs.]

Embarrassment and Suffering [pp. 22-3]

Sandburg was still moving picture reviewer for the
Chicago Daily News at this time [1924]. As on his previous
visit, the movie studios sometimes sent their car for him
and he visited the studio lots. He generously included me
in these explorations and it was fun. It was still the day
of the silent films and we watched the taking of scenes.

On the day of the departure I remember we came in
from a walk to find my rooms burgeoning with flowers.
They had arrived in our absence, and Mother had taken
them from their boxes and arranged them. I turned upon
Carl with an exclamation, for I could not imagine who else
had sent them. Actually they were from friends who wanted
to express their appreciation to me for having shared him.

"Lilla Perry, " Carl exclaimed, "for all your hospitality and courtesies to me I should have sent them. But I
didn't! Truly embarrassment causes more suffering than
crime!"

Paula Could Forgive Him Anything [pp. 23-6]

[In October of 1926, Mrs. Perry made another visit
to her friends in Hinsdale and was driven to see the Sandburgs in Elmhurst.] This time my friends did not leave
their car. They planned to return at five to pick me up.

Mrs. Sandburg met me at the gate. Again I noted
her young face and lovely blue eyes. They seemed to look
always with a smile in them. She introduced me to a woman friend whose name I have forgotten and announced that
Carl was busy finishing a piece of work and would be down
at four.

Meanwhile it appeared we were to stroll in the garden. It was a stifling hot day. I had a coat on my arm
and a very heavy portfolio of Japanese prints which I was

taking to show artist friends with whom I was to dine.   No
one offered to relieve me of them.   I wondered if I were
to sense everything through the haze of an agonizing headache which had come upon me in the drive over.

The garden was a barren looking spot, demanding,
Mrs. Sandburg said, a heavy toll of labor for small returns.
I wandered toward the porch with my burdens, for I was hot
and tired.   The chairs there, however, were bottomless and
evidently discarded.   If there had been any other moment
for seeing the Sandburgs I should have given up this visit at
the gate.   Something of my distress must have shown in my
face, for, after fifteen minutes of conversation about the
garden, the children, and the dog, Mrs. Sandburg suggested
that I take my things into the house.

At the door we met Mr. Sandburg.   "Why, Carl, are
you down!" his wife exclaimed.   "I explained to Mrs.
Perry--"

"Yes, but I heard her voice, and had to see her at
once, " he said cordially, grasping my hand and arm in a
hearty way that almost cleared my head for a moment.   He
had grown grey, looking older than when last I saw him.

"Can't you find something for Mrs. Perry to eat?   I
don't believe she has had dinner, " he said, as he drew me
into a sort of porch dining room, where stood the remains
of a meal on the table.   It was three-thirty, and I protested that I had eaten.   I would, in fact, have liked to
have closed my eyes while the clearing away of the crumby
dishes went on before me.   It was that damnable headache.

Perhaps Carl may have felt I was in the wrong mood
for them, for it was like him a little to make matters worse.
Sitting astride his chair with his arms on the back, he inquired, "Well, how is Los Angeles?   Tell me about Aimee
and the last news of the Iowans. "

I am afraid my eyes flashed.   "The only interest I
have discovered in Aimee Semple McPherson had been since
I arrived in Chicago, " I lied.   "And as for the 'Iowans, '
why need they bother anyone?" I asked tartly.   "You escape
them always by as much as there is in you that is not Iowa.
Why do we always dub dull people 'Iowans' in California?
(That was true in California at that time.)   Such people
exist everywhere.   To which of them did I introduce you?"
I asked, still belligerently.

Sandburg saw I was angry and it seemed to amuse
him mightily.   He gave one of his infectious laughs.   "Well,
that's a fact.   You didn't introduce me to any, Lilla Perry.
There weren't any Iowans in your bunch.   How is Dorothea
Moore?   And Katherine Smith?"   Sandburg disclaimed having
received Dorothea's book of poems which I certainly sent
him.

Mrs. Sandburg had learned from me in the garden
what I had in the portfolio and asked if I would show them
the Japanese prints.   I was glad to.   I had just had marvellous good luck in New York City and acquired some of
the loveliest Utamors that I had ever seen.   It was hard
for an ardent collector to imagine anyone indifferent to them,
but Carl certainly was.   He usually expresses a reaction.
This time his silence expressed one.

He brought out an armful of what he called Chinese
paintings and squares of tinted paper he had found on Grant
Avenue in San Francisco.   We sat for twenty minutes looking them over with more serious attention than had been
given my old wood-block masterpieces.   This was tourist
stuff.   The papers had tinsel designs and colors that rubbed
off on the fingers.   He insisted on giving me a sheet.   I
watched him closely for sign of his perpetrating a joke, but
he was serious.   I began to feel suspicious of his criteria
in other lines.

I was glad when he offered to sing his new folk songs.
This time, however, he took a terribly long time tuning up
his guitar; the dog kept rushing through the rooms, the
children after him, and when he did get the new tunes they
seemed to be in an experimental stage.   It was almost in-
credible that he should try them out on me.   Then he
started a blasphemous one, laughing down Mrs. Sandburg's
expostulations.   "Oh Lilla Perry won't be shocked.   She
has a look as though she might, but she won't."

I called for some of the old-time favorites; Mrs.
Sandburg had risen to leave us for a moment.   "Just wait
a minute till I get back," she asked.   "I haven't heard
these for a long time."

"When Carl sings, Paula can forgive him anything,"
remarked the family friend.

Sandburg and Chaplin [p. 32]

[When Sandburg visited the Perrys in February,
1929,] He missed no chance to be with Chaplin. "He's a
great genius. He is funnier over a supper table with two
or three friends than he ever is on the films. And to see
that fellow work! To see the faculty for infinite pains he
has in him! We watched him on the lot yesterday. There
was a scene where the blind girl puts a flower in his button-
hole. He had it done over nine times, talking to her, directing her patiently all the time. At supper he took off
the deaf-mute Mexican who works around the place. This
man has his own symbolic gesture for each person he re-
fers to, this for Chaplin himself, this for Syd Chaplin, and
this for Syd's wife. Of course, Chaplin bettered the Mexican, and for me to try to imitate for you Chaplin's imitation is--well, it's like trying to play the piano with mittens
on. "

Saving on Hotel Bills [p. 40]

[Sandburg ended his California visit in 1929.] In his
goodbye to me, too, there was a warmth of feeling as if,
after all these years, I had become a real person to him.
He thanked me for the comforts of his visit. I think he
meant the protection from people. He spoke of his earliest
visit. "We were having such a time making both ends meet
that the saving of hotel bills meant a lot to me on that visit.
You took me in then as the pioneer families took in the cir-
cuit-rider--for the love of the Lord! Next time I come I
won't be working. We'll have people again, and make it a
party!"

Umbilical and Other Bonds [pp. 33-4]

Those breakfast hours were my time. I had explained
to him that nothing but the falling in of the roof could inter-
rupt or interfere with my daughter Dorothy's morning practice on piano and violin. Though we closed off the music
room, it went on all the time he was here and was often
the softened accompaniment to breakfast. Once he knew
she had finished working, he would call out requests. De
Falla's "Cubana" was one. "The Tides of Maunanon" by
Henry Cowell was another. He loved to thunder forth the
terrific poem that had inspired Cowell to write that.

He had always given Dorothy a great deal of attention.   She is my adopted daughter, with a lot of musical
genius.   "You made a perfectly safe bet when you adopted
that child, " he said to me one morning.   "You may not
make a musician of her, either pianist or violinist, but she
is going to burst forth in some line or other.   There's a
touch of genius about her.   Maybe she is like Harcourt, my
publisher, who had a great grandmother who went crazy
after she was fifty.   She used to be found pacing up and
down her garden walk, saying to herself, 'I am the most
beautiful queen in the world! I am the most beautiful queen
in the world!'   Any of us who ever amounts to anything
has had a great grandmother or somebody with a queer
twist in her brain.   I think there is someone like that back
of you, Lilla Perry. "   Somewhere in the midst of our talk
about Dorothy he said, "There are bonds that are stronger
than the umbilical cord. "

Interviewers [p. 34]

One day we talked about interviewers, and I reminded him with laughter of Alma Whitaker's interview with
him the last time [prior to 1929] he was here.   "I suppose,
Mr. Sandburg, " she had said sweetly, "that your most popular verse, the one by which you are best known, is that
about the monkeys?"   "How many monkeys are you?" she
had quoted, wrongly attributing to him a poem by Alfred
Kreymborg.   Sandburg hadn't corrected her.

"The worst reviewer I ever had, " he said, "was
once down in Louisiana.   I had said to her, 'When a colored man gets rich he stops singing. '   She quoted me as
having said, 'When a colored man gets money he's no good. '
I am thankful when they pull out a pad and pencil, and take
down exactly what I do say. "

Poetry and Youth [p. 36]

[Of the lines of a young writer, Sandburg remarked:]
"The poetry of youth.   Five years from now he may not be
writing or even reading poetry at all.   Oh, I have such
quantity of verse sent to me.   Unless it is outstanding I
have to send it back without comment.   I used to bother a
good deal with young writers, advising them, trying to help
them.   But I find they peter out in the vast majority of
cases. "

I asked him about our friend Jake Zeitlin, for whose book of verse Sandburg wrote an introduction.

"Judging from his new stuff which he read me the other night, he is going to peter out, too. I found him surrounded by Rockwell Kent's things. He's getting too 'arty'. "

"When I find nothing for me in Rockwell Kent I think there is something the matter with me, maybe. " I commented.

"When I can't find anything in Rockwell Kent, I know there is nothing the matter with me, " he laughed.

On the Use of Education [pp. 37-8]

One morning my son, Richard, who had slept late, had breakfast with him. "What are you intending to do with yourself after college?" Sandburg asked.

Of course, Richard did not know as yet, and one of us asked what had been Sandburg's own first step after he had finished his college days.

"I went into the fire department in my own home town, Galesburg, Illinois, and drove a fire-engine for two years while my family, my relatives, and acquaintances looked on in disapproval and asked what I was ever going to do with my education. They were considerably bothered by my failure to make use of it. I had my own idea about it, however. I had chosen the one occupation I could find which at the same time that I earned my living permitted me to cover a wide course of reading which I had laid out for myself, unassigned by any university. And, you see, except for the two hours a day spent in exercising the horses, good healthy outdoor work, I was free, my time was my own. "

"Did your mother understand? What were her feelings about you at this time?"

"I don't like to recall my relations with my mother during that period. My mother's satisfaction in me rose as the public began more and more to approve of me. "

A Wonderful Host [p. 44]

[When Mrs. Perry visited the Sandburgs in July of
1932, they were established in their new home then at Harbert, Michigan, where the Sandburgs had neighbors on big
estates only during the summer. Mrs. Sandburg drove the
children six miles to the nearest school.]

Its isolation was ideal for the concentrated work Carl
was doing on the Lincoln War Years. The constant visitors
at Elmhurst, so near Chicago, had been a continuous inter-
ruption. At Harbert, none but the most intimate friends
ventured on this day's trip out of Chicago, and for Carl it
was the perfect situation for work and just what Paula
wanted. It made her protection of his time and strength
much easier. Since his fame she had made herself a constant buffer between him and the world of people who sought
him.

I was aware, too, that with their goat farm, vegeta-
ble garden and chickens, they enjoyed a sort of experiment
in "beating the depression. " Their wonderful table was
bountifully supplied with their home grown products. I
doubt if Carl concerned himself with much except to enjoy
and approve it. He kept a stiff routine of work. His breakfast was brought up to him. His first appearance of the day
was at two in the afternoon, when the hearty big meal of
the day was served. At the table and for an hour or two
afterward, he was the wonderful host, full of good talk and
stories. At times he would try out on us something he had
just written.

Had there not been visitors, he might after a while
have gone back to his work. He did the revision of it in
the later hours, he said. But since we were there he gave
generously of his time. Dorothy [Mrs. Perry's daughter]
had brought her violin with her, of course, and it was a
question which he enjoyed the most, her tremendous piano
repertory or her more limited one for the violin. He liked
best to have her play the violin out on the open porch overlooking the lake without accompaniment of any kind.

Sandburg at Work [pp. 52-3]

[On several visits to Harbert during the 1930's, Mrs.
Perry became ...] well acquainted with Carl's own special

quarters on the third floor of his house. It was, indeed, a
workshop. It overflowed with books, housed for the most
part in apple boxes or orange crates turned on their sides.
There was a large sun-deck, and I recall sitting there one
afternoon with the family watching a terrific storm gather
over the lake.

Carl kept to his unvarying routine. He never emerged
from his own quarters till the main meal of the day, around
two o'clock, summoned him to join the family. There were
seldom other guests. Their home was too remote for any
casual visitor.

The guest room in which I slept was called the Lincoln room. Three walls were completely lined, from floor
to ceiling, with the library of books on Lincoln. I was impressed with the quantity of Congressional and other Govern-
mental reports, many of them with paper markers still left
between the leaves.

[In a letter preceding one of her visits prior to 1937,
Sandburg had told Mrs. Perry how welcome she would be
and asked her to tell her friend Gordon Ray Young that the
Civil War material he had sent had arrived in good order.
However, when it came to making an acknowledgment, Sand-
burg found he had lost the donor's address.]

This letter in my files is only a copy of the one received. The original I sent to Gordon Ray Young. I thought
it might help heal his hurt at never having had any acknowledgment of the pile of Civil War material Gordon Ray Young
had sent to Carl. He had compiled it for a novel of his
own.

Working and Bashing [p. 22]

[During Sandburg's 1942 visit to Los Angeles the following incident occurred, causing Mrs. Perry to criticize
his "treatment of our mutual friend, Katherine Smith."]
He had accepted our invitation to lunch with her and a pro-
tégé of hers whom she was trying to encourage in his writing. The opportunity to meet Sandburg would mean a lot
to that young man, she knew. I was aware of the engagement and that she was planning to pick him up at my house
at one o'clock. He and I were sitting over breakfast involved in the wonderful talkfest that always came at that

hour when I realized that the clock hands were moving on
toward one.   Some comment he made led me to realize that
he had no intention of keeping that engagement.   I was sorry
for Katherine.   Her plans were carefully made, and she had
a reservation, I knew, at the best restaurant in town.   I
slipped away from the table and from an extension phone upstairs asked her to call and remind him.   When he was
summoned to answer the phone a few minutes later, I heard
his reply.   He could not keep the appointment, he said.
"I'm working.   When I am in the midst of a piece of work
I have to bash my best friend in the face."   Poor Katherine,
I am sure, felt sufficiently bashed.   Returning to the breakfast table, neither he nor I mentioned the matter, but he
sat for an hour more with me, and leisurely talked.

The Greatest Sea Story Ever Told [pp. 62-5]

One night [in 1943], coming home a little earlier than
usual, Sandburg found me at my big hall desk absorbed in
the reading of some letters.   My niece who worked at Red
Cross had brought them to me.   They had been written by
a naval officer in action in the Pacific, a man named Kenneth Dodson.

"Carl," I exclaimed, "these are wonderful letters!
The man is over there now, going through all this.   These
are letters home to his wife, and written--well, you'll see.
Let me read you some of this."

Carl sat down at the end of the desk and listened,
as only Carl Sandburg can listen.

I began to read just where I had left off:

> One night I worked with my boys until midnight
> transferring 62 wounded men to a hospital ship.
> Some groaned, some talked out of their head.
> One poor kid screamed through grit teeth from
> the pain of moving his terrible bone fractures.
> We worked as gently as we could.   One fine look-
> ing tall boy extended over both ends of his stretch-
> er.   He was shot through the leg and the bone
> was shattered.   For some reason I was impelled
> to ask him where he was from.   He said, "South
> East Oregon" and mentioned a small town near
> Ashland.   I told him my brother-in-law had a

fox farm at Eagle Point. We were just picking
him up to put him in the boat and he smiled in
the moonlight and said, "Eagle Point fox farm.
I know him. He sure had beautiful foxes!" He
gripped my hand hard. Then we picked up his
litter and lowered it into the boat to start him on
his way home. Well, I'd got through all the groan-
ing and the boy who couldn't stop screaming through
his grit teeth, and I'd kept a stiff upper lip, but
as that smiling kid left I had to rub away the tears
with my fist. I hate war.

War leaves a stamp on you. You take a bath and
don't feel clean. You want a spiritual purge of
the whole stinking business. You feel like you'd
like to be baptised and have communion. You want
to lie on the grass on a windy hill in the summer-
time and smell the clean drying grasses and watch
the cumulus swimming by in the blue of the sky.
You want to have your arms around one very near
and dear to you and snuggle your head deep beside your loved one and feel the tenderness of her
lips on yours and the clean warm living scent that
is her. Then sleep. And there shall be no more
war, no parting, no killing, no smell of death.
Just peace.

I had had difficulty getting through that last paragraph.
I looked up at Carl and his face showed all that I had been
feeling.

He took the sheaf of letters from my hand. "May I
have these for a while? I want to get in touch with that
man. He has a gift of expression that must not be wasted."
Did I know who the man was, where he was now, where he
could be reached? I didn't, but I could easily find out
through my niece, Carol, who had brought me the letters.

This was the beginning. Carl never let up in his
interest in Kenneth Dodson, who had written those letters.
Of course, he was a writer, at least, a man who wanted to
write. Carl gave him every encouragement. When at length
Dodson had a novel ready, Carl went to Seattle, near where
he lived, and worked with him for a week on the original
version, offering all that he had in him in helpfulness. When
Dodson's first book, Away All Boats was published by Little,
Brown and Company of Boston, Carl came out in glowing

praise of it that was spread over all the big papers in the
country.   He called it the "Greatest Sea Story Ever Told".
It was for many months on the "best seller" list and was
eventually made into a movie.

Working for M. G. M. [pp. 53-5]

It was in the fall of 1943 that Sandburg was with us
for the longest stay he ever made.   He was with us for
well over a month.   I did not even know he was in town
when he called me up from the Casa Del Mar in Santa Monica.

"Lilla, M. G. M. [Metro-Goldwyn-Mayer Corp.] has
got me out here to write a novel which they want to put into a movie.   I am to meet with them daily till we get the
general skeleton worked out.   But they've put me up here
at this Casa Del Mar at the Studio's expense, and I find I
can't write a word.   Isn't there a corner for me at your
house, Lilla?   I've been here three days now in all this
elegance and I can't do a lick of work here.   I've stared at
the walls unable to get a line on paper.   I've always been
able to work at your house.   Can't you find a spot for me?"

My house was filled with people who were permanent
paying guests.   I didn't know where I could put him, nor
even if he would like it here as he had when there had been
only the family.   I told him to come on in town, however,
and look us over.

Mother and I at the time were using two large rooms
on the third floor, once called the attic.   Carl had always
been put into the best rooms in the house.   I could easily
get Mother to give up her third floor room and take one of
the twin beds in my room, but I was not sure Carl would
like her room.

When I took him up to it, he was exclamatory.   With
the big sundeck leading out of it, it seemed almost to duplicate the working quarters of his place on Lake Michigan.
He was sure he could work there.   He could see it was
practically sound-proof.   He could type if he felt like it till
three o'clock in the morning and disturb no one.   Furthermore, none of the early morning noises, so annoying at the
hotel, would reach him.   So it was decided.   An M. G. M.
limousine brought him, his one bag and a stuffed briefcase

to us the next day. As a joke and to make his workroom
look really homelike, I ranged two empty apple boxes against
the wall for books. He laughed about it. But he used them!

I missed most of our eleven o'clock breakfasts. At
that hour four mornings a week I was out in Brentwood
teaching the Margaret Sullavan-Leland Hayward children.
Our long conversations on this visit took place in the hall of
the third floor beside my big roll-top desk, which had become my working spot during these years. When he came
in too late for me, I left notes on the corner of the desk.
When he knew I would be off in the morning too early for
him, he left notes for me.

He explained why M. G. M. had summoned him to the
Coast. The original idea had been for him to write a "Cavalcade of American History, " not unlike the "Cavalcade of
English History, " which had been put into a movie. There
was, however, to be a fictional element in this, with the
same two characters reincarnated in each historical period.
Carl's ability as a writer of fiction was untested. They
were virtually buying the drawing power of his name for the
hundred thousand dollars named in the contract.

Carl was entering into this project with tremendous
zest and interest. Every day about one o'clock the studio's
limousine called for him and took him off for conferences
over the book. He seemed thoroughly to enjoy the men he
worked with. I heard many tales of Vet Lougin and Sidney
Franklin. His typewriter was busy long into the night.
Often he did not return until late, but there were many
times when he joined us at dinner and entered fully into the
gaiety of it.

Often I found on the corner of my desk in the upper
hall a new or a revised chapter of the book which afterward
became Remembrance Rock. The carbons of those first
versions of the early chapters were given to me when he
left. Once he left on the old desk a sheaf of unpublished
poems which he was carrying around with him, retouching,
refinishing.

Connemara and Remembrance Rock [pp. 66-75]

[In 1945, the Sandburgs moved from Harbert, Michigan, to Flat Rock, North Carolina. Mrs. Perry first visited

there in 1948.   After what she considered "wild wanderings, "
she reached the ...] country lane from which Connemara
Farm leads off; I went by it for a mile or two.   I passed
many other beautiful estates, set far back from the road.
After a little I realized from Mrs. Sandburg's directions
that I had gone too far and turned back.   Nearing the main
thoroughfare again I saw a boy of nine or ten coming along
wheeling his bike up the slope.

        "Do you know where the Carl Sandburgs live?" I
asked.

        No, he had no idea.   I was sure I must be very
close so I tried again, "Do you know where the goat farm
is?"

        He beamed.   "Go right through those big gates, and
you'll find it. "

        Carl, your goats are more important to the country-
side than you are!   I shall get one of your booming laughs
out of you with this story!   Through the gates and around
the double curve of the winding driveway I caught a view
of the house through the tree-lined road.   The white mansion had once belonged to Jefferson Davis's Secretary of the
Treasury, Christopher Memminger.   It was built in the
midst of two hundred and forty acres, Carl had told me,
adding, "Ain't that a hell of a baronial estate for a proletarian poet!"   [Sandburg had been an organizer for the Socialist Party in Wisconsin in 1907-8.]

        Carl, as I knew, was not to be home during my
visit.   Mrs. Sandburg met me with a cordial welcome in
the driveway.   She had, doubtless, seen my car winding up
the hill.   We went up the stone steps to the wide-porticoed
veranda and into the right of the two front doorways.   The
door at the left, as I learned afterward, led into a large
comfortable livingroom, with fireplace, davenport, easy
chairs and the grand piano.   This door at the right led into
what appeared to be a huge office.   There were long tables
and an enormous desk.   They were piled with books and
filing boxes.   There was every evidence of a great deal of
active work going on.   But, as I learned later, this was
where Carl kept his secretaries busy, not where he worked
himself.

        We set my two small suitcases at the foot of the

stairs, then went out-of-doors to meet the girls, Margaret,
Janet, and Helga. Helga, the married daughter, had separated from her husband and was then living at home with
her two young children.

Mrs. Sandburg explained that it was feeding time for
the goats and suggested that I might like to look around
over the goat farm while she and the girls fed them. Helga
was to do the milking, it seemed. The breeding stock was
divided in separate corrals at some distance from the house,
the Saanan, Toggenburg, and the Nubian. I watched and
asked questions while they were fed. The herd of goats to
be milked were in a central building; also, the little kids
had been separated from their mothers.

I did not know that first night of my visit that Saturday being the caretaker's day off, was the one night in the
week when the family had all this work to do. It was the
house-maid's day off, also, and, when we sat later in a
beautiful modernized kitchen and Mrs. Sandburg pulled delicious food out of the refrigerator, I was somewhat appalled
at her hospitality to me when she had so many things on her
mind to do. The next morning the house-worker from the
village arrived; breakfast was served on an immense long
table in the dining-room, of such lavish quantity and such
rich quality that I began to worry as to what ten days of
this was going to do to my figure. The work of the goat
farm and the getting of dinner was only a once-a-week affair.

The room on the second floor on the front of the
house was given to me. It was originally planned to be
Carl's. It looked off over the porticoed veranda, and the
view was breathtaking. In the foreground was a large pool
from which a fountain had once played. This had been removed. Beyond it stretched a long slope of meadow grass
which in the Memminger's time had doubtless been lawn.
It reached far down to the distant road below. A little to
the right was a little lake.

"How perfectly placed!" I exclaimed.

"'Placed' is right," laughed Mrs. Sandburg. "It was
part of the landscaping of Memminger's day, an artificial
lake, made by damming up some of the springs which are
found all over the place. "

Later on I learned that it was stocked with trout.

Some of the villagers came to ask permission to fish there.
Beyond all this lay deeply wooded hills and the outline of
mountains, among them Mt. Mitchell, the tallest peak in
Eastern America.   As I stood in my room looking out upon
all this, I wished I could paint it to carry away with me
and keep for always.

"Carl was to have this room," Mrs. Sandburg continued, "but he said this outlook was too much for him.   He
couldn't write here.   So he has the two rooms on the right
as we go toward the stairway.   I'll show them to you."

They looked very much like Carl's top-of-the-house
rooms on Lake Michigan, a workshop, with desk and bookcases, shelves and filing-cases, all chaotic, yet with order
in it of a sort.   Apple boxes were ranged on top of each
other against the wall to supplement the overflow of book
shelves.   Clippings were pinned about to the edge of shelves
or to the wall-paper.

"Carl isn't really at home here yet.   He hasn't quite
found himself in these rooms.   We have got to do something
about it.   Put in a few more windows, move the wall back
and include some of the hall.   I don't quite know yet."

The hall itself was an immense place.   From my
doorway to the head of the staircase on the opposite side,
I counted thirty-six steps.   The big chimney in the center
was no longer in use, the fireplaces connecting with it having been discarded.   On all four sides of the chimney bookcases had been built.   They were filled, too, from floor to
ceiling.   In all available space between doors, sometimes
even out in the open spaces of the hall, stood huge filing
cases or tiers of apple boxes, filled with books.

From the bedroom door, on the left going toward
the stairway, were two large rooms belonging to Margaret
and Janet.   Margaret's was as filled with books as was her
father's, but in beautiful order.   She was, in fact, the librarian of the family.   Many a time her mother and I talking long over the dinner table would want to refer to some
book.   Margaret always knew where to put her hand on it.
The girls had a large bathroom between their rooms.   There
was one off the hallway which I used.

Mrs. Sandburg's comfortable suite of rooms was on
the first floor: a bedroom, living room and bath.   The bed-

room was huge with big bay windows. Twin beds were lost
in one end of it. There were comfortable arm chairs and
reading lamps. I am sure she used it as her own living
room as well, for the other room appeared to be accepted
as a sort of workroom with sewing machine and an ironing
board left up all the time for convenience. On this first
floor, also, on the other side of the house from her mother's was Helga's suite, a sort of living room-bedroom, the
children's (Paula and John's) room and nursery, and a
large bathroom.

      The dining room was immense, lined with books from
floor to ceiling like all the other rooms. There was room
to seat twenty at the big table. When there were few of us,
we gathered at Mrs. Sandburg's end. Off from the dining
room, separated from it by French doors, was an office,
lined with files and books again, and from which all the
goat correspondence and goat business was carried on. All
here was in neat and easily understood order. This, if my
count is right, made the ninth room on that first floor. I
haven't mentioned a glassed-in conservatory off the front
living room. Just then it did not seem used for the purpose.

      The meals at the long dining table were sumptuous
feasts. Big beakers of goat milk and cow's milk were always on the table, as well as pound slabs of both goat and
cow butter, heaping platters of golden fried chicken, mounds
of sweet corn from the garden, big pans of rich yellow corn
bread, huge baked potatoes. These last were a meal in
themselves when one spared neither butter nor the thick
cream spooned from the pitcher.

      In the corner of the dining room the day I first ar-
rived stood a bushel basket filled with apples of such flavor
that they pulled me back for more. It was a house of abundance, where, I could easily see, an added guest or two
could make no difference. Everywhere was comfort, the
comfort of old arm chairs from which no little hands or
feet had to be warned away. There was the comfort, too,
of every possible convenience and modernity in the kitchen.
In the basement were a washing machine and ironing machine, too. This basement had many rooms, rooms for
storage of enough supplies to withstand a siege. Everywhere was the comfort of things much used and well worn.
This did not link itself to elegance nor even beauty. Of this
there was little, not even the care for arrangement and
orderliness.

The entire household was an expression of Carl's
idea of living. Paula, I feel sure, was not disturbed by it,
had even adopted it as her own. She laughed in unprotest-
ing tolerance at Carl's accumulations. He did not collect
canes; he accumulated them, and his friends, knowing this,
added to the lot. He could never bear to throw away a hat.
Whether his friends gave him those, also, I do not know.
But there were five beautiful new ones in their boxes in the
clothes closet of my guest room. After Paula's mentioning
it, for fun one time I counted Carl's old hats and caps scattered throughout the house. There were seventeen when I
gave up the count. Apple boxes, perhaps because of their
possibility of being converted at any time and anywhere into
tables or bookcases, were another item he collected. I
laughingly asked Margaret one day what her father would
say if we cleared out all the apple boxes in the upper hall
and those scattered through his own two rooms. Her answer was, "I don't think he would like it," in the tone of
doubt expressive of the fact that it had never been tried.

We had known, of course, that Carl would not be
there during my visit. A few unchangeable dates on my
Eastern trip, and the necessity of his being in New York at
the coming out of his new book, Remembrance Rock, had
brought it about that he left Connemara Farm a day or two
before I arrived. We talked over long distance that first
evening. A few advance copies of his book had reached
the family, and I read it late into the night that first evening.

It was arranged that Janet next morning should come
to my room and waken me when she heard her mother stir-
ring. But I was wide awake long before then. For a while
I sat at the open window looking out at that view in face of
which Carl found that he could not write. I was sure I understood why.

Then I got into bed again with Remembrance Rock.
I think I was near the finish of the Prologue when Janet
came into the room. "Why, Mrs. Perry, there are tears
in your eyes!"

"Yes, there are. And if you tell your father so he
will understand that it is my comments so far on his book!"

All through my visit when not involved in some activity with the family, I was absorbed in the book. There

were wonderful passages; it had elements of greatness, but
before I had finished I was deeply critical of it. It was
Carl's first novel. Like Thomas Wolfe he had needed editing. Catherine McCarthy of Harcourt Brace, his publisher,
could have given it to him, but she was in Europe most of
the time that it was taking shape. I had lunch with her in
New York a few years after the book had come out and to
my surprise found that she would have tried to induce him
to make some of the very changes that I would have wanted.
She was in agreement that it should have been a trilogy, not
a single volume. I am not sure that she felt, as I did, that
the book had not needed the framework in which the story is
cast. The old judge is supposed to have written the story
for his children. Carl could better have done the story
straight. I am not sure after this length of time that Catherine McCarthy agreed with me about the rock from which
the book was named. It was the boulder under which were
buried bits of the sand or earth from the various battle
fields in our country's history. This was a touch of sentimentality that was not in the least like Carl and that I, at
least, found hard to take. There were at times magnificent
pages, and for them one read on and on. I did, at least,
though I later found many of my reader friends who did not.
My nearest lending library, a pay library, declared on account of the length of the book they could not stock it. Had
it been in three volumes they would have had a long waiting
list for it.

The reviews were, for the most part, good. The
literary world had somehow come to expect that anything
that came from Carl Sandburg would be good. But today,
as I write these lines many years later, if I were to ask
any literary-minded librarian for a report on the book, he
would say, "It was a best selling novel that is not read
today." I once asked one of the men at M. G. M. (whose
children I was teaching music), one of the promoters of
the book, why it was not being put into a movie. "We
wanted one film from it. Sandburg gave us material for
twenty pictures. Frankly we don't know what to do with
it."

My visit, as Paula said, would have been quite different had Carl been there. But I had been at their home
on Lake Michigan enough to know how it would go. Carl
would not alter his schedule by one iota. I should never
expect to see him till two or two-thirty. We would sit long
at the table and with a visitor there to call forth his best,

all the family, secretary as well, would foregather and join
in the fun. For Sandburg at his own table, as well as anyone else's, was good fun. If he had a guest who could give
him a deep belly laugh he loved it. He treasured from his
own experience the things that had made for laughter and
chortled as heartily as his listeners in the recounting of
them. He was no monologist, however. He was a marvellous, inspiring listener. He drew forth the best from his
guests, at least that is what he did from me. He made me
remember things I had long forgotten. I was asked to his
house because he enjoyed the play of mind we had together.
Yet I was startled once at the compliment he paid me when
he handed back to me my father's autobiography, the published part of it, which he had asked to see.

"That father of yours had the gift of the story teller!
Having read this account of his I shall no more give you
credit for yours than I would give credit to a leopard for
having spots."

"You think me a good story teller?" I asked in genuine surprise.

"You! You are packed with three volume novels!"

That he had that illusion is the reason I have been
so many times a guest at his house. It was fine that he
had it.

It is possible we might have sat over the table until
four o'clock. I doubt if the house-maid would have dared
to intrude to clear the table. Then Carl would rise and de-
clare that he felt the need of a walk. He had always been
a walker, and he then had two hundred and forty acres to
roam over without leaving his own domain. I always suspected that he liked these walks alone, that he worked out
many of his ideas at those times. When he was living on
Lake Michigan, getting very worn and tired and old, about
the time of the end of the Lincoln books, he told me he
had to give up the walks because on them he could never
shake off his work. He had at that time turned to golf, he
said, because he had to have something that would give him
a complete change of thought.

There was one morning during my visit when Mrs.
Sandburg suggested a walk, and I had an opportunity to see
what entrancing territory Carl had to wander over. There

were many springs, sometimes dammed to form little lakes,
rustic bridges, sometimes just roughly made with logs, open
pasture where the herds of goats grazed for as many as ten
months out of the year.   There were wooded glens.   We
did not take the upper pathways which would have given us
a view over the whole valley.   They were the most beautiful,
Paula said, and suggested it for another day.

          As we walked along we talked of many things.   I
asked about the people on the neighboring estates.   Paula
said they had been most friendly and Carl enjoyed them.
In illustration of the inconsistency in our racial prejudices
Paula spoke of the three little cottages belonging to three
colored families, situated just across the road from the
Robert E. Lee mansion nearby.   It did not bother Mrs. Lee,
the III, in the slighest, though in the North it was not tolerated that the houses of blacks and whites exist in the same
district.   Yet at the Flat Rock railroad station there was
separate waiting rooms, one of them marked plainly "For
Colored People. "

          At a tea at Mrs. Robert E. Lee's not long before,
Paula told of a conversation which had amused her.   There
is insistence among these people who could not endure Franklin D. Roosevelt that he is not dead, that, like Hitler, he
has been hidden away somewhere.   It was the first time that
I had heard this rumor, though later I heard it again in
Washington.

          "What reason do they give for such a spiriting away?"
I asked in astonishment.

          "Various reasons.   One, that he had lost his mind,
and that those close to him did not want the people to know
it.   Another, that things had got too hot for him, and it was
judged best that he disappear.   They cite that after his death
he was never seen by anyone, that his coffin was sealed.
While this was being discussed at the tea another Southern
lady burst forth, "There is absolutely nothing in it.   I know
the doctor who attended him, and if he hadn't died that man
would have seen to it that he did.   I know the undertaker,
too, and if there had been any life in him, he would have
finished him!"

A Ten-Year Writing Program [p. 91]

On our drive home [October, 1949] he told me some
of the writing projects he had ahead.

He had a preface to write for a volume of his complete poems which Harcourt was to bring out. In Reckless
Ecstacy, his first book of verse, and The Plaint of the Rose
were to be left out. There would be none preceding the
Chicago Poems.

He had an article to do on Lincoln for the Encyclo-
paedia Britannica.

He was planning a one-volume Lincoln.

He had a mystery story in him which he had titled
"Fallen Leaves."

He had a new book of poems. He gave me a rough
draft of one he called, "Nearer Than Any Mother-heart
Wishes."

He was working on a play which he called "The Laughter of Lincoln." (Paula tried to discourage his attempting
this, I remember. Playwriting, and she is right, takes a
long apprenticeship.)

There was an outline in his mind of two short novels.

There was the book he wants to call "Great Companions." It was to contain chapters on a number of people
whose work and lives had interested him over the years.
One of these was the Japanese print artist Hokusai on whom
he had asked J. D. [Metzgar] and myself to gather data.

There was, of course, always the autobiography.

"These things ought to keep me busy over the next
ten years," he laughed.

The Swedish Call [p. 92]

Once home again [October, 1949] I suggested we go
for dinner to a quiet, good, little French restaurant which
my sister and I frequent.

"Ah, no. Let's stay home. Anything you would fix
would taste better than a restaurant. And if we went there
I couldn't burst out into song whenever I felt like it, or give
the rebel yell!"

While Alice and I were hastily pulling things out of
the refrigerator for an improvised meal, Alice called for
the rebel yell. Actually, he said, a bass or baritone voice
cannot give it. He substituted a Swedish call which he and
his brother Mark used to greet each other with at long distance. It was lusty.

More Fun out of Carl [p. 92]

He had found that the Marx Brothers had a double
feature program, "Animal Crackers" and "Duck Soup," that
night and wanted to go. It seemed he thoroughly enjoyed
the Marx Brothers, whom he knew and whose nonsense is
just as good off the stage, he said, as anything they put on.
I would never have chosen to go to them, but in an enthusiast's company, appreciative of their kind of humor, it might
be different. It was! His laughter led the house. I got
more fun out of Carl than I did the show. The same was
true of my sister, I'm sure.

Watching Combat Film [pp. 92-3]

Carl wanted [October, 1949] to see the war pictures
taken by combat cameramen in the war. Many of these men
had lost their lives in getting these pictures. There were
two parts, "The Building of the Burma Road," and the action
in Europe beginning with the Normandy attack.

We had seen announcements of the showing the night
before. I had said that I thought the pictures would be
pretty hard to take, with the realization that it was no Hollywood stuff but actual action. Carl's answer silenced me.
"I guess if those boys could live through it, we could look
at it."

They were powerful films. Amazing that war could
be pictured for us just as things happened. The next night,
Carl's last, we went again, and took Alice with us. Carl
felt he must see them again.

Arranging to See Dodson [p. 80]

[During Carl's visit of October, 1949 ...] one of my
first questions was about Kenneth Dodson, the man whose
letters from the Pacific fighting front I had once shown to
Carl. Had he ever got in touch with the man, I asked.

"Kenneth Dodson!" he exclaimed. "Why Kenneth Dodson was the reason for my going to Seattle! It wasn't for
that program at Washington State University. That was just
worked in by my agent because I was going to be there. I
owe Kenneth Dodson to you. And was he a gift! I was for
five days with him and his wife. And he is now more than
a friend. He is part of my life!"

Dodson, he told me, was on a place near Seattle,
and in spite of physical disabilities brought on by the war
has gone on with his writing, the same powerful, poignant
stuff we had found in those letters. While he was there,
Sandburg had read everything he had done on his book and
was offering him every encouragement. They had had a
long correspondence before the visit. It was evident from
the deep feeling with which Carl spoke of him that he was,
indeed, part of his life. He inveighed against the attempts
to "manage" Dodson's life by the local moguls of the Veteran's Administration. They were determined to "rehabilitate"
him by the "book," but Dodson was intent upon writing Away
All Boats.

Wearing Well with Paula [pp. 93-4]

As we drove along we talked about Paula. His sister, Mary, and I had talked about Paula and the wonderful
wife she has been for him. She must often have wanted to
change him, get him to pay more attention to his clothes
and his haircuts, or to meet certain demands that he ruth-
lessly shrugs off. Perhaps she early recognized the necessity of his sometimes rather rugged self-preservation,
against the demands of letter-answering, and meeting people.
At any rate, she seems with marvellous restraint to have
accepted him as he is and let him alone.

We were talking of my ten days' visit to his family
while he was away. "It was something to note that you
have worn well with Paula," I put in at one point.

"I like your expression--'worn well.' She has had

lots of occasion for anger at me, " he laughed. "But our
tempers haven't flown at the same time. When one of us
was angry, the other seemed always to be cool. I was
blowing my top soon after our arrival at Flat Rock. I
couldn't work in such conditions! I couldn't find anything
I wanted. My papers were all mislaid. So I raged on.
I'll never forget how coolly Paula said in the midst of my
roaring, 'Well, perhaps it would be better if you went somewhere else!'" How he laughed as he told it! That had, indeed, set him back on his heels.

Reading Spectra [pp. 83-5]

    [During Sandburg's Los Angeles visit of October,
1949,] we found Carl reading from Spectra, the book of
verse which Witter Bynner and Arthur Ficke had years ago
published anonymously, tongue in cheek, a travesty on the
free verse movement. Carl had found the book in J. D. 's
library, a book out of print long ago and hard to come by
nowadays. Our arrival did not stop the reading, though.
Carl went back and read some of the best things over again:
"Upstairs There Lies a Sodden Thing, " and "Sound. " There
were a lot of good ones, hilariously funny.

    Alice had never heard Carl read verse before. His
voice could be velvet. It had organ tones, and modulations,
and two tones on a single word, such as no voice had that
I have ever heard. He might have been a great actor. He
could often convey in just a look some character he was
talking about.

    After Spectra he tried out on us a number of his own
unpublished things, for one, his whimsy of "The Yellow
Paper Horse" which I do not like. It is as crazy as the
most extreme modernistic painting, "Nude Descending the
Stairs, " or worse. When I told him so, he said that was
exactly what he had tried to do, a modernistic painting in
words. But, in addition, it had a mythology of his own, he
said, which he thought he had just as much right to invent
as the Greeks.

    I loved one he read which I dubbed "The Collectors. "
It was about two squirrels who thought only of collecting
nuts. When they met, each asked the other, "Whither goest
thou?" He had another one about a fly, a flea, and a flick.
He used them to comment on books and reading. The fly

he used to represent the reader who counts the pages and is concerned about the length of the book. The flea was the type of reader who looks for pages to skip. The flick sleepily enunciated a policy of beginning to read where the book fell open and preferred to start as near the end as possible. *

He has pages of such nonsense which he reads with great laughter. He has called them, "Fables, Foibles and _____." There is a third word which I cannot remember.

"Publish them? Oh, no," he laughed. "These are just for myself to have fun with. As a matter of fact, some one did ask for them, to publish them, and I found myself drawing back with the strong feeling, Na, na, yer can't have these! These are personal. These are just for my own fun!"

Before we left J. D.'s rooms that night Carl said we ought to send a line, signed by all of us, to Witter Bynner, telling him of the fun we had had on our session with Spectra. Next morning, before Carl came down, I ran off the following on my typewriter:

Dear Witter Bynner,

Three wise men--one of them a woman--sat last night into the early morning hours listening to Spectra. It is true, of course, that Carl Sandburg's voice can make something out of anything. Yet after we had listened to most of them and hooted with laughter over many of them we decided that even if you and Arthur Ficke had written them with your tongues in your cheeks they were good stuff. To this we all subscribe.

Sincerely,

Lilla Perry
Carl Sandburg
J. D. Metzgar

I phoned the public library for Witter Bynner's address, and off the letter went to him. In a few days we got a good answer, "Emanuel sends greetings. How I wish Anne might!" [Arthur Ficke was dead.]

---

*This paragraph has been paraphrased by the editor.

[Spectra, "A Book of Poetic Experiments," was a
satiric hoax, written by Arthur Davison Ficke and Witter
Bynner, using the respective pseudonyms of Anne Knish and
Emanuel Morgan. It was published in 1916 by Mitchell Ken-
nerly and was intended to make fun of such movements as
Vorticism, using the device of the Spectrist Movement, the
explanation of which mocked the serious double-talk of poetic
innovators and faddists. The forty-six poems included use
of metrical-rhymed and free verse, both sorts poking fun
at illogicality in human behavior.]

Taking Chances on Planes [pp. 90-1]

Next day, [October, 1949] we drove downtown to
change his reservations from one airline to another. When
he signed at the desk the clerk asked, "Is it THE Carl
Sandburg?"

"Well, I suppose in a certain manner of speaking it
is."

"Could we have some publicity on this, may I ask?"

"No," said Carl. "I'd rather not. My wife worries
when I travel by air. And in view of those headlines yesterday with fifty-four people lost in an airliner, better
not!"

As we walked away Carl said, "Considering that
frightful airliner disaster a few days ago there have been
times in my life when I would have cancelled this airline
reservation. When I was in the midst of the Lincoln book
I would have taken no chances. I would have had to make
sure that I was around to finish that. Just now, well, it's
an interlude between projects of work. If the plane went
down it wouldn't as much matter as at some other times in
my life."

Visiting Sister Mary [pp. 81-2, 85-7, 88-90, 103, 106, 107, 136, 141-2]

[After a late evening of talk during his October, 1949,
visit] Carl did not appear until twelve. There was a leisurely breakfast. I knew pretty well what he liked. I had
brought sweet butter and dark bread and had squeezed a

beaker of orange juice with the pulp left in. Strange how,
after years, one remembered those things. He spoke with
deep feeling of little mother who, in the days when I would
be away teaching at his breakfast hour, would bring out for
him the things he liked. This was the first time he had
been here since she left us. We sat long over the coffee
cups until, while he went for a walk, I got in a brief half-
hour at the piano. I had a Debussy number half-memorized.

Then we drove to his sister Mary's. I had never
met her before. Though she has lived here a number of
years, I don't believe he has ever made any attempt to stay
at her house. Her son, Eric, and his wife, Charlene, live
with her with their two small children. He may have thought
their household might not fit in very well with his hours of
sleep. I insisted on staying in the car reading during the
afternoon so that he might be alone with his sister. It had
been agreed, however, that we stay to dinner.

The evening was not altogether a successful one.
Eric had asked in a number of friends to meet Carl, and it
was a mistake. "What did they mean to me but a lot of
names!" Carl exploded on the way home.

Next morning, after our twelve o'clock breakfast, we
drove over to Carl's sister's to bring her back here for the
day. I suggested he take her up into his suite, where they
could talk by themselves. In about ten minutes he came
down again laughing. At sight of a comfortable couch Mary
had thrown herself on it and in a few minutes was fast
asleep. "I come to Los Angeles partly to have long talks
with my sister, and I look at her asleep!"

He sat down in the music room near my desk, and
we went on from where we had left off. He had begun his
autobiography and gave me a carbon of the first chapter of
it. I felt certain that his seeing so much of his sister on
that visit was to immerse himself in the atmosphere of his
early days which Mary shared. Through her he would recover much that he had forgotten.

It got to be five o'clock, and Mary was still sleeping. Carl had said when he planned the day that he would
take us out to dinner. Then he declared that anything I
might pull out of the icebox would taste better than at any
restaurant. It was Saturday. I had marketed for Sunday
only. "We can eat up the dinner I had planned for tomorrow!" I laughed.

Carl followed me to the kitchen. My sister Alice
came in, and she and Carl were soon going fast and furious
in a discussion of Ezra Pound. Carl admitted a weak spot
in his heart for Pound and Pound's verse. "And as for his
politics, " he added, "It is just as if a younger brother had
gone all wrong, but he is still an erring younger brother. "

Alice challenged him to read aloud some of the Ezra
Pound verse from an anthology. He started in doing so, in
a corner of the kitchen, insisting on my attention. My mind
was diverted, meanwhile, by getting baked potatoes and a
roast into the oven and with my need of prodding him out of
his corner to get vegetables and fruit out of the cooler behind his back! It was a hectic way to get dinner, and I
would never have gotten it on if Alice had not efficiently
helped me with all the table setting and other trimmings.
We got him to admit finally that Ezra Pound cannot be read
aloud. Even Carl could not compass that.

Mary came down at six-thirty, just as everything was
ready to be taken from the oven. We had a jolly dinner in
which J. D. joined. When we finished, it was time to take
Mary home.

When we reached Eric's, there was a Halloween party
in full swing. Carl didn't want to leave the car but compromised by agreeing to come over the next day if there
would be no neighbors, no party, no people but the family.
Carl growled on the way home about Eric (his nephew) and
Charlene.

"They want me to give up my time when I come out
here and meet a lot of people who are nothing but names
to me; yet they won't take the trouble to read any of my
books. I sent them Remembrance Rock months ago, a year
ago, and they haven't read a line of it yet! I'm not sure
they have ever taken the trouble to read anything else of
mine either. Don't they know that the best of me is in my
books! I can't understand people who lay so much stress
on having me around and won't read a thing I've written!"
He had exploded with much of this to Mary on the way over.

[The next day, Sunday,] we reached sister Mary's
about five. Dinner was soon in order, and this time we
gathered in the breakfast nook. For hours we sat around
the table listening to Carl and Mary tell about old times in
Galesburg.

Carl was inclined to shrug his shoulders over the "birthplace."

"Paula says if the committee which purchased and restored it continues to be without funds for its maintenance it may possibly deteriorate into the condition it was in when we Sandburgs lived there. Now with new sidings and fresh paint she says it certainly doesn't look much like it."

"I hear," said Mary, "that it was your expostulations which saved the outhouse or privy when they were going to tear that down. You're right. It wouldn't have looked natural without that." Sandburg dubbed the inside toilet at the birthplace "The Anachronism."

"I haven't seen the place since the restoration," Carl added. "I'd like to. But I'd want to do it at night--or in disguise. I thought they waited until people were dead before they did such things!"

I quoted something I had read in the paper that he had said when he first learned of the purchase of the birthplace, that he would far rather have people asking why in heck there wasn't a memorial to Carl Sandburg than have them go around asking why in heck there was!

Carl and Mary have little memory of this birthplace. The Sandburgs moved to another house soon after Carl was born. Mary said, to Carl's amusement, that they took her out of the cradle to put him in. There was vivid remembrance of the life that went on in the other two Galesburg houses, however. I wish I could have a transcript of the talk that went on. Chapters of Carl's biography were in the talk that night. When the Sandburgs moved to the last and largest house, Mary was teaching school and had agreed to help with the purchase.

They talked about Carl's coming home from the Spanish war. When the men marched home from the station, the whole town turned out to meet them. The men were a shabby-looking lot. Carl's clothes, like the rest, were worn-out and grimy. Carl told about being given a room in which there was a feather bed at home that first night. He tossed and battled with it for quite a while. Then he got out and finished the night on the good comfortable carpet.

The one who put ambition into the children was appar-

ently the mother. His father, when asked why he did not
learn to read, answered that he was always too busy. He
didn't have time. The mother was a reader, and I remember years ago Carl's showing me a long poem she had
written. After his program at Washington State University,
a student's review in the college paper had said, "Carl
Sandburg said his volumes of Lincoln were written about a
man whose mother could not write her own name by a man
whose father could not write his. Mr. Sandburg added: 'Is
there substance in any thesis about the illiterate?'"

Then Carl and Mary did up the old characters in the
Galesburg of their youth. It was another Spoon River Anthology, which years ago the Sandburgs had encouraged Edgar Lee Masters to write. Carl told of two old town bums.
The school books of that day pictured what hard liquor did
to your liver and the other awful effects of alcohol. Carl,
as a young man returning home after a number of years
away, expected, of course, that these two old bums had
both met their predicted untimely end. He remembers the
jolt he got going through the park to find both of them sitting on a bench, laughing hilariously, still hugely enjoying
life.

Was it any wonder that at this point Mary called for
one of Carl's old folk songs which he always sang with gus-
to. He had no guitar to accompany him this time.

I have led a good life, full of peace and quite,
I shall have an old age, full of rum and riot;
I have been a good boy, wed to peace and study,
I shall have an old age, ribald, coarse and bloody.
I have been a nice boy and done what was expected
I shall be an old bum, loved but unrespected.

In the midst of this the phone rang and it was Eric's
English professor wanting to know if he could come over and
meet Carl Sandburg. In face of Carl's gestures of negation
and his grimaces over the idea, poor Eric had a hard time.
He knew he must put the man off, but he did not want to
hurt his feelings, and he didn't want to lie. He made quite
a mess of it, and there was even danger that the man might
hear our laughter at Eric's difficulties before he got through.

"You ought to have turned that job over to Lilla Perry," Carl said to Eric when he returned to the table. "She's
a practiced and master-hand at it!"

"Gad, I'd better have been, or Carl wouldn't have
continued to come to my house all these years!" I laughed.
There had been plenty of times, I might have added, when,
like Eric and Charlene, I would have liked to have won a
few kudos by showing him off to my friends.

It was one [a. m.] when we started homeward, a half-
hour's ride in the car. Carl was in high feather. He had
had a good time. "You can see, " he said when he came to
leave, "how the intrusion of a strange person would have
completely changed the mood, would have spoiled everything!"

* * *

On the afternoon of his first day here [in November,
1951] I drove him to his sister Mary's. It was to be only
a brief visit this time and again I insisted on staying in the
car, letting him have Mary to himself. But it wouldn't
work. Eric and Charlene came out and got me. Carl was
busy off and on with his autobiography, still in the early
period which Mary, more than anyone else in the world,
helped him to reconstruct. "Its tentative title is 'My Dear
Phantoms, '" he said. (Later when it was published it became Always the Young Strangers.) Recently he had sent
Mary the first big chunk of it. Now he got it away from
her for me to read.

Eric called for Carl next morning [November 12,
1951] to take him back to Mary's. There was to be a last
session with the big carton of clippings. During this quiet
stretch at home I went into the manuscript chapters of Carl's
autobiography. I did not like the beginning. Carl agreed
with me later that it should be changed. But when I got
into the descriptions of his boyhood, the playing in the street,
the characterization of his father, I read with enthusiasm, as
did Alice, also. There was the Carl Sandburg that the people love.

After that we were off for his sister Mary's. She
had promised to get out a big carton of clippings and pictures that a devoted and proud sister had kept way back to
Carl's first writings on his college paper. There it was in
the middle of the living room floor when we arrived, somewhat of a treasure trove, I suspect, for a man in the midst
of writing his autobiography. I watched the scene with
amusement. Every little while at something he picked out
of the box his laugh would ring out.

"You know," he said to me, as I sat on the side-
lines, "I've never in my life subscribed to a clipping bureau. I couldn't see how a reviewer's comments, either
favorable or unfavorable, would do me any good. I decided if anything of any real importance to me was written
it would be sent to me by somebody."

[In an undated letter to Mrs. Perry, doubtless after
the 1951 visit, he asked her for the clippings his sister,
Mary, had given her. He thought there might be an obitu-
ary of his father, among other items. He was then working
on the manuscript of Always the Young Strangers.]

Sandburg's Visit in November, 1951 [pp. 94-7]

The announcement had been in the paper for days
that Carl Sandburg was to give a program in Hollywood on
November 11th.

"We are going to have a visitor soon," my family
announced to me. So it was no surprise to hear his voice
from Houston, Texas, on Friday morning, the ninth, telling
of his arrival by plane that evening.

My sister had offered to give him her suite during
his stay and to come upstairs with me. The fun she had
at these times was worth it, she said.

We were both sitting in front of a brisk open fire
that evening when Carl's taxi drew up. He set a heavy
Gladstone bag, a large brief case, and a surprisingly handsome overcoat down on a chair at the foot of the stairs.
He didn't want to go up just then, he said, and joined us
in front of the fire-place.

"When did you eat last?" I asked. "Alice and I can
quickly throw on a dinner, or I have sandwiches and beer
in the icebox all ready for you."

He said he had just eaten a hearty dinner on the
plane. It was then 8:15, and we sat there before the fire
and talked until after one. Alice faded away about twelve.
That night Carl's talk was at his best. Never with any of
his best old pals could he have been any better. But he
needed just the audience he wanted, else he could be as
silent as he was at his sister Mary's on his last visit when

she made the mistake of asking in her neighbors. Early in
the evening I, too, made the mistake of asking my friend,
Mr. Gilbert Sterling, who lived with us then, as he was
passing through the hall, to come over and be introduced to
Carl. Carl rose and shook hands, to be sure, but he immediately returned to his talk with Alice and me. He em-
barassingly ignored Sterling, excluding him so completely
that the poor man had difficulty beating any sort of graceful
retreat. I have seen Carl do that before, of course.

The next morning I safeguarded myself against a repetition of that occurrence. "Carl," I said, "there are some
of my friends who live here in this house. They have seen
your mail on the hall table. They know you are to be here
during your stay in Los Angeles. They would be hurt if I
did not introduce them. I can assure you, however, they
won't absorb a moment of your time. They will pause just
long enough for an introduction, and that is all." "Of
course. Of course," was his answer. And there was no
repetition of his exclusion act.

The talk of that first night ranged far and wide. "I
wanted this 'farewell tour' (it was the first time he had
ever called it that), because I need at times to get away
from the corner where I work. I arranged to have it hit
Los Angeles and Seattle because I must see my sister Mary,
and I needed good visits with you and Kenneth Dodson."

Mary Austin's name came up. I picked up from a
table Agnes DeMille's Dance to the Piper [Little, Brown,
1952], which had just come out, and read from it a de-
scriptive bit about Mary Austin which had delighted me:

> What did Mary Austin think [about Agnes's dance
> performance at Santa Fe]? She thought a lot of
> things about every fact that came to her atten-
> tion.... She spoke like a sibyl.... 'Never let
> the God be absent from your stage. Say your
> prayers before you dance.' The Spanish tortoise
> shell comb in her bun gleamed in the moonlight
> like a horny crown. She had an arrogant, grey
> mustache, a droopy mouth, and a dictatorial man-
> ner. She did not converse--she issued bulls.
> She had broken the wilderness.

Carl chortled over this, as I knew he would. We had both
known Mary Austin.

With all the work that he has always done, continuous over the years, it amazes me that he knows so well the work of other writers. And he says he is not a fast reader. "From now on I intend to read far less," he said. "My eyes, at seventy-three, are not as good as they used to be. They tire easily."

Perhaps his amazing knowledge of books and writers is because he remembers everything. The highlights of everything remain with him. It always astonishes me that he remembers everything about this household, seemingly everything that I have ever written or told him. For instance, he said, "I've been working in the New York Public Library recently, a really wonderful library, and I said to myself, 'Some day Lilla Perry's journal is going to repose in this place.'" I had forgotten I had told him that my journal, with a release date of forty years hence, is to reside sometime in its archives. I asked him a question I have often intended to, whether he writes his stuff longhand or directly on the typewriter. He answered, as I thought he would, that it makes no difference. "A great deal of the time nowadays I like to write out-of-doors and so do it long-hand. Either way I have my own abbreviations that my typist has to understand." I've seen some of this writing with abbreviations and collected a few examples of it. To me it is quite unintelligible.

Next morning, when Carl came down to breakfast, I could perceive in the cruel morning light, as I did not the night before, that he looked older than he did on his visit here two years before. The outlines of his face were not so firm. There was that perceptible softening of the flesh which comes with the years. Once before on a visit, just after Abraham Lincoln: The War Years came out, he had looked haggard and worn, but the next time we saw him he had recovered from that weariness. My mother had exclaimed about the change in him. "Why, Mr. Sandburg, you look ten years younger than when you were here last. How have you managed it?"

Sandburg gave a laugh. "I'll tell you how, and perhaps it is no secret--by never answering my mail!"

[Currently,] ... he said he had been in fine health and vigor, nothing the matter except the little trouble with his eyes. He did for us some of the exercises he went through every morning. "They are relaxing exercises, not

stimulating ones, " he pointed out, and he had gone through
them every morning for years.

Enthusiasm for Gerro Nelson [p. 101-2]

"That is quite a story!" I replied.   I won't repeat it
here, but, after I had given Carl the few facts I knew of
her [Gerro Nelson, poet and singer] wild career, he suggested that we collaborate on the most interesting tale he
had heard in a long time and call it "Lost Music. "

Next morning at breakfast he asked to see the Henry
Cowell poem [written by Gerro Nelson] again, and read it
aloud again stirringly.   "I wanted to see if it held up to the
first impression, " he said.   "It does.   I would be proud to
have written it. "

My sister now came forward with the two published
poems.   He read aloud "Routine":

> No day can leave its mooring place
>   Without a tattered gown;
> The cloth of tried monotony
>   Is slashed all up and down.
>
> No wind, no tree, is fettered to
>   Tomorrow's little place.
> A rose who wears a color twice
>   Is doomed to see disgrace.
>
> The variable world is full
>   Of etchings finely done
> A cabbage with a bustle on,
>   An apple in the sun.

"Damn that kid!" Carl exploded, as he came to the
finish.   "If I could have discovered her before it was too
late, I would gladly have given the best there is in me to
the development of her genius, as I am glad to give it to
Kenneth Dodson. "

"I don't suppose, " he went on, "that there is anyone
who has received over the years such tons of verse from
aspiring poets as I have.   AND I HAVE NEVER MET ANY-
THING AS GOOD AS THIS. "   He read it aloud again, prob-
ing each line for meanings, an action I stored up to throw
back to him when next he tried any of his "cult of unintelligibility" stuff on me.

> A cabbage with a bustle on,
> An apple in the sun.

"Without the signature wouldn't anyone suspect those
lines of being Emily Dickinson's," he said, "and up among
her best. I don't suppose she had ever read anything of
Emily Dickinson's?"

"At eleven years old? No, I'm sure she never had.
She didn't come from a literary family."

Then he read the lines she had called "Distances":

> All my friends on your long, rough voyages,
> My lost lovers and my children,
> My dead husband, and the adjustments of getting
> Back and forth to the cemetery
> On Sundays, --
> I laugh at your distances.
> Can I not think of Elizabeth in Rome
> Among the ruins,
> And see her red hair blowing in the wind?
> Can I not still feel the first kiss
> On my lips, reconciled?
> My children, though you may run half way
> Across the world,
> I have your fingers at my breast.
> I laugh as I sit by one grave
> And grieve my one grief.
> Maybe William is looking down
> And hating the fading flowers
> And the tears.

Carl read it as only he can read, to bring out the power
and the beauty. When he laid it down he said slowly,
"There is all the mystery of genius here." Then he lifted
the page and read aloud again the lines:

> My children, though you may run half way
> Across the world,
> I have your fingers at my breast.

"Was ever motherhood better expressed, compressed
there in those few lines? Naturally I like best the things she
has done in free verse. I've never been able to express myself in rhymed verse, not effectively. It always twisted
and thwarted my meaning to make the rhyme."

Alice and I promised to find more of the Gerro Nelson poetry before he left.

Audiences Never Seemed to Mind [pp. 103-4]

[During Sandburg's November, 1951, visit to Los Angeles ...] Dinner at the house was a late affair, though Alice turned to and was a marvelous help. Carl asked if we couldn't eat dinner in the kitchen. When we had finished, Alice and Mr. Metzgar, Carl and I, it was suggested that he might like to try out the guitar which he was to use for his program the following night.

"Let's take more comfortable chairs in the livingroom, " I said.

"Oh, nar, the kind of tunes I want to try out fit much better in the kitchen, " was his retort. So there we sat from eight o'clock to nine-thirty listening to his folk songs. I have never heard him keep going so long on them. Perhaps it was because I called for a lot of old favorites he had not sung for a long time. He had lost the words for "Look down, look down dat lonesome road. " But I had it in his own handwriting among my scraps, and found it for him.

Almost all the folk songs were new to my sister, and I could sense her enjoyment of them. Back of it all for me was the remembrance of the rich, sonorous voice of Carl Sandburg in his forties. The amazing thing was that his voice at seventy-three was still so true. His guitar accompaniments would trouble a musician, and I wondered often that he seemed never to have taken the trouble to improve them. Perhaps he felt that an artistic perfection in his accompaniment background would render untrue the folk songs as sung by the people. They strummed their instruments as they felt like it. His audiences have never seemed to mind.

Two Strains in Me [p. 105]

He got his audience [in Los Angeles on November 11, 1951] to laughing when he told of the man who boasted of having heard two hundred Bob Hope programs, and when the program was due he went to it as to his dope. As he said

the last words, he made a jittery little motion with his
hands, and it brought down the house. Discussing the program the next day, he laughed over the putting in of that
little gesture. "If I say it without the gesture, the audience
smiles; if I put in the gesture, they laugh out loud. There
are two strains in me you know, " he added, "one is the
bum, and the other is the vaudevillian. " We have always
recognized the actor in him. Then came the reading of
some "pieces" (he calls them) from his recent, as yet unpublished verse. The program ended with a group of folk
songs. He was generous. His program lasted at least an
hour and a half.

Fifteen showed up at the party at the house afterward.
Carl knew he could ask as many as he felt inclined. It was
a nice number. That evening it was Jake Zeitlin's young
son, David, not Carl, who entertained us with folk songs
sung to his guitar. Carl had done enough. It was the first
time that I had ever seen him really wearied by a program.
He sat close to the fireplace as though he were cold. But
his tongue was unwearied. He told many a good story, and
every little while that great booming laugh of his would
burst forth. It was two-thirty when the last guest departed,
and we had eaten up all the sandwiches.

The Stimulating Guest [p. 107]

The following day he was taken off for his program
in Santa Barbara. It is lucky I have these times of respite
nowadays during his visits or I should go to pieces. I find
him so stimulating, so over-stimulating that there hasn't
been an evening which we finished together that I could get
to sleep without difficulty.

On Unintelligibility [pp. 109-12]

[In spite of the fact that Sandburg usually expressed
himself as being opposed to the "cult of unintelligibility" in
poetry, he at times indulged himself in highly subjective expression. On one of the occasions when Mrs. Perry asked
for clarification, the following occurred:] Then lucidly, in
phrases of real beauty, he paraphrased slowly what he had
just read. "But Carl, " I exclaimed, "that is beautiful!
And I see what you are trying to express. It means something to me! Must it all be so hidden?" He looked at me
questioningly, and did not answer.

There is one particular "piece," "The Triumph of
the Yellow Paper Horse," which seemed packed with meaning for him. I had heard it on each recent visit in different versions. He rolled it lusciously on his tongue. I
think it grew more and more unintelligible. Carl defended
it as though it were the favorite of all his recent output.
He read it aloud with zest more than once on this visit, and
it did not grow on me. I reminded him with what care he
probed for meanings in each line of Gerro Nelson's verse.
"Don't think for a moment that that is not what your readers do to yours. I know you like this yourself. Can't you
give me some clue as to what you want to convey in it?"

He treated my request with seriousness. "I think I
had five intentions before, and I need to mull over them."
"Do you mind if I write them down?" He didn't, and I scrib-
bled on a pad as he outlined them.

"One, to experiment with myth making. The Greeks
made their myths, so did the Norsemen, so do all peoples.
Why should not I?"

"But no one person, Carl, can create a myth. It
takes a whole people."

"But some one must begin it," he laughed.

"Second, to create actions and pictures that would
interest children." Then he added, "I've tried 'The Yellow
Paper Horse' on the children at home, and John and little
Paula laughed at it and enjoyed it. I looked over at Paula,
and she was nodding her head and smiling."

"That doesn't mean a thing! Paula was nodding and
smiling because you were giving the children fun. With
your dramatizations and the inflections of your voice you
could take the multiplication table and make children love
it. But the first time you see any child from five to fifteen
sitting down alone and enjoying 'The Yellow Paper Horse' let
me know about it."

"Third, to form with words and images something
that would parallel the feeling of an abstract painter in line
and color. I rewrote this piece the last time just after I
had visited an exhibition of abstract design at the Museum
of Modern Art."

"In this intention, Carl, I do believe that you succeed."

"Fourth, to convey some moments in the story that would have the spirit of the awful transiency of the Universe. The shelf of the Niagara Falls is slowly wearing back, so many inches a year they tell us.   There will come a day when the Rocky Mountains are no more. "

"I admit, Carl, this is vaguely suggested, but hidden among so much confusion that one would have to be told what to look for.   Who wants footnotes to a poem?"

"Fifth, this is nothing calculated, but I am indulging myself, and I hope the reader will be indulging himself in a blue bath of maroon phantasies, 'spikes of brass married to spokes of gold, ribbons of sleep crossed with battle cries. '"

To this last I could not reply.   I think perhaps he does this for the very few.

Pondering these things and the trend of quite a bit of his later free verse writing I sat down at my typewriter the next morning before he came downstairs to breakfast and wrote off the following:

From the Biography of Carl Sandburg,
by, A. E. Futurus, Published 1990

In his later work he departed from the direct appeal of his earlier verse.   This poet, whose first volume had been carried around under the arms of students, and whose message to the people (yes) had made him the best-loved poet in America, now joined the current "cult of unintelligibility, " and he cared not a hoot that his meanings were known only to himself and God.

There were those among his many devotees who tried vainly to form Sandburg Societies in the spirit of the Browning Societies of the early part of the century where every careless phrase was submitted to microscopic scrutiny.   But the impulse toward greater and greater speed in automobiles and jet propulsion had had its effects upon the human mind.   Whatever poem it failed to solve upon a third reading it cast aside.   It is regrettable to the mind of this critic that the later poems of Sandburg are now read only by the writers of abstruse literary theses.

> For there is value in the effort of those who in
> words have groped with the antennae of the spirit
> into realms through which the human mind has
> never traveled. Through such only are advances
> made. But they must build their lines of commu-
> nication strong, else they take their flight alone
> and none attempt to follow.

Carl laughed at this when he read it. But he folded
the carbon copy, and it went off in his portfolio.

One morning, pawing around among papers for things
to read to Carl at breakfast, I came across a sheaf of scrib-
bled notes which I had written to Norman [her youngest son]
and laid on his desk in the unheated garage room he had insisted on having when he was a college student. It was
probably so he could come and go as he wanted without
supervision from me as to how he looked. It was always
terrible, I remember. I had rescued these notes from his
desk drawer long after he left home. To my knowledge he
never threw anything away. I had recovered my sense of
humor about him by this time, enough to find them funny.

> Norman, if you will empty your pockets and hang
> trousers over a chair at night instead of dropping
> them in a heap on the floor, I'll pay for the press-
> ing. Otherwise, I am going to take it out of your
> allowance. Stockings off floor, please, not dropped
> just anywhere!

> Norman, you have an alarm clock and you've got
> brains enough to use it. I can't ask Beatrice to
> run out to that garage room to wake you mornings.

There were many more. Those days were far enough
away so that I, too, could get a good laugh out of them.
Carl had always recognized Norman's faults as pretty much
what his own must have been in his youth, complete oblivi-
ousness to personal appearance and to comforts. At any
rate, he had always had a particularly warm spot in his
heart for my youngest son, Norman. He took from his
pocket a copy of "The Triumph of the Yellow Paper Horse,"
wrote a note to Norman on it, and said, "Send this to him!"
He had previously asked for copies of Norman's incomprehensible articles on Psychometrics in The Journal of Psy-
chology, and when he asked me to send on this note I said,
"Norman will probably think you are exchanging his work,

incomprehensible to you, for some of yours, incomprehensible to him. " At any rate, I knew that Norman was as little likely to make any reply at all, as Carl himself would be.

Remembering Theresa [pp. 149-50]

Somewhere in that audience [in January, 1953] sat the woman Theresa Anawalt, now as old as himself, who had found herself in his autobiography, Always the Young Strangers. What a surprise and thrill it must have given her to find her name there. For he had written in his book of how he had seen her on his milk route as she walked to her work in a store on Main Street in Galesburg. Though they had never spoken, he wanted her to know, if she should read his words, that she was not forgotten, as was true of many others he had observed in Galesburg.

Theresa Anawalt had found these paragraphs and she had written Carl through his publishers from an address in Glendale, California. She was now married. Doubtless she told him something of her life in the intervening years. I wish I had questioned him more specifically, for the story pleased me. At his program she had sent a little note backstage to him.

> You'd better be good! I'm here in the eleventh row, aisle seat, with ears and eyes alert. I'll come back and see you after the program and when we look at each other after all these years we'll say, 'Well, here we are again!'

It was partly that I might catch a glimpse of her that I watched Carl from the outer fringes of the crowd that thronged backstage to see him [and] to meet him after the program. But Carl told me later that she did not come. When he traced her later over the phone to her Glendale address she made the excuse that there had been too many people. Perhaps with an elderly woman's pride she preferred that he remember her as he had pictured her.

As we came out the stage entrance onto the street I was walking with Carl and had his arm. A beautiful tall elderly woman stood just at the corner of the alley near where we turned into Fifth street. Her face was lit up with an almost ecstatic smile as though she had just been through a moving experience. As we turned he was on her side and

I saw her reach out and touch his arm, so lightly that he
did not even feel it. I turned back to look at her, and for
a moment we held each other's eyes. She was smiling but
there were tears on her face. Up till this moment I have
thought of it as a separate incident. As I write this I wonder if it might not have been Theresa Anawalt.

[The Galesburg Register-Mail carried an account, on
January 12, 1953, of how Mrs. Bernard Wykoff, of Glendale,
had been surprised to find herself in Always the Young
Strangers. Because she remembered the silent meetings
clearly, she had written to him and had received an exuberant reply which she had glued to the front cover of the autobiography. As reported in the Register-Mail, it read as
follows:

> Dear Theresa Anawalt, this you can paste and
> keep in your book--though the years have wrought
> their changes in your face, your words and the
> spirit showing through them have the springtime
> loveliness that so long ago was a beneficence to
> me....]

Can't We Keep Him? [p. 145]

[To celebrate Carl's 75th birthday, in 1953, there
was a gathering of friends and admirers at The Red Barn,
on La Cienega Ave., a book store owned by Jake Zeitlin.]

To celebrate the birthday, there were to be a number of speakers and as Carl's nearest and oldest friend out
here on the Coast I, too, was asked to be one of them.
With all the wealth of material back of me from which to
draw tales and pictures of Carl I readily accepted. I had
no written speech, of course, but I talked for half an hour
from a few topic headings I had on a card. I do remember
the incident I closed with:

"Five or six years ago Carl took me to Ingrid Berg-
man's to dinner. He and Ingrid, both with Swedish back-
grounds, had known each other for a long time. When invited, Carl had asked if he might bring his hostess. This
was long before the break-up of the Lindstrom family, for
little Pia the daughter, was only five. There were just
the Lindstroms, Carl and myself. We lingered long in talk
over the dinner table, and every little while Carl, fearing

that grown-up talk might be getting tiresome to little Pia,
would turn his entire attention upon her, and delight her
with some of his tricks.   Carl has a way with children; I
had many times seen him work his fascination on mine.
When we finally rose from the table it was late enough for
us to take our leave.   Pia sensed that her new friend was
about to depart.   She threw herself pleading into her father's
arms, and exclaimed breathlessly, 'Oh, can't we keep him,
Daddy?   Can't we keep him?'"

A Ready Negative [p. 150]

A prominent preacher of the city [Los Angeles] was
among the guests, [at a post-performance party on the event
of January 30, 1954.]   In my talk with him I learned that
he had come in the hope of inducing Carl to speak at a
Young Peoples' Group at his church the next morning.   I
knew the party tonight would last late, the meeting next
morning was at nine-thirty.   He was asking a good deal of
an elderly man, even if Carl's contract with his agent would
even permit it.   I watched with interest to see what would
happen.   Carl had seated himself among a group of people.
In a brief interval when his attention was not engaged, the
preacher strode toward him, bent over him, and put forward his request.   I saw Carl look upward, fire him an
unadorned "no," then turn immediately to the person beside
him in conversation.

Endorsing a Performer [pp. 150-4]

When we reached home [January-February, 1954],
there was already a houseful of people there, the Swedish
American Society and friends whom Carl and I had asked.
My daughter had arrived early to take my place as hostess.
A refreshment committee of the Swedish Society had taken
over, and I had been warned that I was to have nothing to
do with the refreshments.   Eleanor Remick Warren, the
composer, had brought a singer with her to have Carl hear
songs she had written to some of his poetry.   Young, tawny-
haired William Clauson, whose guitar had been loaned to
Carl for his program, sang us a group of Swedish folk songs.
He had a fine, well-trained voice, was a young Segovia of a
guitarist, and had a strong dramatic sense in his folk song
rendering that woke up the whole party.   He delighted Carl
so much that he, too, reached for the guitar again and sang
with us.

By one-thirty most of the large group had left, but
the folk singers were having too good a time to leave.
About twelve gathered in the music room, some of them sitting on the floor at Carl's feet, and young Clauson's guitar
was handed from one to another until three-thirty.   Carl
contributed his part as much as anyone.   Young Clauson was
easily the star performer with his endless repertory and his
dramatic fervor.   I didn't have to worry about Carl and his
fatigue.   He has as many defenses as anyone I know.   If
those young people stayed on, it was because he wanted
them to.

Long before Carl made his appearance at one o'clock
[the next afternoon], there came a call over the phone to
me.   Young Clauson's father told me what a thrill it had
given his son to have Mr. Sandburg use his guitar and to
have such outspoken approval from him of his singing of
the folk songs.   Bill was too shy to speak up for himself,
but did I think that Mr. Sandburg would be willing to see
his father and let him ask for a short statement in writing
that Bill could use in his publicity.   The young man had had
many years of training both of his voice and his guitar playing.   He was having a bit of a struggle at twenty-three to
get his start.

Knowing Carl and his dislike of meeting people unknown to him, I suggested that perhaps I could do more
about getting a statement from him than his father could.
"I am sure that you could, " was his reply.   I added that
we all had been sufficiently impressed here at 720 [South
Kingsley] with his son's performance to make the effort to
get a statement from Mr. Sandburg an enthusiastic one.

I reported our conversation to Alice, Mary Keller,
and Dorothy.   They were keen about my getting a word in
writing from Carl that would be a help to the young man.
I groaned, however, remembering all the work Carl had
confided he had before him while staying with us.   (I have
often suspected that there were hours of work behind Carl
before he appeared at twelve or one for breakfast.   When
he spoke once of making powdered coffee in his room, I
was sure of it.) He had to finish the careful reading of
Kenneth Dodson's 508-page book.   He had a review to write
of it for the Herald Tribune which must be the best thing
of its kind that he had ever done.   He had to contribute
"words" that were to be inscribed in bronze over the door
of a Swedish hospital.   "When they are to be in bronze, you

know, " he laughed, "it's easier to write a book!" He was
to give a talk on his way home at a new Chicago high school
which was to be called, "The Carl Sandburg High School. "
There was plenty to be done while here to account for his
fending off people or any new problems.   Yet we wanted
that word for young Bill Clauson.   "Perhaps if we worked
out a statement ourselves, something we know he would be
willing to sign, it might make it easier. "   This was my
sister Alice's suggestion.

Alice, Mary Keller, and Dorothy got into a huddle
on the front porch.   What they evolved was good, but it did
not sound like Carl.   I had to whittle it from that angle.
Nothing was satisfactory.

Mr. Metzgar and I had an errand in Pasadena that
afternoon.   It was a beautiful day, and Carl asked if he
could come along for the ride.   As I started up my car,
Alice gave me an appealing look.   I might have answered
her that I did not intend to try anything on that ride.   But
when, midway of our trip, Carl burst out enthusiastic comments on young Clauson's performances of the night before,
I seized my chance.   "The boy has had lots of good preparation and he's now all ready to go.   If you would just write
out one statement of the opinions about him you have been
expressing, he could use it in his publicity, and it would
be of immense help to him. "

"I'll do it, " said Carl.   He tore off the margin of
the newspaper he had in his hand, and began to write.
When he handed it to me I was surprised and pleased.   In
it he had said much more than we would have dared invent
for him.   It read:

> William Clauson is a Viking of song, to me irre-
> sistible, one of the most colorful and versatile
> singers and accomplished guitarists I have ever
> heard.

When we reached home and showed it to the girls I
put a white card in Carl's hand and said, "Don't you want
to copy that in more permanent form?"   "Aw, no, I done
'writ' enough, " he drawled.   "Type it out if you like and
I'll sign it. "   "We'll give Bill this, as is, " I answered.   I
wanted Clauson to have it all in Carl's own writing.   So it
was the newspaper margin note that Bill Clauson got.   "Paste
it onto something, " I suggested.   "I'll get it photostated at
once, " he beamed.

Not Working [pp. 159-60]

On Saturday, the last day of his stay [in 1954], Mr.
Fahlstrom and Mr. Anderson of the Swedish American Committee called to ask Carl, my sister Alice, and myself to
go with them to a Swedish Smorgasbord. It was a small
place, not well known; in fact, we would have it almost to
ourselves, they told us.

"Sounds good to me.   Let's go, " said Carl.

There were only seven of us at the dinner.   The food
was good; the talk was good; Carl was in one of his most
amusing and entertaining moods.   The Swedish woman who
owned the place fluttered anxiously around, excited at having so distinguished a guest.

Two other patrons, a father and his young son, lingered long at their table, delaying their departure as long
as they reasonably could.   The young boy's face was beam-
ing.   He had probably learned Carl's poems in high school,
"The Fog, " at any rate.   He had recognized Carl's much-
pictured face and was not actually within ear-shot of the
great man's stories.   As they left the room, emptied now
of all save ourselves, the boy stood for a moment shyly
beside Carl's chair.   When Carl looked up, he held out a
card and asked for his autograph.   "There are times when
I have to say, 'I'm not working tonight. '" Carl replied.
And the boy moved off, looking crestfallen.   Carl hadn't
seen the boy's face as he sat at the table.   Had he done
so, he would have answered differently.

The Dinner-Interview [pp. 154-6]

Carl's stay this time [January-February, 1954] lasted
twelve days.   To the people who called up before his program, he had not arrived; to those who called afterward, he
had already left town.   I was used to being this buffer.
Many of the people insistent on seeing him were from the
press.   "Why should I be interviewed?" he protested.   "I
had enough of that sort of thing in Chicago at my birthday
celebration.   What do they think I am, a prophet, an elder
statesman?   Should I know whether we are likely to be
attacked by atomic bombs?   Who do I think is the most
promising young writer in America today?   Have I got to
decide that? Jesus wept!" he exploded.

He did consent to letting Mildred Norton of the <u>Herald</u>
<u>Express</u> come out to the house.   She had written a report of
his program which he liked.   Instead of the walk which he
had suggested to her when she arrived, she took him in her
car up into the hills, and they walked there.   He came home
all enthusiastic about her, her fine mind, her penetrating
intelligence.   He did not mention her beauty.

He had invited Norton to have dinner with him somewhere on the night I had told him I had an engagement else-
where.

"I hate a restaurant!" he commented.   (Didn't I know
it?   Hadn't I had to get dinner for him here at the house
every night, I who have forgotten how to cook?)   "It would
be so much nicer if we could find a place where we could
find cheeses, cold cuts, and salads and could eat them right
on your kitchen table. "

"Why don't you?" I laughed.   "The coast will be
clear, everybody out of your way. "

"We could sit there and talk, annoyed by no autograph
hunters, " he added.   But in a few minutes an unpleasant
thought crossed his mind.   "But we'd have to clear it up.
I couldn't ask Miss Norton to wash dishes. "

"Leave your table just as it is.   It won't take me a
minute when I get home.   You need not tell her that I will
do it.   Just make a sweeping gesture when you get ready
to leave the kitchen and say, 'This will all be taken care
of!'"

"You are certainly a good sport, " he chuckled.

When I reached home from my evening's engagement,
I thought Norton would be gone, but I could hear their
voices in the lighted kitchen.   For a moment I swung open
the kitchen door to laugh at them and to greet her, "Did
you ever have a man take you out to dinner this way before?"

"No, I never did, " she smiled, "but it's fun!"

I retreated up into the living-room of my sister's
suite, now given over to Carl.   I found Alice there, reading.   We were both getting in every minute we could on

Kenneth Dodson's book, <u>Away All Boats</u>. Alice had gone
there to find Carl's advance copy. We read until Carl himself appeared, Miss Norton having departed. "You won't
need to go near the kitchen," he announced. "It's completely ship-shape. Miss Norton insisted on doing the dishes
and I wiped them!"

"Carl, it's the first time in my life that I knew you
could wipe dishes!"

On Answering Mail [pp. 163-4]

[During a visit to the Sandburg home in 1959, Mrs.
Perry observed] Carl had a pile of mail, the interest of
which he shared with us. There were several batches of
poetry sent in by would-be poets. One group of verses had
been typed in that beautiful printing you get with an electric
typewriter. It was on vellum and between each two leaves
was a protecting page of tissue. "This poor lad must have
thought very highly of these poems," Carl commented.
"And listen to them!" He read one or two of the short
pieces. They were utterly without promise.

"Are all the poems you get as bad as that?" I inquired.

"No, many are much better. I told you once that
of the tons of verse that have been sent to me over the
years for my comment I never had received anything as
good as Gerro Nelson's."

"Now, what will you do? Send these back?"

"If they send me an addressed stamped envelope,
Margaret takes care of them for me. But they seldom do
that thoughtful thing. If I answered all this mail, I would
never get any time for my own work. I once thought of
writing a sort of form letter to return to them. It would
be something like this: 'If you are a real poet, nothing I
could say would discourage you. If you are not a poet,
nothing I could say would really help you.' I should have
done it, I suppose, but I never have."

UCLA's Program Honoring Carl [pp. 169-72]

In November of 1958 came Carl's big program in the

auditorium at the University of California at Los Angeles.
In the interval since I had last seen him, his constant appearances on television had made me feel that I had kept in
touch. At first he had felt that the price offered him for
these television appearances was fantastic. He had so expressed himself to both Catherine McCarthy and myself.
Later he made no demur when his agent asked outrageous
fees for him. He came to take them for granted, I believe.
A letter of my own which I find with a brief reply of Paula's
tells of the important event of this visit.

                                The day after Thanksgiving, 1958

Dear Paula, -

    Carl, as of course you know, is at Norman
Corwin's this time. He has deserted me for the
first time since 1920, but it is quite forgiveable.
I drove out to see him day before yesterday and
found him hard at work on some sort of script in
a fine little guest house beside a big swimming
pool. It must be quite ideally isolated from the
household activities, a fine place for getting work
done.
    Carl had sent me tickets for the show Hollywood
put on for him at U. C. L. A. I had gone wondering
whether it would be the kind of thing he would like
or would be at all worthy of him. It was wonderful! I doubt if any poet in all history has ever
had such a tribute. The big auditorium at the
University was packed. Mr. Frank Baxter, the
college professor who has put back Shakespeare
and other classics on radio and television programs, was master of ceremonies. In his hands
it could hardly go wrong. He sat at a table--
just as he does for his radio programs--and talked
off the script which I suspect was Norman Corwin's. But you would never know it was not his
own, with his many ad libs.
    There was an empty throne-like chair in the
center of the stage with Carl's guitar beside it,
books piled high at its foot. Carl came in and
took this seat to a rising ovation at the start of
the program. Grouped across the stage were
other empty chairs which were gradually filled as
one by one leading actors and actresses of Hollywood came onto the stage, recited or interpreted
whichever of Carl's poems had been assigned to

them and took their seats.   Some of them were
thrillingly good, others not.   'I am an ancient reluctant conscript, ' one of my favorites, which I
always hear in Carl's own voice, was not satisfactory.   No wonder that did not satisfy me.   I
had heard Carl read it so often.   One could tell
when Carl was pleased.   He gave the performer
a salute.

At the finish came Carl's part.   He talked to
us a little, sang one folk song, which made us
want more, read some new verse, and then it was
over.   People thronged the stage, of course.

Carl had seen to it that I got an invitation to
the party at the Edwin Pauley's afterward.   I knew
the family well because I once taught their children
music, and to my surprise there were a lot of
other people whom I knew.

When Carl and I were talking it over at Corwin's later I was saying that I wished you could
have been there.   You have had many occasions
of being proud of him, but there young people reciting his poems would have given you a new kind
of lift.   I said as much to Carl and he said, 'Why
don't you write Paula about it.   You can give her
a better idea than I can. '   (The rascal!   I doubt
if you hear from him except by phone or wire
once he gets away and is caught up by the rest
of the world.)

I had driven out to Norman Corwin's because
people, expecting Carl to be with me, had been
bringing in books to be autographed.   Quite a
stack of them had collected.

Carl said he would try to get over to see me
before he left for home, but he and Corwin seem
to be very busy and I doubt if he manages it. . . .

Yours,

Lilla

Carl's stay at the Norman Corwins' extended over
several weeks.   Together they were working on the script
of what later became "The World of Carl Sandburg. "   The
germ of that successful bit of theatre came surely from the
university program where Carl's poems were interpreted by
the people of the moving picture world.

During those days of work I saw Carl several times.

Once he had Mildred Norton, who was doing some secretarial
work for him at the Corwins', drive him here for the afternoon. Once Mrs. Corwin phoned and asked me over to dinner. This was at Carl's instigation, I am sure. I am not
certain she was too happy about it, for she was her own
cook. No matter what the financial means available, a
hostess seems to have that role thrust upon her these days.
Good household help is a great rarity. There was a nurse
for the two children, I observed, who fed them and put them
to bed before our own dinner. Before Carl came in from
his guest house work shop in the garden, Mrs. Corwin spoke
quite feelingly, I thought, about Carl's unwillingness to be
taken out to dinners. I was laughing inside. Didn't I know!
Dinner was a gay affair, however. Carl can always make
it so. I was amused at his calling forth my own funniest
tales. He was determinedly not being the star on this occasion.

Soon after this dinner party Carl called up to say
goodbye. He was leaving for home. Mr. Corwin was driving him to the airport.

The World's Estimate [p. 177]

Carl surprised me next morning [during a visit to
Los Angeles in 1959] by asking if I would let him have
copies of portions of the old journal that I had read him.
I was reluctant. They were so frank, so personal, those
sections I had read him. Reading them to him was different, letting him have the typed sheets to use or lose
was something else again. He saw my reluctance and was
quite visibly hurt or vexed. Next morning I handed him the
pages, tailored a bit in their preface so they could never
be traced. He had so often wanted for himself things I
have read him that I suppose I should have felt pleased.

While talking about Norman [her son], I had described
the disorder in which he kept his desk and tables and still
did. Carl laughed. "I'm the same way myself. Papers
and memoranda just pile up in my workroom, and I won't
let anybody touch them. I never destroy anything. My
manuscripts all go to the University of Illinois. They have
a Sandburg room there. I have sometimes thought of stuff-
ing all my loose papers and memoranda into envelopes and
turning them in, also. What a wonderful thing it would
have been for me when I was writing my Lincoln books if
the notations made at Lincoln's desk had been saved."

Carl, what is the implication here? Yet it must be hard not to take one's self at the world's estimate. We all watched television while Carl gave his Lincoln talk before the Joint Session of Congress [February 12, 1959]. The place was packed with dignitaries from all nations. All rose when Carl's turn came on that Lincoln Memorial Program. A storm of applause greeted its close.

Carl Edits a Manuscript [p. 180]

That evening [in 1959], seated comfortably in a big arm-chair, Carl demanded to have a look at the manuscript of my forthcoming book, Chinese Snuff Bottles, The Adventures and Stories of a Collector. The book had been accepted by Charles E. Tuttle Co., but there was to be a final typing and minor corrections of my own.

After a few minutes of reading, Carl looked over his glasses and said with a smile, "Would you think me a friend if I wanted to put my pencil marks through some of your phrases and interpolate a word here and there!"

"Go to it! Mark it up! It has all got to be typed again." Carl must have spent two hours over those first two chapters, which were all I gave him. It was mostly the beginning over which he worked; the latter part he said he did not want to touch. Any writer, certainly any unknown writer like myself, would rate high such a service. I have carefully put away those pages and their annotations, the pencilled corrections and the crossings-out. A few I could not use. They sounded so completely Carl, not Me.

Losing to Youth and Beauty [pp. 181-3]

For days now [March 1, 1960] I have been realizing that Carl must again be in town. Phone calls and mail kept coming for him, and the papers had continuous publicity about the opening of his show, the one he had made with Norman Corwin, "The World of Carl Sandburg." It had already toured much of the country to much acclaim. At the opening in Los Angeles Sandburg himself was to appear.

When he phoned me a few days ago I was not at all surprised to learn that he was again at Mildred's [Mildred

Norton]. It came out that he had been there since last
Wednesday, almost a week. He was now calling to ask me
to be his guest at the opening of "The World of Carl Sandburg" and to attend with him the party to be given for him
after the show. For time and place of meeting he turned
me over to Mildred.

"The party Carl is asking you to," she said, "is to
be one of those huge Hollywood affairs that my husband and
I would like to skip. Since you will be coming in your own
car could we turn transportation of Carl over to you after
the show?"

"Why, of course," was my answer. "But instead of
driving Carl way out to Inglewood to your house at that late
hour and having the long drive back alone, wouldn't it be
better," I asked, "if I brought Carl home with me?" She
seemed to think so, and thus it was arranged.

There was little to do to get ready for him. I had
learned that two days following the opening he was to take
a plane home. Convenience had thrown him my way for
the last two days of his visit.

I sat at the phone after the call--thinking. Never
again would this house be "his home in Los Angeles," as
he had so often called it. I had lost him to Youth and
Beauty. Mildred is a lovely woman in her early thirties,
and he has always liked her. I think as I sat there at the
phone table there was a smile on my face--a sad little
smile, perhaps, but not too sad. "Conrad in Search of his
Youth" I thought. Having once been admitted--no matter
how hesitantly into her household--how natural that he should
have called her up from the airport on his arrival rather
than me. She represented all that within himself he knew
to be slipping away, that at eighty-two a man still wants to
hang onto: youth, vivacity, energy. What, in comparison,
did I, a contemporary, have to offer, with disabilities, no
matter how carefully concealed, reminding him of his own?
No, I wasn't hurt, just saddened a little.

I turned away from the phone with just a little feeling
of relief that I had not had the stimulation of him since last
Wednesday, not having to pay for it today with the complete
mental and physical exhaustion in which his last visits have
left me. This was the core of my sadness--too sharp a realization, brought out by my feeling of relief--of what old age
does to one.

Surely I would once have been hurt. When I, too, had had youth and vivacity I had had the strength to glory in those mentally exhilarating visits. Would I have relinquished them with the ease of today? I am sure I would not.

Accepting the Throne Symbol [pp. 184-5]

The whole program ["The World of Carl Sandburg"] was well conceived and carried out [March, 1960]. There was an enthusiastic audience and the papers later carried rave reviews. At the intermission a line of movie folk came down the aisle to speak to Carl, some to get books autographed. Groucho Marx, Edward G. Robinson, Kirk Douglas, were among the long-famous actors whom Carl knew, but when the new, younger faces appeared Carl could not remember their names.

At the end Carl himself was brought onto the stage. Bette Davis led him to the throne seat which had been placed back of the performers, a sort of symbol with his guitar upon it and a pile of books on the dais where it stood. Once Carl would have violently objected to this throne symbol, but then he took such things in his stride. The standing ovation given him by the audience when he rose from his throne to speak was something I am sure he had long been accustomed to.

The reception behind the stage afterward seemed unending. The house lights finally began to blink to put us out. Bette Davis was a surprise. I had expected her to look young in her beautiful costuming on the stage, but, even when I was within a few feet of her, she did not look more than thirty. She must have been fifty-five.

When we gathered later for our supper at a restaurant nearby, the official family of the production and Carl's friends, there were just twelve of us. The supper was only mildly interesting. Too many talked at once. There was no general conversation; no one person held the floor. Talk was mainly about the show's astonishing reception in 58 cities to date. It had been given to packed houses everywhere. Financially and in every way it was considered a success.

Enjoying Hollywood [pp. 186B-8]

On July 18th [1960] the Los Angeles newspapers were
full of Sandburg's arrival. I had skipped reading the papers
that day. I had no awareness that Carl was in town. I had
gone to bed early to read, as I often did, when at nine
o'clock the doorbell rang. My housekeeper answered it and
presently appeared in my bedroom. "There is someone here
who you will want to see," she said smiling.

"Oh no-oo!" I protested.

"Oh, yes! It's Mr. Sandburg!"

I was out of bed before she left the room. I got into
an all-enveloping house-coat and, without stopping to even
run a comb through my hair, I rushed out into the hall.
Carl greeted me warmly. Then to my surprise and a little
to my consternation (considering my appearance), he turned
to the man who was with him. "This is George Stevens,
who's got me out here to do some collaborating with him.
He picked me up at the airport today, and tonight I insisted
he bring me over here. Strange, as often as I've written
this house number and been in this house, I couldn't give
him your address--yet I directed him straight to this house."

"Do come and sit down," I said, leading the way into the living room. "But tell me, Mr. Stevens, how in the
world did you come to choose this old agnostic to help you
with the life of Christ?"

In his answer he parried my question, "I've been
after him for more than two years."

"On the drive over I've been telling Stevens a lot
about you," Carl went on, "and all my happy connections
with this house. It has always been a stimulating place in
which to work. Just now, Lilla, on account of the daily
conferences to which I'll have to be accessible, they've put
me up in a suite in the Bel Aire Hotel. We'll see how it
works out. But I'll be phoning you. You'll be hearing from
me."

Before they left, an hour or more later, Carl asked
me to show Mr. Stevens some of my Japanese netsuke collection, little masterpieces of wood and ivory carving, mini-
ature sculpture, one might call them. I brought out my best,

of course. Mr. Stevens had apparently never seen them before and his interest seemed genuine. He struck me as a
very genuine person in every way. "We want to come back,"
Carl said in leaving, "some day when we have more time.
I'd like Stevens to see some of your other collections. "

     It was heart-warming that Carl had wanted to come
over to see me on the very first night of his arrival. But
many weeks went by before I heard from him again. The
papers, however, were full of his activities. He was a
natural for newspaper stories. They made a lot about his
refusal to stay in a $45 a day suite in which 20th Century-
Fox had put him up. They compromised by setting him up
in a $25 a day one. There appeared an amusing article,
headlined, "Carl Sandburg Scores Hit in Funny Iconoclastic
Press Conference. " There were articles about his meeting
the movie stars.

     There were constant appearances on television. Reg-
ularly I was being called up by my family and my friends,
"Watch television, Channel so and so. Your friend, Carl
Sandburg, is on. " It was evident he was enjoying Hollywood.

Working and Playing [pp. 190-2]

     [The year] 1961 must have been a busy time for Sand-
burg. He was working on the film ["The Greatest Story
Ever Told"]. Through the papers I continued to hear of his
activities and a number of times watched him on television.
It was apparent that he flew back and forth across the country a good deal. After my one bid for an invitation to drive
over to his hotel, I never mentioned it again. I was deeply
curious to know something about his work. Once, when
some books had arrived here at the house to be autographed,
he asked me to bring them over. I could gather from the
glimpse I had of his large room that there was much activity
going on. His desk and tables overflowed as at his home
with books, papers, and memoranda. There was a corner
where one could see that his secretary, Betty, an old family
friend (whose last name I never knew), was kept busy. The
place must have begun to look like home to him. There
were no orange crates nor apple boxes to extend his library
space, but he had purchased some crude unmatching shelving to hold the overflow. I knew he must have given forth
his orders that no cleaning woman was to touch that orderly
chaos. There was work being done, plenty of it.

One day he called me up to say that at his request
a film he had missed was being run off for him in one of
the studios. "Bring anyone you want to. I could have
forty guests if I wanted." It was too late to get up a party,
but I did have some house guests whom I took. Besides my
own group there were only himself and a few people from
his studio. The film itself was one that I, too, had missed,
"Treasure of the High Sierras." Carl greeted me with expressive warmth, and we talked briefly at the end of the
show. "Mr. Sandburg is evidently very fond of you," my
friends said. "Yes, I think he is," I laughed.

He sent tickets to me when he received an honorary
degree at U.C.L.A. He asked me to drive out to the hotel
and go with him and "Betty" to a Bowl concert. Kostelanetz,
an old friend of his, was the conductor that night, and we
met for cocktails at the apartment of the Kostelanetzes in
the Beverly Hilton before the program. It was a popular
program, and the Bowl was sold out. Our progress toward
the Bowl, Kostelanetz driving, was a bumper to bumper
affair. The opening moment of the program arrived, and
we were not there. Kostelanetz leaned out the window and
hailed a policeman directing traffic. "I'm conductor at this
affair at the Bowl tonight. We are late. Aren't there any
side streets through which you could guide me there?" The
policeman assured him there were not. "Anyway they can't
begin until you get there," he added.

At last we arrived. Our car was seized and spirited
away at the entrance to the stage. Two attendants made an
opening wedge for us through the throng of people to the
Kostelanetz's box. The preliminaries began. The announcer
declared that there was a very distinguished visitor among
the thousands in the Bowl that night. Would Carl Sandburg
please rise and let the spotlight reveal him for a moment?
We were immediately blinded with light, and Carl, a somewhat surprised Carl, rose and bowed to thunderous applause.

Kostelanetz gave a spirited conducting of a program
of the almost-too-familiar. At one point, Carl leaned
toward me and whispered, "There seems to be almost everything here except 'Turkey in the Straw.'" I had long realized
that Carl, musically, had been steadily becoming a more sophisticated person. "Come with us next week," he added as
if in apology, "to an all Tschaikowsky program."

This first evening at the Bowl there was a gathering

afterward of many of Kostelanetz's and Carl's friends in the
room behind the stage which perhaps is still dubbed "the
green room." There was much gaiety and laughter. I
missed most of it in the babble of voices and for the most
part sat in a corner with Betty and drew out her interpretations. Once or twice there was silence created around
Carl, and he got off one of his amusing stories. Carl held
his own in any group.

On the night of the second program there was a
supper party afterward at one of the palatial estates in Bel
Aire. After both these occasions, when I picked up my own
car at Carl's hotel (Betty had been our chauffeur from
there), Carl seemed as unaware as I that at three in the
morning I had a long drive before me alone through dark
lanes and untraveled streets before I reached the traveled
safety of Sunset Boulevard.

The Kennedy Autographs [pp. 193-4]

Toward the end of 1961 the papers announced that
in the book department of one of our stores Carl Sandburg
and Harry Golden would autograph the recent biography written by Golden [see his reminiscences on page 152] of Carl
Sandburg. I had read the book, in fact Carl had seen to it
that the publishers had sent me a copy. I had a feeling
that a biography, written by a close friend, had best be
written after the man was gone. Otherwise, it loses a certain objectivity. I am sure many other biographies of Sandburg will be written.

I had heard nothing from Carl for some time except from the constant newspaper reports of his doings and
his appearances on television. I decided to surprise him
at this autographing session. I found myself in a long line
of people streaming toward a table where Sandburg and Golden sat busily autographing the books. After each signing
I saw Carl look up from his writing, smile and make some
comment. I waved to Betty who was standing on the side-
lines with the store manager. She pointed me out to him
and they both laughed. What she said (as she told me later)
was, "Watch that woman in the blue coat. She is an old
and dear friend of Mr. Sandburg's and he isn't expecting
her here. There will be some little explosion when she
reaches his table!"

The line of autograph seekers inched along and at

last I stood at his desk. Carl was speaking to Harry Golden
at the moment and didn't look up as I held out my book.
When he took it I held onto it firmly and he glanced up.
Surprise and laughter! He jumped up from his seat, reached
out both arms and grasped my shoulders. He shook them a
little as he exclaimed his pleasure at seeing me there. We
talked only briefly for there was that long waiting line behind me.

"I'll be seeing you. Has a big package of books
come to the house for me?"

I assured him the big package of books was standing in my front hall. He passed on my book for Mr. Golden
to sign with some comment which I did not hear. I joined
Betty then on the side lines and we chatted for a while. She
explained about the box of books. A friend of Carl's and of
the Kennedy's had sent on Carl's books to be autographed
for the Kennedy family for Christmas. They were to be
sent to the White House after inscriptions had been written
in each of them. Sandburg would be over shortly to inscribe
them, get them repacked, and have them picked up by Express.

Carl seems to have been kept busy with work and
play by the studio. He knew the books had come. They
arrived the last of November. There were frantic letters
to me from the sender in New York, a telegram and finally
a phone call. Had the books been inscribed by Carl and
sent on to the Kennedy family? I phoned Carl just once
about the sender's deep concern.

A few nights before Christmas Carl arrived with
a secretary--not Betty. This woman unpacked the heavy
box (there must have been twenty books), and Carl went to
work on them. The person's name to whom each was to
go was on a slip of paper inside each volume, all members
of the Kennedy family. I sat beside Carl on the davenport
as he wrote. After each inscription he handed me the book
to hold open for a moment lest it blot. I got my chance
thus to read the inscriptions. They were very fine. Carl
would sit for a few moments in thought before he wrote.
The inscription for the books which were to go to President
Kennedy (they were the war years of Lincoln) was given the
most thought and came out like an inspiring prose poem.
These were moments when my admiration for him was deep.
I kept silent until he was all through. He complained be-

cause there had been no book for Caroline. "I wanted there
should be a book here for Caroline." I remembered Carl's
particular fondness for his children's books.

Somehow he and the secretary got the books out
into the car. He had arranged to have someone pack and
send them for him.

[Mrs. Joseph P. Kennedy had decided to give her
children signed and autographed copies of books by well-
known authors (according to a letter, dated Feb. 9, 1977,
from Gertrude Ball, Joseph Kennedy Enterprises, New York).
Thus, late in 1961, seven books were sent to Sandburg for
autographing.

Six made Christmas presents for the following:
President John F. Kennedy, Robert F. Kennedy, Mrs. Sar-
gent Shriver, Mrs. Patricia K. Lawford, Mrs. Stephen E.
Smith, Senator Edward E. Kennedy. One was for herself.

Mrs. Robert F. Kennedy, McLean, Virginia, has
verified the possession of the book sent her late husband.
The undated inscription made reference to friendly greetings
of "years ago," but Mrs. Kennedy could not throw light on
that friendship. Sandburg mentioned Robert Kennedy's wisdom and courage and signed himself "fraternally."

The inscription for Jean Kennedy Smith, dated
1961, simply offered her Sandburg's good wishes. Both
Eunice Kennedy Shriver and Jacqueline Kennedy Onassis
verified their possession of the autographed books but could
not find them to give the text of the inscription.]

A Last Talk with Carl [pp. 194-6]

[After Sandburg dispatched the books for the Ken-
nedys,] he came back to talk for a while. He told of the
many activities which had kept him busy and of his great
admiration for George Stevens. He was now within a few
hours of taking a plane for home.

"In some way your book on Chinese snuff bottles
has gotten away from me, Lilla. I must have loaned it to
someone who did not return it. Do you have another available?"

"Remembering the many books of your own which

have come my way, I can assure you another of mine is
available, " I laughed.

When I returned with it, he asked to once more
have a look at my netsuke collection. "Why don't you write
a book on these?" he asked. You might even make it a
children's book and make the legends and stories so often
shown in the netsukes delightful to them. "

It would never have done to have told him that
there had been many books written of netsuke. He would
have reminded me that there had been hundreds of lives of
Lincoln before he wrote his own.

He looked at each beautifully sculptured piece with
careful scrutiny. "Haven't you got some a feller could buy?"
he asked. "I'd like to get a few, and no one seems to know
where any can be found. "

"I've a few duplicate types put away for a dollar
to take. Would you like to see if there are any among them
you would like? You were certainly a wood-carver in some
previous incarnation, " I laughingly reminded him. "These
wouldn't haunt you so if you weren't. "

He looked the netsuke over and selected two of
the very best. The prices for the dealer had been put on
each, and he pulled out his checkbook. I wanted much to
give them to him. I hesitated, but they were so expensive.
I thought of his $3600 for six poems to Playboy, of his
$3000 for a 20-minute reading of the Lincoln Preface, of
the heavy sums his agent now demanded for television appearances. As for me, for these coveted things of beauty,
I drove an old car; I made a good suit do for more than
one year; I did without many things to save for them. This
expenditure meant little to Carl; yet I took his check re-
luctantly. I wondered if he was getting them for Margaret,
who loved them as much as he did. Christmas was only a
few days off.

"No, not for Margaret, not just yet anyway.
These will join for a while the little carved dog which has
sat on my desk at home ever since you gave it to me years
ago. "

We said goodbye as though we were going to meet
again next week.

How well it is the future is hidden from us. I was
never to see Carl again.

Paula's Secret [pp. 196-8]

The year 1962 went by without any communication between us. I learned only through the newspapers of his
activities, his programs in different cities, and his television appearances.

A new volume of verse, Honey and Salt, was to come
out on his birthday in January, the following year, 1963, but
I was receiving none of the experimental versions of the
poems to be published in it as I had often done in former
years. I began to wonder if he were angry at me. It was
years since there had been such continuous silence.

Two things might have vexed him, my expressed
criticism of his selling poems to Playboy, my withheld permission that he have access to my voluminous journal now
in the archives of the New York Public Library. There
was a forty year release on it. Carl had asked me to give
him a note to the librarian, breaking the agreement for de-
ferred release of it in his own case. What he wanted to
see, of course, must have been the portions relating to himself which he was sure were among them. They would be a
help in writing the second volume of his autobiography, Ever
the Winds of Chance. But how could I? To find these portions he would have to read through much not written for
anyone's eyes. Yes, how could I?

These two possible rifts in our friendship troubled
me. His new book, Honey and Salt, would soon be out.
He had been so thoughtful in the past to see that my Sand-
burgiana was as complete as possible. If I did not get
Honey and Salt, I would know there was something wrong.
The date of publication came, the weeks went by, and I got
no book. I was certain now that he was angry at me. It
was the first time in almost fifty years [1919-1963] that I
had failed to get any newly-published book of his, even the
expensive four volumes of the Lincoln War Years. Disturbed by this certainty of Carl's displeasure, I wrote Kenneth Dodson. His answer came:

Dear Lilla,
        Letha and I think you should know some things

which may at the same time sadden and comfort
you. Yes, we got an inscribed copy of Honey and
Salt but if Paula had not reminded him we are
sure the book would not have come. This only
means that the C. S. of 1963 is a very much older
man than your friend of years past. He is getting
very forgetful and confused about details.

Kenneth Dodson's letter went on to describe Carl and
Paula's visit with them at the time of his program at the
Seattle World's Fair. His condition was such at that time
that Paula--against his will--made the trip with him. Both
Paula and his agent had advised against that appearance, but
Carl had to prove something. He had to assure himself that
he could still do it. On the drive to Seattle from the Dodsons' home, he asked if they were going to the Dallas airport and what he was supposed to be doing there anyway.
As Dodson described it, he and Letha and Paula sat in that
audience close to heart failure when Sandburg came out onto
the platform, not knowing what would happen. But there
was a capacity audience. They rose and greeted him with
thunderous applause. They took him to their heart as they
always have in late years before he uttered a word. He
fell into the old groove. He got away with that program
magnificently. He read his poems as no one else can read
them. He ad libbed between his readings with nonsense that
delighted his hearers. At the end the Dodsons and Paula
had difficulty in extricating him from the crowds that wanted
to meet him, speak to him, get his autograph.

Back at the Dodsons' home he stayed in bed for
twelve hours. At no time during that visit was he the night
owl he had always been. His mail lay unread, as I suspect
it does at his home today.

No, Lilla (Dodson continued), you and I will
never get letters from Carl again, but be assured
he has no anger against you. Whenever your name
came up he spoke of you with deep affection.
Paula tries to keep the Press and the merely
curious away from him. She does not want his
failing condition known. So, dear friend, please
understand, join our conspiracy of silence, and
keep Paula's secret.

PART II

Sandburg [standing, second from right] at Cornell College (Iowa), December, 1920. [Photo courtesy of Carl J. Allen. By permission.]

A HOST OF ENCOUNTERS

Introduction

This writer knows of perhaps a dozen persons (in addition to Mrs. Perry) who could prepare book-length manuscripts about Carl Sandburg. The number of persons who had brief but exciting experiences involving him is probably incalculable but certainly great. The second section of this book includes a sampling of encounters with Sandburg, describing his exciting personality and often throwing important light on his life.

The Funeral and Remembrance Rock*

When I went to Boston University, I sort of lost contact with him, because he wasn't in Boston much. Then when I was transferred here (California), I found out he was doing his column for an editor I knew.

Then I saw a story saying he was coming to Los Angeles.

I wrote to him at Harbert. I told him I was at Lynwood and wanted to know how we could get together.

In February, 1942, I was sitting in my study at five minutes to eleven on Sunday morning, meditating, as was my pre-sermon custom. The phone rang. Carl's voice said: "I am in Laguna Beach. There are some girls from the University of Chicago here. They have lost their mother. They want to have the service at Laguna Beach, and they want me to conduct the service. I thought you should conduct the religious part." When I agreed, he told me the service was the next morning at 10 and told me where to be.

---

*Interview with Carl Allen, February, 1970.

When I got there, he was in the guest house with the
Bible in his hand, in case I did not get there. We conducted
the service together. Sandburg got up and talked about the
mother of the girls, including what a good mother she had
been. Then he took his guitar and sang three Negro spirituals, including "Go Down, Moses."

I then took him to his home in Lynwood, stopping on
the way so he could cash a check.

[Sally Kaye, whose mother's funeral is referred to
above, had lost her father in the same month. Sandburg
wrote Allen from Harbert in March 12, 1942, to say that
she was still in the wilderness of that experience. He commented on her rapport with her parents and her vulnerability.
He suggested she was possibly too sincere and imaginative
to be an English teacher.]

The next year (1943), Allen went to Mrs. Per-
ry's, where Sandburg was staying. "I am waiting for Metro-
Goldwyn-Mayer to send a car to take me to meet the president," Sandburg said.

A Lincoln with a chauffeur came for him. Sandburg
and Allen went in and went to the studio. He went in and
sold the privilege to use Remembrance Rock.

He gave Allen something to read while he waited.
He came out and said he had signed a contract for $100,000.
He said they agreed to "buy the book."

He talked about living with the Allens. He wanted to
have the contact but did not do it.

He had lived with some people the last year he was
in Los Angeles. Allen did not know who they were.

Sandburg Hypnotized Him*

Since the introduction of printing and the fatal development of reading among the middle and lower
classes of this country, there has been a tendency

---

*Anonymous, "Carl Sandburg: Poet and Newspaper Man,"
An Institute of Modern Literature. Lewiston, Me.:
Lewiston Journal Co., 1926.

in literature to appeal more and more to the eye
and less and less to the ear, which is really the
sense which, from the standpoint of pure art, it
should seek to please and by whose canons of
pleasure, it should abide always.
    --from Oscar Wilde's The Critic as an Artist.

Life goes faster than Realism; but Romanticism is
always in the front of Life.
    --from The Decay of Lying, Oscar Wilde.

Carl Sandburg made me turn to Oscar, Friday evening, after I arrived home close to midnight from the stirringly emotional evening with him at the Bowdoin Institute
of Literature and Poetry.   Perhaps it was need of a counter-
irritant; perhaps it was a lingering desire to pursue Mr.
Sandburg's definition of Art a bit farther.   Perhaps it was
because Mr. Sandburg with his guitar is not, as was Oscar
Wilde, in Oscar's days of greatness, clad in pallid greens
with a pale lily in his button-hole.   And I wanted a heart-
depressent.

And so I sat far into the night and read The Decay
of Lying; Pen, Pencil, and Poison and the Critic as an Artist
and finally got back to a middle-class normalcy.   And so to
bed.

* * *

Sandburg makes newspaper people proud because he
is a product of its life and its action.   Like the rest of
these poor devils, he has been a long, long time coming
into his own, being today an impulse to a Renaissance of
American Literature and Poetry.   The Sandburg trail is
coming to the end of the various and devious paths of its
Pilgrim's Progress.   For him the trumpets will surely
sound on the other side, if not sooner.

He is hardly 50 years old; he was born in 1878, but
his hair is grayed like that of all hard-working editors
and true poets, and it falls down straight and untroubled on
either side of a countenance that looks like the Great American Desert--arid, sun-browned, silent, swarthy.

He came in full "act in one" for he has long been a
favorite recitalist of American folk songs with audiences the
land over, bringing his guitar which he strums in minors

and handles as one croons over a tired child. He dressed
to his part also--Smoke and Steel; Corn Huskers, Rutabagas,
Chicago of the South Side cutting out North Shore boulevards.
No "soup and fish"; no white tie and white vest; but dressed
like a city editor during a tough week on a murder-mystery.
He could not have sung as he did or talked as he did, with
half the unction, in an evening suit. For Sandburg has been
an adventurer; a man of action and a student of men. Just
to look at him suggests songs by the firelight of lumber
camps, hoboes gathered about the red-flickering camp fires
in the "lots" behind freight train yards, roar of cities, silence of deserts. For Sandburg has been a soldier, editorial writer, foreign correspondent for newspapers, lecturer,
and singer.

He said a bit before he went to the platform--"I
bring this guitar and I sing my songs because it rests me.
I like this part of it; I do not like the speaking. I don't
want to break down as do so many other workers. These
songs I love. "

The audience was the largest of the series. The
stage was filled with students and extra chairs filled the
hall almost to the stage. Among the audience were Mr.
and Mrs. Robert Frost, Mr. Frost having returned from
Orono where he spoke to the students of the University of
Maine.

Mr. Sandburg referred to Mr. Frost once or twice
in his talking.

Now, I wish I could convey a fairly truthful and pictorial appreciation to our readers of the sort of a talker
that Mr. Sandburg is; for he is unique.

It is his voice, chiefly. Mr. Frost who spoke on
"Vocal Imagination" the evening of the opening of the Institute, should travel with Mr. Sandburg, and use him to illustrate the emotions of the voice as a spur to imagination.

It is all in minors--this voice, meaning by that not
exact musical notations but the croon and the lullaby of a
voice. His level speaking is majestically powerful and
effortless. It is a voice of rich and mystic music. It had
the touch of nature about it--music of seas on shores, the
aeolian harp of pine-trees; an organ note in a cathedral
where colors from stained-glass windows play on sculptured

friezes; fireside and folk-song notes all through it, as though
men and women who had suffered were telling stories to
make themselves more placid.

       Now this is not "bunk" on my part. I shut my eyes
and that is how it left me. I am not to blame that Sandburg
hypnotized me. Darn him--that is probably what he means
to do to anybody that he can get. Once or twice, if he had
called me to the stage to go through a common variety of
hypnotic act, I should probably have come along. If he
should read me more Jazz Fantasy, I might even try to
dance--which would be pathetic. That is what may be called
Vocal Imagination and Romanticism and using a particular
sense of hearing to convey Poetic Art. And Oscar Wilde
says that "lying, the telling of beautiful untrue things about
nature is the proper aim of Art." It is like what Sandburg
said in his exquisitely delivered tale of the old "Lie" about
the man who took the colored silks from the woman's work-
basket; closed them in his hand; opened his hand and lo! the
room was full of the most beautiful of butterflies. And then
sweeping his hand again into the air he took the butterflies;
again closed his hand and put them back again into the work-
basket, as skeins of colored silks.

       You don't believe that! Well, you do not have to be-
lieve it; but God pity you if you don't love it, just the same;
God help you if you despise that tale. How do you know?

       So this voice--it makes me dream and wander in
strange places and see. And that was what Carl Sandburg
was showing us--and he has surely a very proper organ for
playing upon. Experience has made him perfect. He is no
tyro in public speaking--nor is this anything but art, re-
fined. He stands just outside the reading-desk; puts his
hands in the pockets of his old suit and plays the part of
what he has been--porter, scene-shifter, truck-handler,
harvest-hand, college-man, newspaper man, poet-laureate
of the industrial classes, emotional democrat, with a face
as immobile as a "broken gargoyle."

       Mr. Sandburg attempts no analytical definitions of
his subject "Realism and Romanticism." He evidently trusts
an intelligent audience to perceive, by illustrations. He
told several very clever humorous stories to illustrate his
points; he interjected a bit of suggestion of fondness for
Longfellow and he told us that Bill Reedy liked Longfellow
and believed that he was equal to Keats in certain ways.

And when a newspaper man quotes William Marion Reedy, he is quoting from the Holy Writ.

About all he said about Realism and Romanticism was conveyed in two stories. One was about the wise men who condensed for the King, all of the books of the world. The King had no time to read. They condensed, first, all knowledge into a book. Then by orders of the King they put it into a page and then a single word. That word was "PERHAPS"--Maybe.

Nothing real is real--it MAY be real. That's all we can say about it. Perhaps.

Romanticism, he illustrated by the story we have mentioned about the silks and butterflies. Pure romanticism--how lonely is life; how empty if we can not believe in it. If you can believe that story of the butterflies, you are an honest-to-God romanticist. It is worth believing.

This led to Mr. Sandburg's definition of Art which seems to be with him a matter of personal taste. Two men were coming from Tia Juana which is a smart town where the ponies run, down beyond the Mexican border out of San Diego, and they were talking about a horse. One man said, "He may be all you say, but I can't SEE him." That's it. Debate as much as you like over matters of poetry, taste, sculpture, music. If you can not SEE it, it is not Art for you. That's the gist and summary of many a noisy controversy--one man SEES it, the other does not.

Again, what is art? Here Mr. Sandburg talked baseball--Ty Cobb, where Ty Cobb began to decide when he could slide to the second and what kind of his eleven different sides he would make. Ty says, "I just slide."

What makes a pitcher good one day and no good another? It is what they call "Smoke." If you have "Smoke" when you deal in Art, you get it over--if you do not have Smoke, you may have all of your technique and fail as does the pitcher batted from the box.

Then Mr. Sandburg began to talk about reading his poems. With deliberation and fantastic meanderings of speech, he approached his readings--just like a wanderer. He said that he would read from Chicago Poems. They were like a railroad in Texas--the Houston Eastern Western Texas,

not much of a road, despite its long name.   The people
down there take its initials H. E. W. T. and call it "Hell
Either Way You Take." His poems reminded him of egging
houses in Chicago.   They take a carload and in the morning
they are all classified.   Special, Extra Fresh, Fresh, Special Fresh and Eggs.   And then they take the Eggs and grade
them as Checks, Spots, and finally "Broke."

Then he began to read.   Then our eyes began to open
and we lost ourselves in the measureless labyrinths of Mr.
Sandburg's voice and in its strange melodies and nuances.

He read "Jazz Phantasies" so it sounded like an or-
chestra; the "Wilderness" in a creepy sound, just as Jim
Riley used to do his "Ghosts will get ye;" "Kahoots," like
a gangster; the "Young Sea," like the sound of many waters.
And so on and on and on.   I loved his fragment on Nancy
Hanks and the coming of the young man-child Lincoln, as
Nancy sat by the fire--it will always be remembered.

Mr. Sandburg could read

> Simple Simon went a-fishing
>   For to catch a whale,
> And all the water that he had
>   Was in his mother's pail

and you would feel damp all over and see fishes in the eye
of the mind.   I can't read his verse that way from the book.
He ought to go along with every copy.

Then he sang with his guitar--just as a hobo would;
as a lumberjack; as the gang around the furnace fires would;
as the rough world with its singers always sing--and others
sit mute by the wayside while the stars shine and the winds
laugh.

And it made me hunger.   And it made me dream.
Hunger and dream for company of these waifs of genius,
singing by camp-fires; world-wide, by sea and shore; toss-
ing their bundles of colored silks into the air; to make them
butterflies about the heads of children of Romance.

And alas--and this may be the best of it after all--
again reaching out their hands into the star-shot dusk, to
catch their butterflies and put them back again into their
work-boxes as silks.   This is Romance and Romance is a
memory of Carl Sandburg.

Alfred Harcourt Remembers Carl Sandburg*

During his long and successful career as one of the
most colorful and dynamic figures in American book publishing, Alfred Harcourt discovered and promoted many authors.
A number of them became his personal friends. But in all
his years as an editor and seller of books no man impressed
him more than Carl Sandburg, America's great biographer
and poet. Sitting on the shady terrace of his fine Montecito
home, the retired publisher recalled many instances from
his 40-year association with Sandburg.

"When Sandburg had completed his writing of The War
Years--the last part of his Lincoln biography which grew
under his hands and took him sixteen years to complete--
he came to me and said 'Well, Alf, here it is--a scroll and
a chronicle.' And then he made two extraordinary comments. He said 'I feel sure that now that it's done no one
need look anywhere else for any authentic piece of Lincolniana except for verification' and he added 'it's the first six
volume biography about a man whose father couldn't write
his name, written by a man whose father couldn't write his
name.'" [Harcourt has here confused a remark often made by
Sandburg, correctly cited on p. 37 of this book.] Harcourt related the following when asked to tell of his most memorable
encounter with the author who first attracted his attention
when his verses appeared in Poetry magazine in 1910:

"At that time I was a traveling salesman for Henry
Holt and Company and whenever I hit Chicago I would visit
Harriet Monroe whose Poetry magazine was reflecting a
true renaissance in American poetry. During one visit I
was impressed by some of Sandburg's poetry which she
showed me and told her to send him to me when he was
ready to publish a book," the publisher recalled.

In 1912 Miss Monroe's assistant, Alice Corbin Henderson, paid Harcourt a visit and brought him the manuscript of "Chicago Poems." Harcourt was greatly taken by
the hefty volume which exhibited all the aspects of the 34-
year-old poet's talents.

"I've always thought it to be a mistake for young
poets to start publishing with a slender volume. Here was

---

*Anonymous, "Alfred Harcourt Gives Interesting Account of
Carl Sandburg's Life," Santa Barbara News Press, 1951. By
permission of the publisher.

somebody whose collection would make a dent in the mind
of the indifferent public, " Harcourt said.

Soon editor and author became fast friends and when
Harcourt started the firm Harcourt, Brace and Company,
Sandburg became one of his most promising authors.   Since
then this firm has published the Lincoln biography, An
American Songbag, Rootabaga Stories, The People, Yes,
Good Morning America and many other Sandburg works.
Harcourt has gotten to know the author as "an ingrained
newspaper man, a scholarly biographer, a wandering trouba-
dor and somewhat of a hobo. "

Sandburg's parents came to the United States in
1873 and settled in Galesburg, Illinois, where he was born
five years later.   His father was a railroad blacksmith.
Carl attended school until he was 13 when he struck out on
his own and left home to work in brickyards and potteries.
At 17 he was working in the West on railroad construction.
From these experiences came the inspiration for parts of
the Cornhuskers, Smoke and Steel and Slabs of the Sunburnt
West.   After a while he returned to Galesburg and his milk
route and in 1898 he enlisted as a volunteer in the Spanish-
American War.   A number of people in Galesburg had spotted Sandburg as an extraordinary youth by then and when he
returned from the war they helped him to enter Lombard College.

According to Harcourt it was his milk route that got
Sandburg's lifelong interest in Lincoln started.

"Every morning Carl would take a shortcut across
one corner of the college campus where he would notice a
tablet commemorating one of the Lincoln-Douglas debates,
with a quotation from that debate which had taken place on
this spot.   He became so absorbed in it that he read all the
debates and began collecting items regarding Lincoln's life
which he was to picture so vividly later on. "

When the two men met, Sandburg was working as a
reporter on the Chicago Daily News, married to Paula
Steichen, sister of photographer Edward Steichen and members of an extraordinary family, from Luxembourg, who understood what Sandburg was up to.   He was writing a daily
feature, "Carl Sandburg's Notebook, " living in Elmhurst and
writing quite a bit of poetry.   Soon he was telling some
lovely American fables to his daughters Margaret, Janet
and Helga.   There was one telling of a skyscraper about to
have a child and another about "a village where nobody

worked unless he had to and nearly everyone had to. " These story tales were collected in Rootabaga Stories and Rootabaga Pigeons, which have become children's classics in this country.

"After we published Rootabaga Stories I received the only request for advance royalties which I have ever gotten from Carl. He asked for six hundred dollars so he could buy the lot next door. He wrote 'it has the biggest lilac bush in Illinois and a sunny lying-in corner where our cat has her kittens, '" Harcourt recalls.

In 1923 Sandburg told his publisher that he would like to write another book for children. Harcourt, who knew of his interest in Lincoln, suggested that he write a life of Lincoln for teenage boys and Sandburg agreed that might be fun and returned to the Middle West planning to write one volume of about 400 pages.

"Three years later we received the manuscript of the first two volumes of Sandburg's biography, which deals with Lincoln's early years. Incidentally, they contain the finest description of the way poor white trash lived in Kentucky and Illinois in the early nineteenth century I have ever come across. Sandburg submitted no title and it was Van Wyck Brooks who suggested that we call these volumes 'The Prairie Years. ' It is the most amazing picture of a man who was fundamentally influenced by his environment and then stepped out and reshaped it, " Harcourt says.

A prominent magazine offered to run excerpts from the biography for a consideration of $3500 but when its editors had concluded negotiating with Harcourt and his staff they agreed to back their faith in Sandburg's work to the extent of $30,000.

"Carl was in Texas and I never felt better than when I sent him the telegram telling him the good news. He wired back: 'Now I can ride the pullmans and I don't always have to look at the right hand side of the menu. ' It did not take us too long to convince booksellers that this Midwestern newspaperman and poet was really doing a beautifully written but scholarly biography of a great figure. Carl had left most of his financial worries behind and he moved into a new home on the shores of Lake Michigan complete with a third story studio and library. Paula began breeding goats on this field. When the family moved to the plantation at Flat Rock, North Carolina, where it still resides, the goat business moved right along with it, " Harcourt says.

In 1939, Sandburg completed his "Lincoln job" and in
the first year Harcourt, Brace, and Company sold over
40,000 six-volume sets.   The authenticity of his work with-
stood all challenge and the beauty of his writing made his
book one of the most widely read biographies of our time.
He continued to write poetry and tried his hand on a novel,
called Remembrance Rock, which Harcourt characterizes as
"an account of the American idea."

Only last week the publisher received a letter from
his 73-year-old friend who is now "slowly getting together
his autobiography" which, in Harcourt's opinion, will be a
"noble book."   In the history of American letters few associations have been so fruitful and heartfelt as that of these
two men.   Hearing Harcourt talk about his friend, Carl Sandburg, gives you the feeling of having met this great American
writer face to face in the sort of friendly, informal chat they
had so often.

An Intense College Audience*

I sat up in the balcony peering down upon a pool of
heads.   College heads, with college educations inside them.
Carl Sandburg appeared and the heads gave a show of hands.

From the first the heads gave attention, these blasé
heads with the college educations inside them.   Not only
attention but concentration.

His voice was rich and deep.   It drawled now and
then, but it was musical and colorful.   He stood hands in
pockets, his feet together, swaying slightly.   No gestures
to illustrate what he said; only words and his voice, Carl
Sandburg's voice.

The heads leaned forward expectant, interested.   This
was unexpected; this quietness, this force.   The man was
peculiar, but he was colorful.   He was telling of beauty and
of the appeal which must be innate or there is no response,
and the heads leaned a little forward.

Then came poems, dropped one by one, like mist
particles in a rolling fog, and they fell on the heads.   Some

*Anonymous, Oregon Daily Emerald, Feb. 25, 1923.

of the poems split lights into many lights; and some of the
poems shot sparks like yellow-hot iron. The poems settled
on the heads and the heads smiled and grew wistful. But
there were other poems, shake-up poems, drops of hail;
they fell on the heads, and the heads grew stern.

Rootabaga stories, the balloon country, the bibbed
pig country, the Blue-Wind boy, and the heads smiled and
laughed and showed dream-emotions, and answered the end-
ings sea-breaker-like. "Phantasies," the heads turned to
each other to say, "but ... yes, phantasies."

Mammy songs, hobo songs from jungles; the heads
who knew the south, and the heads who had beaten their way,
leaned forward.... Lumpy throats and laughing throats the
heads had, as they listened to the voice, Carl Sandburg's
voice, create little visions, great visions, longings.

Today, tomorrow, Carl Sandburg can come and tell
all over again his stories and his poems; his blood, vulgar,
steel, pictures, jagged, sober poems; his chimera stories;
his American songs of the cotton fields and the railroad
rods. And the heads, the blasé heads with the college educations inside them will go back to hear with him, to see
with him, and to feel with him.

The Return to Lombard College*

Carl Sandburg's bow at Lombard College Chapel is
one never to be forgotten by those who attended. The reader
was introduced by President Tilden, who expressed the sentiment of the audience when he said that Lombard was more
than proud to be honored with so notable a personage, and
one who had graduated from that institution.

To pave the way for his unusual, yet true poetry,
the author cited a number of humorous incidents of people
who had not been able to interpret other people's thoughts.
He told of one lady, who, after reading a poem of Browning's, which she was not quite able to understand, asked
the author just what he meant. He replied: "When I wrote
it I knew what it meant and so did God. Now only God
knows."

---

*Anonymous, "Carl Sandburg Reads Poems to Large Audi-
ence," Lombard Review, March 14, 1921.

The first poem on the program was the poem from his latest publication, Smoke and Steel. This was a most picturesque piece of poetry, and was read with sentiment and feeling that only the author could express.

Probably the most enjoyable was a "Jazz Fantasia." This was undoubtedly due to the fact that it was light and the more easily understood. All the instruments of a jazz orchestra were brought in, in a very unique manner, and the inflections of the reader's voice were so true to the real thing that it made one want to dance.

The city of Kalamazoo portrayed in poetry was re- markable, and was so horrible that in fact the audience felt as though they did not wish to hear any more, but as the verse stated, the very same things were going on in one's own surroundings and one could marvel to think they had not been noticed in that way before. Mr. Sandburg in all his poems shows what a wonderful and keen observer he is of human nature and what an extraordinary power of inter- preting human nature he has.

The program was closed with the last poem in the volume Smoke and Steel entitled "For You," which very fit- tingly concluded this hour of entertainment.

While Mr. Sandburg's poems are deep, so to speak, they are not above the people's heads. They are unusually written in a finished style of his very own. Some of them seem terrible and gruesome, but when analyzed they are found to be wonderful and true interpretations of humanity.

A very large number of city people attended this pro- gram which is probably the finest ever given in Galesburg.

Life at Lombard College*

Ye editor and scribes decided to take a little time out to publish an American Magazine story. For truly, the story of Carl Sandburg is one of a rise to fame from some- what unpropitious beginnings. The students of Lombard

---

*Anonymous, "Carl Sandburg's Life at Lombard," Lombard Review, March 8, 15, 22, 29, 1928. By permission of the publisher.

should be interested in his life story, for it is not every
small college that boasts such a famous alumnus.

Over a quarter of a century ago, Carl Sandburg,
then called Charles August Sandburg, returned to his home
in Galesburg after having seen active service during the
Spanish-American war in Porto Rico. His traveling companion, another doughboy, declared his intention of entering
Lombard. Although Sandburg had in his possession little
more than a hundred dollars, he too decided to enter the
local college. He gave fifty dollars of his money to his
parents and with the remainder, he paid part of his tuition
at Lombard, a tuition quite small when compared with that
of today.

Sandburg's early education was received here, there,
and other places, and we can well believe that much of it
was acquired in the school of experience, for he left school
at thirteen, not to return for any length of time until his
college days. During the following six years, he engaged
in various occupations. In rapid succession, he drove a
milk wagon, was porter in a barber shop, scene-shifter in
a cheap theatre, truck-handler in a brick yard, turner ap-
prentice in a pottery, dish-washer in Denver and Omaha
hotels, and harvest hand in the Kansas wheat fields. Surely,
this was a varied and unusual career for a youth not yet
twenty years of age.

Then came the war with Spain, and as we would have
expected, Sandburg, perhaps on the lookout for adventure,
joined the forces and served in Company C, Sixth Illinois
Volunteers. He saw active service with the infantry.

Sandburg's college days are highly interesting, but
we know fewer anecdotes of his life than we might wish for.
Of his social life, we know practically nothing. We can
only wonder if some nights may have seen him and his
guitar serenading some fair Lombard Hall damsel. We
can only wonder how often his studies were neglected. However, the reporter had no occasion to write of the "happy
culmination of a college romance. "

His first duty as a Lombard student was that of bell-
ringer at Old Main, his duty being to ring the bell indicating the five-minute period between classes. Legend has it
that he spent this interval between bells reading old theo-
logical books then stored in the belfry. He undoubtedly

read some of the books now stored in the back stage rooms of the chapel.

Bell ringing was one of the jobs by which Sandburg worked his way through school. Besides other odd jobs around the campus, he worked at the Brooks Street fire department.

Carl Sandburg won distinction while in college as an athlete. He was a baseball player and a basketball player. These, too, were good old days of championship basketball teams, although we often think of Paul J. Schissler as bringing championship athletic teams to Lombard. The students of today can admire Sandburg for his playing in a [basketball] game against Knox, the score of which was 19 to 9. The Review says: "The small score of Knox is due to the magnificent guarding of Sandburg and Andrew who allowed neither forward a single point." Sandburg played guard as a rule, although he was sometimes used as a forward. In 1901, he captained a championship team. His baseball accomplishments were just as note-worthy.

Sandburg's scholastic record at Lombard is not the record of a "grind," a "bookworm," or even of a Phi Beta Kappa. If he burned the midnight oil, it was probably to "cram." At least, his grades in the college files are barely average, maybe somewhat low. However, he never flunked out of college, contrary to a consoling tradition that has grown up on the campus. He remained in school four years, but was never awarded the coveted sheepskin. For some reason, the college did not see fit to reward his efforts with that usual token of commendation and approval that follows the completion of four years of collegiate study.

Sandburg was not a scholar, although he probably profited more from his studies than certain other students who basked in the approval of the faculty. He passed in all his subjects with grades averaging from 78 to 90 except the subjects of mathematics and sociology. As for mathematics, he simply seemed to lack a mathematical mind. At the end of his freshman year, he attempted to enter West Point, and he successfully passed all the physical and mental tests with the exception of arithmetic. In sociology, there was a different explanation of his failure. He received no grade in this subject. The incident related is that at one time during a classroom discussion he and Doctor G. R. Kimble, the instructor, engaged in an argument, and a violent discussion. Suddenly, with head held high, Sandburg proudly stalked out of the classroom and never returned. This is the reason he never completed the course.

Carl Sandburg was connected with the Lombard Review, a monthly publication, describing himself as a "live college journal," almost throughout his college days. He was business manager during the years 1899-1900, and he served as the Editor-in-Chief in 1901-1902. The "terrible Swede," as it is said he was called, could have been given these honors because of his literary ability.

For the most part, Sandburg's first writings were labor discussions, and discussions of sociological principles. His knowledge of sociology seems extensive although he did not receive any credit in his college course. In February, 1900, he published "E Pluribus Unum," a labor discussion. Sandburg showed a sympathetic interest in the workingman, and an interest in the strike phenomenon.

His sociological interests were the basis for his oration, "A Man with Ideals," with which he won the Swan contest of 1901, an oratorical contest which is still held annually and is now known as Swan-Lawton contest. James E. Bowles was the winner of second prize. "A Man with Ideals" is a tribute to Ruskin, a eulogy to the moralist, artist, and reformer. Ruskin's sympathy with the workingman aroused in Sandburg an admiration for him.

Among the other works of Sandburg which we find in the Review is a column called "Sidelights." It contains mostly comments on happenings of the day. In scanning the Reviews we uncovered an article on literature signed Charles August. This was undoubtedly written by Sandburg, in those days when every Review article appeared above a signature. He says: "One thing is certain. That is that the best and highest literature is opposed, stands against greed and capacity of commercialism. That literature which will be handed from father to son five hundred years from now will surely not be that which when boiled down is 'Do others or they will do you.'"

In the Review's joke column, we find an interesting sidelight on Sandburg's college life. It is entitled "Statistics--Some Lombard Celebrities." Charles Sandburg, age--Augustan; Nationality, Schnorky; Pet name, Cully; favorite study, College annuals; manner, calm; chief virtue, pipe;

pastime, jollying; ambition, "Foot-prints on the sands of
time. " A little prophetic perhaps.

While at Lombard, Sandburg began to understand
literature, and to think in terms of literature. In addition
to his Review associations, he had many other literary con-
nections--Professor Philip Green Wright, a professor of
English and Astronomy, organized a Poor Writers' Club at
Lombard. Sandburg and two other students met at his home
on Sundays and talked about literature, read and criticized
their own works, and in general made literary progress.
Professor Wright was a writer of ability, and one can read
many of his poems in the Review. He is also remembered
as the composer of the words for the "Lombard Hymn, "
and the "Lombard Field Song. " Two years after Sandburg
left Lombard, Professor Wright published some of the poems
and prose writings of Sandburg in a pamphlet, "In Reckless
Ecstacy. " One critic has said these poems, with the exception of the rimed verse, are strangely like the work of
the mature Sandburg in feeling, and could be placed without
incongruity in the midst of any of his later books.

Sandburg left college without his degree in the spring
of 1902. In 1923 the college honored him by giving him the
honorary degree of Doctor of Letters. In this score of
years, Sandburg had accomplished much, and had become
justly famous. In fact, he is rated by critics as one of the
six greatest living writers of America.

The story of these intervening years is by no means
uninteresting. Sandburg's occupations after leaving college
were almost as varied and numerous as those of his early
life. He worked as advertising manager of a department
store; for a time, he was in politics; then he was successively a salesman, pamphleteer and a newspaperman. As
a safety-first expert, he went to the various factories,
wrote articles on necessary safety precautions, and came
before various conventions of manufacturers as a lecturer
in accident prevention. In the meanwhile, he was still Carl
Sandburg, the poet, and even in his busy business world he
did not lose his former ambitions.

It was not until 1914 that Sandburg became known as
a poet. He received one of his first recognitions when
some poems, a part of "Chicago" were awarded the Levin-
son prize of two hundred dollars. That is to say, Sandburg
did not "arrive" until he was thirty-six years old. Then,

his works met with a storm of protest. He met more than
his share of the criticism aimed at the "new" poetry. But,
he has weathered all storms of protest, and his true greatness is recognized. Cornhuskers, and Smoke and Steel are
among his best works. Sandburg entered another field when
he published his now famous biography of Abraham Lincoln.
It is a great biography of a great man, and as such has
been highly praised.

Carl Sandburg's latest book is The American Songbag,
a book in which he has gathered together the original songs
of Americans, songs gathered from every walk of life. The
ballads are those of the pioneer, the cowboy, the negro, the
farmhand, and the railroad worker. It is an interesting collection, and the first in its field.

We offer no criticism of the works of Carl Sandburg:
we merely stand back, admire them, and to some extent, at
least, appreciate them, although it will probably be left for
succeeding generations to truly realize his greatness. "Fog,"
is a favorite among his poems.

A Soviet View: People's Poet of America*

These days a meeting with Carl Sandburg, an outstanding American poet, follower of Walt Whitman's traditions in modern American literature took place. Sandburg
came to this meeting with a guitar: at home he is known
to be a specialist in folklore who has collected and published
many songs. Hundreds of times Sandburg performed these
songs for workers, farmers, students and schoolchildren.

Here he is singing in the Central House of Men of
Letters. His voice sounds so youthfully and passionately,
that it is difficult to believe that the poet and singer is now
81 years old.

I'm going to sing to you a song which has been sung
by me for seventy years, he says.

A chord of the guitar sounds and we hear a song
familiar to us having been performed by Paul Robeson.

---

*Anonymous, Literature and Life (U. S. S. R.), Aug. 5, 1959.
p. 4.

This is a Negro spiritual, "Let My People Go," and Sandburg sings it with a special feeling.

The Negroes composed it when they were slaves, explained Sandburg. This is a song about the faith in a better future. Probably, serfs in Russia used to compose similar ones.

Sandburg's words, his songs and brilliant verses--everything proves the fact that in the person of the elder of the American poets the Soviet people have a true friend and this is but natural. Carl Sandburg was born on January 6, 1878, in a worker's family. When a boy of thirteen he began earning his livelihood. He used to be a worker, a farmhand, a door-keeper and a newspaperman.

Sandburg got to know his country perfectly well, her common toilers, workers and farmers. And in poems he speaks on behalf of common people, he struggled to protect their rights. Sandburg took an active part in the working movement of the U. S. A. and in the years of WWII he was in the first ranks of antifascists.

The collections Chicago Poems, 1916, Fog [sic] and Steel, 1920, Good Morning America, 1928, The People, Yes, 1936, and others brought him the world fame. Abraham Lincoln's biography written by the poet is an outstanding work in the democratic literature of the U. S. A.

Like Whitman, Sandburg writes free verses known for the vivacity of a genuine conversation, rich folk humour and keen observation. The most particular feature of the poet's writings is the combination of folk wisdom with the vital problems of the contemporaneity.

A Loving Handshake*

Just as Carl Sandburg was impressed by the many children he saw and spoke to last Thursday, so the children were impressed by the tall, white-haired poet.

As Sandburg left the new school named in his honor

---

*Anonymous, "Handshake Conveys the Message," Independent-Register (Libertyville, Ill.), Oct. 22, 1959.

following an assembly in the Carl Sandburg school auditorium, a young boy, crowded in with dozens of other curious youngsters, looked sad for a moment as he realized he would not get the poet's autograph. Sandburg, to avoid the fatigue that would follow unlimited autographing, had said earlier that he would sign only books in which his work appeared.

This particular boy did not have the necessary book.

Then the youngster was heard to say, "I'll be just as happy if I shake his hand."

Eighty-one-year-old Sandburg caught the remark as he passed, turned and stooped down to shake the boy's hand.

Both smiled happily.

Another still younger boy, Charles Valkenaar, 7, son of Mundelein trustee Charles E. Valkenaar, related the poet's genuine interest in the many children who cheered and greeted him that day.

Charles, a second grader at Washington school, went home Thursday afternoon and told his father how Sandburg had shaken his tiny hand.

"Daddy, do you know, Mr. Sandburg loves children?" the boy said.

"Did he say so?" Valkenaar asked.

"No, but he does," answered the seven-year-old.

A simple handshake had told him so.

Sandburg Among the Swedes at Rockford*

Wooden carvings in the Erlander Home museum impressed Carl Sandburg so much Wednesday that he paid an unscheduled visit to their sculptor, Axel Farb, 1602 S. 5th St.

For half an hour, Sandburg sat and praised the wooden

---

*Anonymous, Rockford Morning Star, April 9, 1959.

carvings, depicting Swedish men and women. Given two of
them, he promised to put them on the mantel of his living
room.

"I'll write about them and their maker, " Sandburg
promised. He said he would have his wife's brother, Edward Steichen, one of America's foremost photographers,
take pictures of them. He also promised to have his daughter, who had "gone in for painting, " see what she can do in
"painting these two. "

"What a visit in Rockford I have had, " Sandburg said
as he left the Farb home.

At the Erlander museum, where a group of 80 officers and directors of the Swedish Historical Society of Rockford gathered with members of their families to greet him,
Sandburg dedicated a bronze plaque on which is inscribed,
in his handwriting, a tribute he wrote in 1954 to the early
Swedish and Norwegian pioneers of the middle west. He
asked for an enlarged copy of the plaque and said he wanted
to frame it and place it in his study in Flat Rock, N. C.

Explains Tribute

Sandburg said that he thought principally, when he
wrote the tribute, of the record of the Swedes and Norwe-
gians in the civil war and of how they cleared the wilderness and put the plow to fields not touched for thousands of
years.

"The Swedes are extravagant in vitality and strength
when there is something to be done, " he said.

As a postscript to his talk at the museum, the poet
and Lincoln biographer said some people ask him, "What
kind of a Swede are you?" He said his answer is, "I'm
one of those Swedes who until he was three or four years
old knew such words in Swedish as 'mjolk' before he knew
'milk' and 'far' and 'mor' before he knew 'father' and
'mother. '"

In private conversation, he turned often to Swedish
to express himself.

David W. Johnson, president of the Swedish Historical Society of Rockford, presided at the museum. Herman

G. Nelson, past president and currently secretary, expressed
the society's thanks to the visitor for having written the tribute.   Dr. Leland H. Carlson, president of Rockford College
and host to Sandburg on his visit, praised Sandburg as one
who had "deeply inculcated himself into the hearts and affection of the people of this broad land of ours. "

Students Present

The Swedish club and classes at East High School
were represented by Chris Vale, president, David Westin,
vice president, Lynette Carlson, and Sandra Berglund, 1958
midsummer queen.   They received autographs from Sandburg,
who also autographed copies of his books.   He was shown a
scrapbook about himself and remarked, "Half of what's here
I haven't seen before. "

He was greeted by Adolph Germer, who knew and
worked with Sandburg years ago in Milwaukee.

"Your museum is marvelous; I only regret Galesburg
doesn't have one, " Sandburg said.   Sandburg was born in
Galesburg and his home there is maintained as a museum.

It was when he toured the museum, interesting himself in almost every item, that he spied the Axel Farb carvings and remarked spontaneously:

"This man is an authentic artist.   I'd like to shake
his hand. "   He continued to praise one figure after the other
for their lines and simplicity.   "They are cartoons, " he
commented.   The museum has 14 of the Farb carvings, including two he made a month before his 87th birthday.   He
is now 94.

At the Farb home, Sandburg and Farb exchanged
their own brands of humor:

"Will you do a wooden head of me ?" Sandburg asked.

"I'm too old, " Farb replied.

"There are people who say I have a wooden head, "
Sandburg said.

"I have another, " Farb answered.

When Sandburg tenderly held the two wooden figures--

one of a man and one of a woman--that Farb gave him,
Sandburg said.

"This is done by a young man."

"Me?" Farb asked.

"Your heart was young," Sandburg said.   "Your bones
may have been sixty years old, but you saw these people
through youthful eyes."

Farb had said he didn't start carving until he was 60,
after he had retired from farming.

Referring to the grin and mouth of the woman figure,
Sandburg commented, "That took a delicate touch.   I have
met sculptors who are hypocrites."

"This man," Sandburg said, "has had a good life ...
one of laughter; that I can see."

Sandburg was surprised to hear that Farb had used
only a common pocketknife for his work.   He commented:

"If I had ever gone to prison for twenty years, I
would have been a wood carver and a good guitar player."

Farb also showed Sandburg a carving of Lincoln.
Sandburg said, "That belongs in the museum.   There is
something authentic about this Lincoln when you know about
Farb."

Every so often, as he looked at the figures he fondled
lovingly, Sandburg would burst into hearty laughter.

"They make for good laughter," he told Farb.   "It
was good for your head and heart to make them."

Referring to a Swedish cartoonist and artist about
whom Sandburg said he wants to write a book, the poet told
Farb, "You do in wood somewhat like what Albert Engstrom
did in drawing, black and white."

Farb told Sandburg that when he quit farming, he
made a visit to Sweden and brought back two carved figures.
"When I came back and had quit farming, I had nothing to
do, so I started to carve these figures."   He said he fed
the furnace with quite a few before he was satisfied.

"In my mind they are like the people looked when I grew up," Farb said. He told Sandburg, "I have read your works but I never expected to see you."

Sandburg Was a Wonderful Experience*

Dear Editor:

Fog came on little cat feet Wednesday and brought us Sandburg. I'm inclined to think that the majority of people have based their conceptions of the poet on just that line about fog, judged from what I've heard around and about. The way to criticize a work of art--and it applies to the artist, too--is to determine what it sets out to do, then decide whether or not it does it, or so I have been taught. When you put Sandburg through that kind of a mill, he comes out whole--did for me, anyway. For did he not pose (most poets do pose a little) as a man of the people? And wasn't he speaking to "The People, Yes," in their idiom for the most part, and in their interests? The proverbs were folksy, banal, someone said, but aren't a great many people that way, and weren't they miles away from E. A. Guest folksiness? I realize, of course, that few of us will come out and say we are People. The Mills of the gods grind exceeding fine.

The casting of a wet blanket on Mr. Sandburg's program frankly incenses me. Perfection, we've discovered by this time, is impossible. Our education cuts off its own nose if it doesn't teach us primarily to realize the good parts in people, then to recognize their flaws and forgive them at our own discretion. I don't advocate unqualified praise, but to find flaws first of all shows a kind of negative appreciation. If we are merely to pick at our intellectual food, can we expect much in the way of nourishment? A seasoning of tolerance wouldn't be at all amiss.

Every written word's a kind of propaganda, of course, but I trust it's not shouting from a soap-box to say that Sandburg was a wonderful experience.

---

*Anonymous, Mills College Weekly (Oakland, Calif.), March 1, 1938.

A Negative View in Charleston*

Carl Sandburg, whose free verse has been the fore-
front of the rebel group and whose sonorous and melodious
[voice] persuades even the enemies of free verse to be at
peace with him, declares in round terms that men, and particularly poets, must act in the living present, that the
poet's duty is to paint a picture of the world around him
and to try to preserve the spirit of the age in which he
lives.

This, unfortunately, was not said in time, and great
poets, unguided, have failed to do it, beginning with the
author of the Book of Job, coming down by way of Homer
and his Odyssey, Virgil and his Aeneid, to Dante and his
Jolly Hell, Milton and his Satan, Shakespeare and his Caesar. It may be that covertly each of these notable men of
genius depicted the earth and its situation in his age; but
this is not transparent. Yet, says Mr. Sandburg, in accord
with his statement, our new age must necessarily and inevitably be interpreted by a new poetry, for the old is hope-
lessly out of joint and totally dislocated. "A few poets," he
says, "still persist in writing of such long forgotten things
as the hearth and fireside, not recognizing that these ancient
poetical institutions are now obsolete and replaced by hot
air furnaces and steam heat radiators."

Wait till I put some more coal on my fire and I will
take this matter up!

No doubt, beyond that parlous groove along the earth's
arched stomach known as Mason and Dixon's line, the hot
air furnace and the steam radiator and Rootabaga stories
have taken place of the old gray stone hearth and the ruddy
fireside of Grimm's Fairy Tales and Aesop, his fables.
But, praise God with honest reverence, south of that line
there still exist, here and there, in many a town and thriv-
ing city and almost universally throughout the countryside,
still hot and happy, both hearth and fireside. And when the
day is ended and the night is wafted downward like a buzzard
in its flight toward the bleak roosting tree, we, down here
in Dixie Land, maugre the many drawbacks which appear to
beset us in the eyes of our Northern poets, still may put
our feet up on the fender, stir the red hot embers to a

_____
*Anonymous, The State (Charleston, S. C.), Feb. 18, 1923.

blaze, chuck on a chunk of riven oak, and fall into a toasted
peace, envied by registers and by radiators ... the while
our perfectly satisfactory families peruse the evening paper,
the youngsters cypher busily upon the lessons of the approaching morrow, the good wife reads the recent books which
teach us how uncomfortable all the world should be were it
just like Chicago; and, there, in our obsolescence and an-
tiquity, archaic as our good green hills and wholly out of
fashion, we still read classic volumes of standard English,
and from the bottoms of our hearts are grateful that our
life is not as their lives who have no hearthstone and no
open fire, but must find their inspiration in piped heat.

A Swedish Impact*

        His influence on us youngsters when we as the group
of Five started in 1929 was very important. I saw his
name first in 1923 in an anthology called "Ungt hav" (Young
Sea) after a poem by Sandburg. It was translated by the
Finnish-Swedish important poet, Elmer Diktonius. The
poems by Sandburg translated in the book were "Steel-
prayer, " "Joy, " "A Little Bit of Love, " "Anna Imroth, "
"The Washerwoman, " "Under a Telephone-pole, " "Style, "
"The Last Answer, " "Baby-toes, " "Window, " "The Fog, "
"Statistics, " "Choice, " "The Dog's Head, " "Testament, " and
"The Young Sea. "

        I read these poems over and over again and about
1928 I tried to translate some of his poems. It was harder
than I had originally thought it would be. My comrade
Artur Lundkvist was more successful, and he wrote his first
article about Sandburg in the Stockholms-Tidningen for December 2, 1938, and I think it was one of the first good
articles about Sandburg in a Swedish newspaper. He has,
too, as you know, translated many of Sandburg's poems, and
he has written a sort of portrait of Sandburg, which is published in his third book of poems, called Svart stad (1930)
or "Black City. "

        [A translation of Lundkvist's poem, "Sandburg, Amer-
ika, " prepared by the author from a rough draft by Asklund
follows:]

---

*Based on a letter of March 24, 1970, from Erik Asklund.
Translated and edited by the author.

I am coming from wheat-tossing prairies,
from morning-red hills and evening-blue valleys,
from cities, streets, rivers, timberforests--
    I am bending over the typewriter
    and am taking down the hoarse laughter of Chicago.

Give me a thousand sheets of paper!
I have the pockets filled up with people's lives,
I have a sunrise of love and a night of hate,
I have rain and wind for a hundred springs and autumns,
I have two blue oceans and a handful of small glittering--
    twinkling morning stars--
    I am bending over the typewriter
    and am taking down the hoarse laughter of Chicago!

Two years later, 1932, Artur Lundkvist wrote a book
of essays, called Atlantvind or "Atlantic Wind," and the
first part was called the "Modern Literature of America,"
an introduction, and there he began with Whitman, and after
a short introduction (8 pages) there came as the first poet,
Carl Sandburg (12 pages). This was a very good essay (it
seemed to me) with many translations of Sandburg's poems.
I think it was the first serious treatment of Sandburg's work
in Sweden. This book was very important for the identification of a new generation of writers in Sweden.

To me Carl Sandburg was one of the most important
poets in the States. I loved him and I still love him. I
am not a poet, you see, but I and my comrades under this
first years in the thirties have got many influences from
Sandburg, first of all Lundkvist himself and our comrade
Harry Martinson. But it would take a lot of time to point
out where you can find lines, pieces of Sandburg's style, in
their poems. But they are there. Sandburg gave us a
free, open sight, so to speak; he was very close to life, he
was (and is!) very warm. He came from the common people
(like we did!) and I guess his book, The People, Yes! was
a sort of signal even to us. We were very sorry that Sandburg didn't receive the Nobel Prize, and we did all we could
for him in that way, but in vain. And now when I am reading his books, I feel the same warm feeling that I had in
my youth....

Sandburg Blasts Forces of Darkness*

The greatest figure in the field of American letters today was talking.... "That 'Chicago' poem of mine was a literary curiosity. It thumbed its nose at those New Yorkers who say Chicago has no culture. To me, those snobs have always represented the Forces of Darkness--the Forces of Evil. They are tearing down our cultural and social standards. They got us into two world wars. They have much to answer for."

His tired eyes lighted up as he added: "For many years I never agreed with THE CHICAGO TRIBUNE on anything. Now I thank God that it can and does maintain its integrity--on the subject of books, on everything worthwhile. For that I am deeply grateful."

Carl Sandburg will be 80 years old next January.... But he still has the mental vigor he was endowed with when he was writing the life of Lincoln, the midwestern poems, the volumes that brought him world-wide acclaim. And he still sings those ballads and strums that guitar.

"You're busy, and I refuse to take up your time," I said over the phone.... "I'll give you twenty minutes," he replied. "The postmaster will tell you how to get here." ... "I'll stay ten minutes," I said.... The visit lasted nearly an hour, and I didn't ask half the questions I wanted to ask him.

The road from Flat Rock wound over the hill to his 260 acre farm, fenced for the 72 goats prized by the poet-biographer. Clad in the garb of a farmer, Carl greeted me from the porch of his 120 year old home. It was one of the many reunions we have had thru the years.

My first question was the one inevitably posed to authors: What are you working on now? He's working on a continuation of his autobiography--a sequel to Always the Young Strangers. He hopes to deliver the manuscript to Harcourt, Brace next winter, for publication the following fall... "Originally it was to end in Chicago in 1912; now I

---

*Frederic Babcock, "Sandburg Blasts 'Forces of Darkness,'" Chicago Sunday Tribune, July 28, 1957. Part 4, p. 6. Reprinted, courtesy of The Chicago Tribune.

plan to go beyond that. " Next question: What's its title?
Answer: Ever the Winds of Chance. Q.: May I announce
it in my column? A.: Sure.

"But I have another book coming out in the mean-
time--November fourth of this year," he continued. "It's
to be called 'The Sandburg Range,' and it ranges over just
about everything I've ever written: poems, songs, biography,
autobiography, children's stories, excerpts from such things
as Remembrance Rock. It even includes the song, 'The
Colorado Trail.'" ... "Never heard of it," I said.... "Then
I'll sing it for you," he said. He did, in his resonant baritone.

"I have lots of time for writing down here in North
Carolina. No phone calls, no crowds, the way there were
in Chicago and later up there in Michigan. And I have
plenty of time for reading. I've read Jessamyn West's To
See the Dream three times. Have you?

I thought her The Friendly Persuasion was terrific,
and I got a wallop out of the way she described, in To See
the Dream, how she, a Quaker, had gone to Hollywood and
helped turn The Friendly Persuasion into a movie....

"But To See the Dream is much more than that,"
Carl protested. "Her philosophy of life, her love of nature,
her sincerity, her craving for the simple life, shine all the
way thru it. She's my candidate for the successor to
Thoreau." I looked and listened, and wondered if Carl
himself wasn't the logical successor to the author of Walden.

He was not so complimentary about some of his and
Jessamyn West's contemporaries. He mentioned two of them--
both highly touted by the critics and both obsessed with sex-
ual themes--and said they were no better than Mickey
Spillane.... "But don't quote me," he cautioned. "Somebody might think I envied them for their ability to pull in
the cash."

Reaching back a quarter of a century, he chuckled
over some introductory remarks I made as master of ceremonies at a dinner in honor of Oswald Garrison Villard, the
then editor of the Nation. That was in the days before so
many of the professed liberals had gone illiberal and totalitarian and intolerant--if not intolerable. My remarks were
an attempt at both humor and sarcasm, and Carl commented

at the time: "Babcock writes and talks like a gargoyle, not
knowing whether to laugh or to cry. " Then, kindly soul that
he was and is, he sent me a note of apology.... Now he
was chuckling once more. "I still have a clipping of that
speech of yours, and I still say it was darn good. " ...
"You're entitled to your opinion, " I said.

It was time to go. "Have you seen Ben Hecht's new
book on Charlie MacArthur?" I asked. He hadn't, but he
would like to. I went to my car, reached into my brief
case, and pulled out my copy of Charlie. I wrote in it:
"Stolen by Carl Sandburg with the permission of his friend,
Frederic Babcock, " and handed it over to him. His booming laugh was the answer.

As we drove away I turned to my 11-year-old daughter. "Now you've met one of the finest authors of this or
any other time, " I told her. "That's something you can remember all the rest of your life. " ... "Yeah, " she said,
"but don't forget: I met Sinclair Lewis when I was only
three years old. " I'll not forget either meeting ... And
neither will she.

Lesley Frost's Introduction*

[Some time shortly after September 15, 1925, Carl
Sandburg went to Pittsfield, Massachusetts, to give a reading at The Open Book, the store operated by Robert Frost's
daughter, Lesley. When she introduced him, this is what
she said:]

There are two kinds of beauty in the world always:
two kinds in almost direct contrast; two kinds that have always had and always will have each its own apostles and
followers. They are the smooth and the rough, the polished
and the unpolished, the finished and unfinished, the cut and
the uncut, the civilized and the primitive. Nature has them
in the flower and the precious stone: one perfected to the
utmost detail, breathtakingly outstripping the imagination;
the other hidden and hinted at, showing a gleaming facet
here and there; firing the imagination to do things with it.
The human race has them: one the cosmopolite, completed
and well fitted to every slant of living and learning; the

---

*By permission of Lesley Frost Ballantine, New York, N. Y.

other the person who clings to simplicity, simplicity of
manner of dress, of speech, of adventure. And because of
these opposing forces in man--art has them: the glory in
finished detail of a Botticelli, the suggestive uncouthness of
a Cezanne; the glittering sophistication of an Edna Millay
against the rough word settings of a Carl Sandburg which
allows for contrasted flashes of idea, of feeling.   There is
no question of ultimate choice between the two kinds. Of
course we all tend to one form or the other: we like to
model life or let life model us, to reform or let well enough
alone, to change the setting of a flower or leave it standing,
to handle jewels in the rough or shape them and back them
with filigree gold, to listen to music swung a thousand
miles through space, or to the dark laughter of a Sherwood
Anderson, to fashion a pattern of words or let the words be
almost maltreated by the idea; to go into a garden of Eden
or into the diamond mines of the Klondike.   Tonight it happens to be the latter.   Mr. Sandburg gives us the jewels
out of the earth, out of the rock! Or rather in the rock,
and you, the hunters after beauty fall forward on your knees
suddenly over a flash of color of light of idea of meaning.
Mr. Carl Sandburg.

          [After the appearance, Sandburg wrote (letter of No-
vember 9, 1926) Lesley that a "glint" of her was in a poem
he had written about New Hampshire.   After Remembrance
Rock appeared in 1948, he inscribed a copy for her in
friendship and admiration.   Recently Lesley Frost Ballantine
told the writer that she and Sandburg were "excellent friends,"
as were Sandburg and Frost.   She noted "certain contradic-
tions" and the fact that they were both "hardheaded."   Good
humor, caustic wit, and mutual and permanent respect were
inter-mixed in the relationship as she saw it.]

A San Francisco Enthusiast*

          From a correspondent who lives in San Francisco
I've had a letter protesting against the treatment accorded
the American poet, Carl Sandburg, during his recent visit
here.   A week ago, Sandburg gave a reading from his own
work and, in addition, sang a group of American folk songs
to his own accompaniment on the guitar.   I don't know

*John D. Barry, "Sandburg in San Francisco," San Fran-
cisco Call, March 26, 1921.

whether it's true, as my correspondent says, that Sandburg
"ranks as one of the three or four most distinguished American poets"; but I do know that during the past few years
his work has been widely published and has been warmly
commended for its unconventionality and its vigor.   Though
I didn't happen to hear him at his single public appearance
I did meet him and I found him an extremely interesting and
agreeable man, seemingly free from self consciousness and
with a spontaneous humor.

     From what my correspondent says and from what
other people have told me it's plain enough that Sandburg is
an unusual figure on the platform. He's among the few
writers who read as well as they write and he has a dramatic gift and a singing voice that enable him to be effective in
public.   It's a pity he didn't have a larger audience than the
"175 people who were fortunate enough to attend the reading"
and that he didn't attract more attention from the newspapers.
As a matter of fact, the scant notice that is complained of
with some warmth must have been a great disappointment to
him and to the friends he made and to all poetry lovers
here.   I agree, too, that a man of his quality ought to have
been heard at the university.   "Under the circumstances, "
says the writer, after referring sarcastically to the general
neglect,

          all that I feel justified in doing is to plead rather
          bleakly that the newspapers and universities really
          ought not to rub it in.   Not justice I ask, but
          charity.   San Francisco, which has a lively and
          sentimental memory of such figures as Stevenson,
          Bret Harte and Frank Norris, likes to pride itself
          on being polite to the servants of the arts.   In the
          present instance I cannot help feeling that such
          pretentions have not been sustained.   Why not?
          How did it happen?   There are plenty of people
          in San Francisco, in the newspapers and in the
          universities across the bay, who are quite aware
          of the significance of such men as Sandburg, in
          whose work America is struggling to be conscious
          of itself and to express itself in terms of art.
          Why did they not bring about some public expres-
          sion of that awareness?   When San Francisco has
          answered that question it will at the same time
          have found the answer to another haunting query:
          Why do San Francisco poets leave home?
               In conclusion, I am left with the melancholy

reflection that San Francisco's discourtesy will in
all probability go unpunished unless it is capable
of feeling the pangs of remorse for a lost opportunity. Indeed, I look forward with keen anticipa-
tion to Sandburg's next volume in which San Francisco may find itself quite undeservedly immor-
talized in a beautiful companion piece to 'The Sins
of Kalamazoo. '

It's plain enough that any one who can write so point-
edly and so eloquently is himself a writer. I suspect that
he's a poet, too. Most of us can sympathize with his state
of mind. But I don't think he's wholly fair. The trouble
wasn't altogether due to the neglect of the people who might
have known better. It was due in large part to mismanage-
ment. Sandburg came for his first public appearance here
virtually unheralded. Gifted as he is, he hasn't as yet
reached the place where people spontaneously proclaim his
coming. Besides, the poetry reading public is small and
comparatively uninfluential. Even those lovers of poetry in
San Francisco who knew Sandburg through his published work
didn't know anything about him as a reader and as a singer
of American folk songs. They didn't know that he was
"equipped with a beautiful voice" and that he used it "with a
mature artistry" and that he could sing admirably "the
finest trophies" gathered "during his long period of adventur-
ing as a wanderer and laborer. " If he had stayed here
long enough to make his talents known I believe that they
would have won appreciation. As every one who has had
anything to do with public works is aware, there's an immense amount of ability that is lost to the world simply because it isn't properly managed. I happen to know that
during the brief visit here Sandburg made at private houses
several displays of his gifts and had a huge success. The
chances are that when he comes back he will get a much
better reception. But he could hardly expect to win acclaim
before his merits became recognized. His reputation as a
poet wasn't sufficient to draw a big audience. Many a poet
with ability to charm through the printed page has been a
bore on the platform. Sandburg is so fortunate as to pos-
sess the qualities that, even if he couldn't write at all,
would make him a popular entertainer. Some of his new
friends here have been urging him to make an appearance
in vaudeville and some others have been shocked by the
suggestion. A poet in vaudeville--what an idea! Well, it
seems to me an excellent idea and I wish it might be carried out. There are plenty of people in popular audiences

that would be interested in the kind of thing Sandburg does
and a man of his quality would do much to improve the tone
of vaudeville entertainments.

It's true, I believe, that San Francisco is considerate
of the people described by my correspondent as "the servants
of the arts" and takes pride in her association, not only with
Stevenson, Bret Harte and Frank Norris, but with a great
many others. ... As for the question why San Francisco
poets leave home, it may be answered that those of them
who do leave home seek the wider opportunities provided in
the East. But they don't all leave home by any manner of
means. In spite of a dazzling social success in London,
with showers of appreciation from many of the greatest
people in the English speaking world, Joaquin Miller preferred to live close to San Francisco, where from the
heights behind Oakland he could survey one of the most
glorious panoramas in the whole world, including the San
Francisco bay. George Sterling, by many people regarded
as California's foremost poet, lives in San Francisco and,
for this reason, isn't denied the recognition that is his due.
And Dr. Edward Robeson Taylor is one of the few poets
that ever had the distinction of serving as the mayor of an
American city. Perhaps this writer didn't happen to know
that we once had a poet mayor.

However, the truth remains that most of us who are
interested in people with talent have missed something in
failing to hear Sandburg. When he comes back I think he
can feel assured of a better reception. The chances are
that he won't come back this year. Just now he's in Salt
Lake City and headed for the East. But there will be
another tour, perhaps next season. When he returns it
won't surprise me if he becomes the rage, not simply because he's a poet, but because he has something to offer
in the way of entertainment that is interesting and dramatic
and altogether unique.

21 Hours with Carl Sandburg*

My 21 hours with Carl Sandburg began on November
14, 1960, at Fort Wayne's municipal airport. I was calling

---

*Letter from Robert B. Belot, Fort Wayne, Indiana. By
permission.

on an insured and was informed that Mr. Sandburg was
somewhere in the terminal building.   Hoping to see this
famous American, I inquired as to his whereabouts and was
informed that he was in the rest room.   Entering the rest
room, I opened the conversation by asking him if he was
Carl Sandburg.   He replied, "Yep, taking a pee."   Noting
that he had two pieces of luggage, I offered my services,
which he accepted.   He subsequently asked me where he
could find a taxi, and I suggested that he allow me to take
him to Fort Wayne.   On the trip to downtown Fort Wayne,
he noted that he was there to make an appearance on behalf
of the Art Academy.   He suggested that I take him to a hotel that would be in close proximity to the location of his
appearance.   In the course of his conversation, he noted
that he did not care for hotels.   On this statement, I offered my home, which he immediately accepted.   It is interesting to note here that there was no reception committee
at the airport, since he did not announce his time of arrival.

There was little conversation during the auto trip to
my home.   In our home, he asked to use the telephone and
he called his wife in North Carolina.   After the phone conversation, he suggested that we contact a representative of
the Art Academy in order to confirm his arrival in Fort
Wayne.   It was approximately five p. m. and he was scheduled to appear at eight.   About the only information that he
had was that his appearance was to be held in Fort Wayne.
Our dinner consisted of ham and eggs, which was on his
request.

After dinner, he changed shirts, and we left for his
appointment.   Prior to arrival, he asked me to bring his
coat to him at eleven, indicating the time that he wished to
depart from the Academy.   My wife and I were permitted
to watch his performance, which consisted of dialogue and
songs.   There was a reception following and precisely at
eleven I presented him with his coat, and we left shortly
thereafter.

We returned home, arriving at approximately eleven-
thirty.   We sat at the kitchen table until three in the morning.   During this time, Mr. Sandburg controlled the entire
conversation.   He discussed many topics.   He talked about
his farm and his seventy-two various animals.   He was
quite humorous, laughing greatly at his own jokes.   There
was a wide range in the tones of his voice, from the very
mild to a great booming and tremendous enthusiasm.   He

noted that he preferred Kennedy to Nixon, since this was
the presidential election month. He talked about his days in
the wheat fields of Kansas and his experience of hitching
rides on freight trains. He talked at length about Lincoln
and his collaboration with George Stevens in the movie
"Greatest Story Ever Told." He stated that he didn't care
for television (because of the commercials), roadsigns, and
cosmetics. He also noted that he did not like to see women
smoking. He was humorous, gentle, humble and precise in
his convictions. Since I am a cigar smoker, he also asked
for one. He pulled out a small knife and cut the cigar into
equal portions of about one and a half inches. For snacks
that evening he preferred melted ice cream, and he asked
us to put it on the stove so that it would melt more quickly.

Incidentally, prior to leaving for the Art Academy,
he allowed my wife to assist him in dressing.

The following morning, he came out of the bathroom
and stated, "What is that classic phrase? Is the coast
clear?"

It was noted that, in the morning, he was singing in
the bedroom.

He was scheduled for a tour of the Lincoln Museum
in the Lincoln National Life Insurance Company with departure from Fort Wayne scheduled shortly after 12:00. We
arrived at the Lincoln Life, where he was met by the Lincoln Life representatives as well as the press and TV people.

The tour of the museum completed, he was notified
that the Lincoln had provided a few automobiles for his trip
back to the airport. I was fairly close to him at the time
the statement was made and was rather surprised when he
stated that he would travel back to the airport in the same
car in which he arrived, which was my old, rather tired,
compact car. And the two of us left for the field, from
which he departed.

Upon leaving my home, he gave my wife a rather
grateful embrace, removed a ring from his finger and gave
it to her. In addition to this, he gave us two books which
he had authored and which he suitably inscribed. He also
gave us a copy of his speech before the Joint Session of
Congress.

Walks and Talks with Sandburg*

Eleven years ago we took a three-day trip in Indiana
and Kentucky, with several hours at "Santa Claus" about
which Carl wrote a Christmas piece for one of the popular
magazines. He took copious notes of the nature of the ter-
rain, the kind of trees and plants that grew there, and what
time in the year certain flowers came. He talked with old
settlers and studied old maps. We stopped at a small post-
office in Indiana nearby where Lincoln had trudged miles to
school. Carl had a lazy, indolent way of interviewing, not
the crisp, direct staccato of a busy newspaper man. He
proferred tobacco to the grizzled post master, passed the
time of day with him, and led gently to his subject. The
post master, the third or fourth in his line, dug up musty
old ledgers and maps, marvelous first source material.
"Friend," said Sandburg, in a slow drawl, "could I borrow
these if I return 'em?" Invariably, he got what he wanted.
We paced off distances. We looked at the clouds and the
sky. We smelled the new mown hay and tasted the air.

Night came, and we found ourselves at midnight at
a crossroads, miles out of our way. A farmer finally
roused pointed to a vacant farm house on a distant hill.
"You're welcome strangers to stay over yonder if you like.
You'll find some beds. But the windows are out mostly.
There's a good pump. Make yourselves at home." So we
spent the night in an empty farm house on the hill with the
wind blowing through the broken windows.

The Unexpected But Welcome Guest†

The W. Harold Brentons were not expecting to have
Sandburg as their house guest in October, 1955, in Des
Moines, but they greatly enjoyed having him. Mr. Brenton
went to the airport to meet a Mr. Burgess, whom they were
expecting to have as their guest during the Iowa Bankers
Convention, at which Sandburg was to appear. He encountered Sandburg, carrying a guitar and small black oilcloth
shopping bag, in the airport.

---

*Letter from Paul L. Benjamin, Saratoga Springs, N. Y.
By permission. (See Sandburg's "There Is a Santa Claus!"
Pictorial Review, 32 (December, 1930) 24-6.)
†Based on a letter, dated Aug. 20, 1970, from Mrs. W.
Harold Brenton, Des Moines, Iowa.

After Sandburg had accepted Mr. Brenton's offer of
a ride to his hotel, Sandburg turned to the other passenger
and asked him where he was staying. He replied that he
was to be the guest of the Brentons. After a silence, Sandburg told Burgess how lucky he was to be staying in a private home; he was envious, because he did not like hotels.
His remark, which Mr. Brenton thought of as "plaintive"
and "amusing," immediately brought forth an invitation,
which was accepted. Mrs. Brenton, though she thought
Sandburg's luggage unusual, was used to extemporaneous
invitations.

After he had been assigned his room, Sandburg asked
Mrs. Brenton to walk with him through the trees on the
lawn of the house. He was excited and wanted to talk as
they strolled. He said he felt footloose and that the reason
was he had finished his biography of Lincoln, had just sent
it off to the publishers, after all the years of preparation.

Further, he told her that Lincoln was a man of many
humorous stories. However, because the biography was intended for a family audience, he had many "earthy" stories
which he had not been able to include in the work. He
asked Mrs. Brenton if she would object to hearing one.
She readily assented. She thought later of the conversation
as "gay" in tone. Though she was an obliging listener, she
could not accommodate his request for goat's milk when they
returned to the house.

That evening, at a reception, still in a lightsome
mood, he told the same story, but only after checking with
Mrs. Brenton to make sure no one would think it offensive.

When he left the next day, Mrs. Brenton thought he
had been the ideal guest, one she still thought pleasantly
about fifteen years later.

My Guest, Carl Sandburg*

"The new jet liners are wonderful; the engines almost silent, but the hundred people inside chatter incessantly; you couldn't hear them before, but now no one can

---

*Contributed by Prof. F. S. Bromberger, Univ. of Redlands,
Calif. By permission.

sleep. " Thus Carl Sandburg described the first East-West
American Airline jet flight, which flew him to California
after he had dedicated the commercial jet age in New York
on 25 January 1959. He was sitting at our long, knotty red-
wood kitchen table dunking toast in coffee on a rainy afternoon before one of his now rare lecture-recitals. What
would it be like to have Carl Sandburg here for two days?
we had asked ourselves before he came. Would he be sul-
len or gloomy? what would he want to eat? what would he
want to do or not do while he was in Redlands?

Sandburg and I grew up in Galesburg, Illinois; we
attended the same grade school, and our families had known
one another. My grandmother's sister had been the midwife
who delivered him on 6 January 1878. When I knew in November that he was to lecture here the next February I offered to act as his man Friday while he was in the area,
and he accepted graciously: he'd be glad to chat again about
Galesburg, and Knox and Lombard colleges, and the friends
and institutions that we had known in the little "Swede town"
redolent of coal smoke in winter and basking in a forest of
corn leaves in the sultry summers.

Of course many people wanted to see him. Could
the Los Angeles and the local papers interview and photograph him? would he speak at the Lincoln Dinner before
his lecture and give the prizes for the Lincoln Essay Contest? would he come to the Lincoln Shrine? could students
ask him questions? would he visit some classes? would he
attend a reception? I was anxious for all those who wanted
to see him; so I wrote again asking how much he was willing to do besides lecture. He replied on 8 February that
he knew he should not attend the Lincoln Dinner, for his
work for the evening audience would be as great as pitching
a fourteen-inning game in August. He was anticipating his
address to the Joint Session of Congress and a rush of
other events. He mentioned a stock ploy, that all he really
had to say was in his twenty-two books.

He had turned eighty-one in January, and after out-
lining this wilting schedule (with two more immediate lectures after the one here) we could not expect him to jump
at social, journalistic, or classroom invitations. On his
arrival I'd ask him exactly what he wanted to do; I knew
that Carl Sandburg was not a man who could be pushed
around.

He called from San Francisco first on Saturday, 14

February, to say that he wanted to see Ed Murrow's "Person to Person" television show at 6 p. m. on Sunday: he, Senator Dirksen, and Northcote Parkinson from different parts of the world were debating the question, "If Lincoln Were Alive Today Would He Be a Republican or a Democrat?" No one had seen the show since it had been recorded. His voice was soft and warm like the purring of a contented lion. I assured him that we'd find a TV set and see the program if he arrived on time.

He called later in the day to say that he was having lunch with Admiral and Mrs. Chester Nimitz on Sunday but that he'd arrive in Los Angeles at 6:41 p. m. Had he forgotten the telecast? He seemed perfectly relaxed on the telephone in spite of the strenuousness of the "campaign," and we tried out a few Swedish phrases on each other; when we both admitted to having forgotten much he said, laughing, "I'll see you tomorrow night, and we'll compare our deficiencies and talk about Galesburg." The Swedish language has an immediate warmth and intimacy about it and especially for those who learned their first prayers and songs in its rich inflections.

At two o'clock on Sunday afternoon Mrs. Nimitz called from Berkeley that Mr. Sandburg was taking an earlier plane so that he'd arrive in Los Angeles at 5:41, just in time to see the telecast. On the way in from Redlands I heard a broadcast of a part of his tribute to Lincoln before Congress. It was pleasant thinking that within a few hours Carl Sandburg would be in the same car skimming over the Los Angeles traffic on the Harbor Freeway. His plane was fifteen minutes late; so I didn't see the tall, heavily overcoated bard until 5:55, barely in time for us to be whisked by an airline receptionist up to the plush TWA Ambassador Club for VIP's. There he chuckled at his adroit handling of his part in the discussion. I was amazed at the temerity of any two men who would appear in a Lincoln-Sandburg debate with the man who wrote the longest biography that has ever been written about any man. Mr. Sandburg enjoyed the program both as a participant and as an onlooker.

Because he arrived at supper time, my brother Bob in Los Angeles provided a light smorgasbord and suggested that his company, Los Angeles Airways, be responsible for Mr. Sandburg's transportation back to Los Angeles and arrange later for getting him on his way to Salt Lake City.

The drive from Los Angeles to Redlands was through

rain the whole way. He was surprised that we were in the
City of Angels for the first fifteen miles and was happy to
leave the freeway traffic. Thousands of cars were returning from the mountain areas at the end of the week, and
the oncoming traffic with its dazzle of lights and reflections
on the wet pavement was a river of light that kept him fascinated: he had never seen so much continuous traffic on
a highway, and he shook his head at the statistics about
Californians and their automobiles. He asked about Redlands, the University, and the purlieus and proved himself
an excellent listener, never forgetting the answer to a question. Perhaps the one thing that all great poets have in
common is a superb faculty for remembering details. If
Carl Sandburg lives to be a hundred he'll probably be able
to recall his visit to Redlands in remarkable detail. He
had heard about the Lincoln Shrine and would like to see it.
Remembering the Lincoln Dinner, he said, "There seems
to be much Lincoln interest in Redlands; so, since I'll not
be at the dinner, maybe I should go heavy on the Lincoln
material in my talk. "

Because I had promised so many people that I'd ask
him what groups he'd like to meet with before and after the
talk, I said straightforwardly that I needed to know whom
he'd see so that arrangements could be made. He said,
"Let the newspaper men make notes from the lecture. I
always lie down for an hour before a talk, and I'll be tired
afterward. Of course students want to ask questions, but
nearly every question that any student has asked me has its
answer written as carefully as I know how to write it in
my books. One student the other night said, 'Mr. Sandburg,
what was Mrs. Lincoln like? Did she really make life hard
for Mr. Lincoln?' I wrote a whole book on Mary Lincoln.
If people are interested in a writer they'll read his books.
I'm coming to Redlands as a lecturer and recitalist. "

Anyone who has heard Sandburg's many phonograph
records, especially his readings from The People, Yes,
knows his mastery of the change of pace and his dramatic
range of delivery, his voice at one moment a soft wind
soughing through the grass and an instant later crackling
with fury like a wind-blown forest fire. His mood can be
ephemeral too. We had been talking quietly in the soft rain
when I asked what seemed an innocent enough question, "What
does Mrs. Sandburg think of your continuing to go on lecture
tours like this?" He was silent for a few seconds, and then
he came back in a loud gust, "Mrs. Sandburg knows that I'm

a platform artist who has a great deal to offer audiences.
I'm doing the colleges a favor at my age to come out and
talk to them; I don't have to lecture any more, but she
knows that an artist has to be heard. She's a Phi Beta Kappa from the University of Chicago. That's all I have to say
to your question!" We both listened to the rain for a few
minutes after that; I had apparently touched him at a sensitive point with an obtuse question, and I was happy when his
voice came back rich and warm, "Did you find a guitar for
me?" Our contract with him specified that we were to fur-
nish a "six-string guitar with nylon strings." A week before
I had borrowed Noel Quinn's excellent Martin and fitted it
with nylons which were now well stretched; it was at home
waiting to be tried. "Good," he said, "I'll get used to it
a while this evening."

The great slender height of the Mexican fan palms
caught his eye when we came to Redlands, and he remarked
about the gray skirts on the heavy-torsoed filiferas, but he
was most taken with the grotesque trunks of the old pepper
trees. We stopped by one near a familiar mailbox and got
out.

Corrine, my wife, had a crackling fire, hot coffee,
and chocolate waiting for us inside. I assumed that he'd
want to go right to bed after getting acquainted with the guitar, but we realized that Galesburg hadn't been mentioned.
He was pleased that I had twice enjoyed Always the Young
Strangers, the autobiography of his first twenty years. It
was published on his seventy-fifth birthday, a rich book,
full of sadness and laughter, a thousand detailed memories
of his sensitive early life in Galesburg. Any one who grew
up in a small town is surprised to find his home's name in
print, much less a whole book written about the section of
town where he grew up. I had devoured the anecdotes about
the neighborhood streets, the gangs and games, the people,
the schools and shops and relived the pleasant warmth of
my own youth in his moving pages about the scenes and
situations which had seemed so ordinary. We had both
grown up in families, among neighbors, friends, and relatives nearly all of whom were Swedes. While he sat strumming the guitar, we traded stories about the "green Swedes"
who spoke half-Swedish, half-English.

He laughed until the tears came at the story of the
old woman who came to see my grandmother one day: her
nephews from the city had come to visit her and wanted to

milk the cow; they said they knew all about it, but they
didn't. They squirted milk on the wall; the cow kicked the
pail and broke from her stanchion and was so discombob-
ulated that she couldn't be controlled for a couple of days.
The old woman's summary was, "När de comes to mjölkin
de ku de anta no monkey bissness." (When it comes to milking the cow there can't be any monkey business.) He re-
joined with his father's "nearly off color" story that appears
on page eighty-four of Always the Young Strangers. We
laughed even when the stories were not funny, but they
seemed like home and we were young again. Occasionally
we found ourselves in Swedish sentences, thinking in the old
language. When we were children we had both dreamed in
Swedish. We should have gone to bed before two o'clock
that morning, but he felt like singing and talking. "We only
live once," he mused, "and the dawn is so fine when you've
waited for it all night!" and he threw back his head, closed
his eyes and sang in a voice that was deep gold:

> It's all the same where you go when you die,
> It's all the same where you go when you die;
> You've got friends in both places
> And you'll see friendly faces--
> It's all the same where you go when you die.

Then the haunting melancholy came back, in Swedish this
time.

The evening of songs and memories was rich and
evocative, but anyone but a Galesburg Swede who couldn't
join in with the language, stories, remembrances of place
would simply have been amused at two people who were lost
in their youths. I was touched to find, after he had left,
that he had written in my copy of Always the Young Strangers, "... so very truly min Svenska vän." (my Swedish
friend.)

"I usually sleep until about noon," he had said when
we discussed plans for the next day, "but I may get up
earlier." We showed him where things were in the kitchen,
since all of us would be gone until noon. I returned home
after my eleven o'clock class to find him contentedly squeez-
ing orange juice; so we joined him in a two-hour breakfast;
he was not perturbed by the almost continual ringing of long-
distance calls. When he's away from his study at Connemara Farm in Flat Rock, North Carolina, he likes to move
leisurely at his own pace talking about myriad topics: "This

Freud stuff is bosh. " "<u>Exclusive</u> (pronounced deliberately
and with long, high accent on the second syllable) is the
ugliest word in our language. " "A few things are important
in life, " he said with great forcefulness; "I want to work
(long pause), have some love (longer pause), and sing, and
stay out of jail. " I remarked that while he had described
many people that his autobiography noted no physical details
about himself. "All right, " he chuffed, "let's fill in: five
feet ten and a half, one-hundred sixty-two pounds; white hair
was once dark brown; sea-gray blue eyes. "

Since I was to introduce him that evening, I had
made some rather elaborate notes; I knew many anecdotes
about him, could tell about his early days, his rise to fame,
his contributions to so many aspects of American culture--
"Let me tell you a story, " he broke in. "After <u>The War
Years</u> was published in 1939 offers for honorary <u>doctoral</u>
degrees began coming in from several colleges and universities, Harvard and Yale among them. Yale came first
that next June. I stood for many long minutes while Billy
Phelps extolled everything known about me. It was boring
and nobody learned very much. The next day came the
honor at Harvard. The citation took ten seconds to read,
said everything: 'Carl Sandburg, whose poetry captures the
American rhythm and who has fortified national morale by
serving as Washington correspondent for the Lincoln administration. '" My introduction would necessarily be short
now: the range of his work, the Harvard citation ("Some
bastard stole that piece of sheepskin soon after I got it!"),
and mention of his greatest honor, the invitation, four days
before, to address Congress on Lincoln's one-hundred fif-
tieth birthday. ("The president was the only man in the
government not ambulant that day. ") He had lost his comb,
and when I gave him mine he said, "Why don't you say tonight, 'Mr. Sandburg offered to help me with this introduction if I would give him my pocket comb'?"

The rain stopped for a few moments as we rolled
down Center Avenue, and a bright sun shot a gorgeous rainbow over the town. "Oh, look, " he said, "there's the pret-
tiest rainbow I've ever seen. " Who could forget one of his
definitions of poetry in <u>Good Morning America</u>, as an explanation of the appearance and disappearance of rainbows.
But it disappeared and the rain was insistent when we got
to the Lincoln Shrine. He was photographed many times
as he moved slowly around the cases of Lincolniana, and
he much approved the collection, but said that the documents

in Lincoln's hand should be stored in fireproof vaults and
reproductions set out for public display.

The rain precluded seeing very much of the old
houses in town; so he suggested that instead of more driving
around we return home so he could run over the songs he'd
sing that night and think about his speech. He invited all
five children to be his audience while he practiced. They
had learned several of the songs from his Decca album "New
Songs from The American Songbag"; so he pretended that he
had forgotten the words, played the guitar while they sang
the songs that he had collected and made famous, and then
he applauded them. After "I Ride an Old Paint" he said,
"I'd better go upstairs and think about my speech." He
asked that supper be early; so we called him at almost five
o'clock, and he ate quickly this time, with his famous green
eye-shade under the flowing white forelocks. He asked specifically if he could have all the children there for supper;
he seldom saw small people any more and liked to be with
them, as anyone who had read the Rootabaga Stories and
Early Moon would know. But he wanted to rest; so he excused himself after some joking and banter. ("Here, Cor-
inth, let me show you a new handshake. You lock little
fingers, then touch thumbs and pat hands. Show that to
your friends, and it will be all over California in a few
weeks.") "Call me at the latest possible moment," he
called as he went upstairs again.

His lecture was scheduled for 8:15; so I called him
at 7:40, and we were at the Chapel by eight, he feeling sorry for the long line of people who were standing in the rain
hoping for standing room. He didn't want to arrive too
early because he knew that the photographers and reporters
would be there. They were, and he got rough with a radio
man who insisted on taking a tape for later broadcast. He
said he didn't want recorded what he was saying to a living
audience. His grimness disappeared instantaneously, however, when he saw waiting to greet him Mrs. Gold from
Pomona who had been his secretary in the twenties when he
worked for the Chicago Daily News. He had a few minutes
of old days and old friends with her and was in a good mood
for the audience when he went out on the stage. A standing
ovation will move the most hardened lecturer, and he gave
his best that night to a responsive audience which he con-
gratulated when his hearers were moved to intense silence
after he read the same words that he had spoken to Congress. The Daily Facts and the San Bernardino Sun printed
good accounts of what he said.

He was weary after autographing his books but suggested at home that we sit for a while before the fire. "I
think I never told the Spicknoodle story as funny as it went
tonight. " He left his overcoat on but took off his shoes
and chatted as he munched strong Camembert cheese on
crackers. "The critics have forgotten so many good writers;
if ever I do an anthology Edwin Piper Ford of Iowa will be
there with his 'Sweet Grass. ' ... How many people today
know Steinbeck's wonderful To a God Unknown? ... I'm
about to break ground for a new book on Lincoln when I
finish the next volume of the autobiography, Ever the Winds
of Chance. " He asked to hear chapter XIII of Saint-Exupéry's
The Little Prince. No matter how slowly I read he wanted
to hear it more slowly. "That's so delicious that I want to
savor every bit of it. It's a classic and has new implica-
tions for the space age. Read it all again. " He regretted
that Burns was not being memorized and recited as much as
before. Of his method of writing: "I have notes on slips
of paper and pin them on a bulletin board under two heads,
'perhaps' and 'weave in. '" He wove in more Galesburg
yarns, though I wished that he'd have said something about
his family, the new poets, the world situation. He likes a
big audience but does not hob-nob easily with those who just
want to be near the great man. When he's traveling he
uses several defense systems: a man sees him on a plane
and sits down saying, "Aren't you Carl Sandburg, the poet?' ...
"Oh no, " he replies, "I'm the president and chairman of the
board of the North American Pawpaw Society. "

His first paper-back will be out soon, Fiery Trail, a
section of his huge novel, Remembrance Rock. "It will cost
thirty-five cents. The publisher and I get seven tenths of
a cent a piece from each copy. "

My brother was to pick him up in the helicopter in
San Bernardino at 10:25 the next morning; so he got up unusually early, at nine, and enjoyed an adagio breakfast while
James Sloan and I fidgeted hoping that there would be some
time for pictures. Mr. Sandburg complimented Jimmy as
"a most uncommon photographer" when he took twelve pictures in about ninety seconds. Some of them are the finest
I've seen of the wonderful-voiced man whose "face spoke of
granite. "

Remembering a Vital, Touching Force*

The news of Carl Sandburg's death came to me through
the evening paper. And even though all of us here who were
his friends in Los Angeles had expected news of this sort
for more than two years, it was still a shock and a great
sadness.

I had been friends with Mr. Sandburg. He had lived
as a house guest in my small Brentwood apartment in the
last months before I was married in 1960.

Norman Corwin, the noted writer, had called me one
day to ask, "Would you put Carl up?" I had to turn to my
future husband, Mark Sandrich, and say to him, "Can I put
Carl Sandburg up?"

Norman, on being told this, said, "Carl won't mind,
if you don't."

So it was settled. We picked up the great man at
the airport and stopped at the Beverly Wilshire for a drink.
There a woman who came up to our table for Sandburg's
autograph was told by him, "I have an incurable disease,
madam, which prevents me from writing my name."

The woman looked at Carl Sandburg, her eyes bulging, and finally retreated.

Carl was an undemanding guest. I discussed with
him what he could and could not eat. There were few, if
any, restrictions. He took large oranges into his room at
night. I made goulash. He ate everything that I fixed. In
the evenings he read from his poetry to Mark and me. I
took some marvelous photos of him reading; there was an
unreality to me about this period, and the pictures today
bring back these moments. Carl would not wait for someone to express an interest in his work. He assumed it and
opened one of his books and read.

He chose poems he thought would have meaning to us,
putting small pieces of paper in his books as an endless

*Vanessa Brown, "Some Personal Memories of Carl Sand-
burg's Landlady," Los Angeles Times, July 14, 1968. By
permission of author and publisher.

series of reminders.   He rambled when he talked.   There
was a remote quality about him as if he talked to himself
and only related to you in some peripheral way.   As we got
to know each other better, he became more personal and
almost direct, but much of the time he was a character, a
man inbued with his own thoughts.

I think affection for others came slowly.   He certainly expressed those feelings more easily in written words.
He was extravagant in his praise on paper.   I have a score
of flyleaves of his books (that he sent subsequently) and
letters that show that another person did make an impact on
him even though he did not always show it immediately.
For years afterward he sent me clippings on Adlai Stevenson and Ed Murrow, mutual friends we had rather heatedly
talked about.

Probably the evening we talked the longest was one
when Mark, too tired of hearing Sandburg read, had decided
to stay home.   Carl and I walked up to the roof of the Meri-
dian apartment and looked out to the west to watch the sun
setting.   There was some rather pointed talk about how "we"
were going to miss Mark.   And should we go to see so-and-
so, a lady with whom he had stayed before and whom he had
not called yet.   I did not really feel like going out and said,
if he wanted so badly to see her, I would be happy to drive
him.   After a kind of pointless back and forth, we settled
that we would stay in.

In the apartment, I put on some music.   Carl said
rather testily, "Ah, Chopin.   In honor of the dear departed ... " (meaning Mark, who plays and composes).
Then, somehow, the mood changed and we talked intensely.
I cannot remember what.   I guess it had to do with purpose
and how you express purpose and intent in writing and in
art.   Carl had been taken by my paintings, as very strong
abstractions.

He was trying to tell me something profound; important; intense and personal.   And all that stays with me
now is an inchoate feeling of "Have faith ... have courage ...
strong feelings ... force does overcome you ... stay with
it. "

That is somehow an intensely personal memory.

I have others, not quite so intense.   These memories

go to make up my own personal mosaic of the man and what it was like when he was living among us.

From the photos I had taken of him on the evenings he read to us, I had made a painting. When Carl came back to Hollywood later, under contract to George Stevens, he allowed me to come to the studio for several days to sketch him. One day I brought along the big painting of him that I had been working on, setting it up in the corner of the elegant suite he occupied at 20th Century-Fox Studios in Beverly Hills.

The morning of that day, George Stevens called to find out if he could come over to see Carl Sandburg. As soon as Stevens arrived, I offered to remove myself and my paints. I was very surprised by Stevens' reply:

"No, No. I don't want to stop creation."

I was rendered beet red with embarrassment, because the painting I was doing was by now so worked over and so far from what I had envisaged it should be that "creation" was very far from my mind. But, numbly, I was grateful, and I continued working while George Stevens and Carl talked over the script of "The Greatest Story Ever Told."

This was the time Carl was living at Hotel Bel-Air. The elegant hotel had made the extraordinary concession to let him have a small portable stove in his room. As his former landlady, I took the liberty to look into his closet at the state of his suits. Well, you would have thought a pauper lived there! In the entire long and elegant wardrobe hung two ratty jackets with spots on them.

Mrs. Corwin and I talked over the phone, afterwards, trying to figure out a way to get Carl to buy some suits. We also discussed his extreme parsimony.

It was pathetic, at times, when it was not downright funny. There was the time my husband and I took him to the Frascati Restaurant in Santa Monica. The manager, very impressed, came up to our table to talk to Carl.

On our way out, Carl, as if in correct response to the manager's elegant solicitude, asked him, "Do you know, sir, if that pawn shop is still near here?"

Turning to us, he said, "That was a dandy pawn shop...."

I guess nothing one person observes about another ever comes close to being an accurate whole person, but each observation adds to the sum total of a man ... somewhere.

Carl Sandburg was not the remote, austere figure the obituaries would make him. He was vital, moving, touching force, and we who are left behind cling to the remembrances of himself that he gave us.

Words Which Will Belong to the Ages*

[This is the recollection of Carl Sandburg by Fanny Butcher, "a retired Tribune literary editor and his friend from long ago," which appeared in The Chicago Tribune on July 23, 1967, the day after his death.]

The fires of Carl Sandburg's spirit were lighted not only by man's inhumanity to man--a common fuel for many who have stirred the thoughts of their fellow men--but by the certainty that man could make a world worth living in if he wanted to, as he had made for himself a good world.

Such fires burst into flame in his poetry, rebellious against the old forms and contexts, iconoclastic of thought and style. When the poem "Chicago" was first published in Poetry, a magazine of verse, it elicited cries of agony from some critics. A few of us saw in it a sort of mirage toward which some young poets would struggle.

Many did, to find that its honesty, its freshness, its strength, its flexibility was no mirage, but reality.

It was when the book Chicago Poems (1916) was published that I first met Carl Sandburg, the slow-spoken, often bellowingly laughing newspaper reporter who "wrote" in his spare time. His family--a wonderful, quiet, gentle wife, whom for some reason he called Paula altho her name was Lillian, his little girls, his Golden Retriever which had been the gift of the widow of another poet, William Vaughan

---

*Reprinted, courtesy of The Chicago Tribune.

Moody--were an island of serenity to which his fellow reporter, the late Lloyd Lewis, and I sometimes were wel-
comed.

Sometimes he and Lloyd would sit with me after our
work was over, two marvelous, happy arguers about life to
whom I listened and whom I seldom interrupted, for their
talk was like the fastest game of tennis anyone could imagine,
with slamming service, and bullet-like return. Sometimes
there were fireworks of words, oftener roaring of laughter.

Carl often would pull out of his pocket bits of paper and
read us something he had just written, for "the heiresses,"
as he used to call his daughters.

He may have had dreams of the future, but they
could not have approached the fulfillment that came to him,
honors piled upon honors, all this and the heaven, too, of
becoming, while he lived, a monument.

In it all, he never lost a sort of childish wonder at
how things had turned out for him, and a kind of naiveté
about the ways of the world.

We saw him one time in Hollywood, while he was
working on the script for the movie about the Bible, and he
sat behind an enormous desk in a suite that had been Mari-
lyn Monroe's (which pleased and amused him), pushed buttons, talked into each of the six telephones in turn while he
laughed at playing the tycoon.

He had no sense of time. He could often, and did,
he said, work for days practically without stopping. But he
could also talk for hours without stopping, and often, when
he would come to Chicago from Harbert, Michigan, where
he wrote a large part of Abraham Lincoln, he would spend
the night with us and sit up until 3 or 4 o'clock talking.

One of those almost all-night sessions included a
young poet, Jesse Stuart. The old poet and the young one
discovered a bond besides their passion to write--like Carl's
father, Jesse's could neither read nor write. Carl put his
arm around the shoulder of the boy (then in his sailor uni-
form from Great Lakes) and roared with laughter, "We're
just a couple of illiterates." There was a fierce pride in
the man who had climbed his private Mount Everest.

Sandburg, the man who went around the country singing the songs of his land, strumming his guitar (to help support his family while he worked on the endless Lincoln biography) was known to many who didn't, and in many cases couldn't, read his poetry or his biography--for which he won the Pulitzer prize as a historian.

His long historical novel, Remembrance Rock, never became a best seller, but it proved to its author as well as to the critics that he could write fiction as well as fact.

And the stories he wrote for children were as different from the popular tales for children of the past as a missile is different from a carbine, and his essays had the quality of a missile. He was the literary phenomenon of our day in versatility.

The 75th year of his life was celebrated in Chicago-- the city which had been so much a part of his life. The great from near and far came to wish him long life and happiness. It pleased him that the king of Sweden sent his country's highest decoration. For his 80th birthday his publisher gave a party in New York to which 80 were invited from all the world. One hundred and fifty insisted on being there.

Every birthday until this year's I talked to him on the telephone. This year he was asleep. I remembered with what pride he had once told me that the President of the United States had just called to wish him good luck, and with what unfailing friendship over a half-century had passed, the lean years, the fruitful ones, the honored ones. I am glad that he left the world with no struggle physically. To all of us he has bequeathed words which will belong to the ages.

Riding to Tampa*

When The Rollins Sandspur reported a "lecture" by Carl Sandburg in Knowles Hall on the evening of March 30, 1928, it characterized him as having a "quiet and retiring

---

*Based on letters from Mrs. Dorothy Emerson Doggett, Atlantic Beach, Florida of April 15, 1970, and September 26, 1977; and from Mrs. Stella Weston Chapman, Maitland, Florida, of February 21, 1970. By permission.

manner. " It said further that the audience was attentive
throughout and came to feel, as the program progressed,
that they had known him a long time.

As far as it goes, that account is useful and interesting. Fortunately, however, two Rollins students of that
time have a much fuller and more accurate record of Carl
Sandburg. To start with, Dorothy Emerson noted that
"... he wore a blue shirt and looked like a clean laborer.
His lock of hair fell over his brow. He sat on the side of
the platform rather than in the middle and sang softly to
his guitar. It was mostly students and teachers who were
listening. ... "

Afterward six or eight selected students went to the
home of Professor Willard Wattles, who had had Sandburg
as his house guest on similar campus visits in Oregon and
who was responsible for the Rollins visit. A few sat in the
softly-lighted living room and a few on the darker porch.
"It seems to me that the men were the ones who found something to say and that the talk was not much of poetry but
more of prize-fighting. A young, nationally-noted boxer had
been enrolled at the campus about this time. "

Stella Weston was "quite positive" in her recollection
that Professor and Mrs. Wattles had students in for breakfast the next day. (Sandburg had stayed at the Wattles
home.) Stella also remembered that "... Carl gave me a
bag of money--bills, loose change, etc. --the loot from his
appearance the night before--and asked me to take it to the
bank and get it put into big bills. He apparently had not
counted it and had never seen me before in his life, except
for the prior day. So either I had an honest face or he a
trusting heart. "

Though neither of the students has recalled how it
came about, arrangements had been made that Sandburg was
to ride approximately eighty miles across Florida to Tampa
in Stella's car. Also to make the trip were Dorothy and
Stella's aunt, visiting from Massachusetts. On the afternoon
of March 31, the air was sufficiently chilly that the following
took place: "Stella Weston and I, in her car, stopped near
the campus to speak to Professor Willard Wattles ..., who
was host to Sandburg. 'He wants to borrow a sweater to
take to Tampa, ' he said. 'I'll never get it back. ' He
seemed both amused and begrudging. "

"The next morning, " Dorothy has written, "loading

Stella's car for the trip to Tampa, sure enough, there was
Carl Sandburg wearing Mr. Wattles' nice grey sweater. He
had on a cap much as men often wore in those days. He
sat up in front with Stella; I sat in the back with her aunt,
who went along as chaperone. "

As she thought about the trip in 1970, Stella (known
as Boots) remembered two things outstandingly. "One was
walking down one of the ... main streets--Carl was in the
middle and he was holding Dorothy's hand and mine--swing-
ing along with the three of us singing, 'Poor little violet,
covered all over with snow.' I remember it was from his
Songbag, and I'm sure he told us it was a baseball song. "
When she wrote to a friend on April 12, 1928, Dorothy said
of the trip she had made with Sandburg to Tampa: "We had
a glass of beer together and he taught me a ridiculous song.
I wish that he could be here again to talk to me. " Writing
in September, 1977, she remarked that she wished she
could "remember that 'ridiculous song. '"

The glass of beer was Stella's other outstanding
memory: "(we went) ... with him to a speakeasy for a
glass of beer. As this was during Prohibition and neither
Dorothy nor I had ever been in a lounge, much less a
speakeasy, I can remember my heart pounding with excite-
ment. I ordered a Coca Cola but then asked Carl if I
could have a sip of his beer, as I had no idea what any al-
coholic drink tasted like. He shoved it over to me, and I
took a sip, discovering it to be so bitter that I never have
liked it to this day. But I can still brag that my first in-
dulgence in this field--and illegally, too--was sharing Carl
Sandburg's drink! My New England aunt about died. "

Dorothy recalled that, during the trip, she got an
occasional chance to talk with Sandburg:

> At one point, Stella's aunt suggested that Sandburg
> advise me to write poetry more fitting for my age
> of nineteen. He gave me an intent look and re-
> plied, 'I can tell her nothing about writing poetry. '
> I immediately felt his respect for person and for
> creativity itself. (I had published in The Flamingo,
> Rollins' literary magazine, a long poem that had
> been toned down considerably but was rumored to
> have lost Rollins an endowment from some frown-
> ing Northerner.)

Dorothy recalled the journey as a "pleasant mingling

of green landscape and sunny expanses." Hearing Sandburg
and Stella speaking quietly occasionally, she would fall into
reverie. Then Sandburg would suddenly address her: "I
bet you didn't see that we entered Polk County [near Lake-
land]!" Then he said, "I bet you didn't see that Alligator
Farm sign!" He even alleged: "I bet you didn't see that
cow in the field!"

She recalled "his serious face turned toward me as
he warned: 'To be a poet takes great sacrifices ... great
sacrifices.'"

Stella captured her impressions of the trip in two
pages which were written soon thereafter:

> Thump ... thump ... thump ... thump ...
> thump. ...
> 'S--ay! What's that God-awful noise, Boots?'
> 'I'm afraid it's a puncture, Mr. Sandburg.'
> 'Well, well. So wildly wandering wobbly Willy,
> the Weevil has a flat tire. Never mind. [This
> very briskly.] All punctures are on me.'
> 'Fine! We can have four of them in that case.
> But now that we've got to wait while Willy gets
> fixed, tell me your honest opinion about the writing
> game.'
> 'Well, if you and Dot want to write, you've got
> to do two things. You've got to work hard and
> you've got to work steadily. You both ought to
> write at least two hours every day. Of course,
> it won't all be good. G--osh! The God-awful
> bunch of manuscripts I've torn up! S--ay! What
> do you think of this piece?'
> 'Well, I like it but I don't understand it.'
> 'G--o--sh! Well, to get back to writing. As
> far as poetry is concerned, there's practically no
> money and very little thanks in it. But what of
> it? I write because I like it. Some of my best
> stuff has had no audience except myself. What
> others say about my writing makes no great dif-
> ference. The satisfaction comes in pleasing your-
> self. G--o--sh! Guess Willy's ready to travel.'
> 'Righto, Mr. Sandburg. But how do you go
> about breaking into print?'
> 'Now, Boots, --and you, too, Dot. You young-
> sters don't want to break into print for a long
> time. What you do now, is work hard and work
> steadily. S--ay! Look at that Rootabaga church!'

Five minutes silence. Then suddenly, 'What county are we in now, Dot?'

'I don't know, and care less, Mr. Sandburg.'

'Ah-ha! And how can you expect to write poetry if you don't know your geography?'

'Huh! You wouldn't know yourself if you hadn't just read that sign back there.'

'Is-that-so! G--o--sh! There's a Rootabaga cow in the road.'

For thirty-seven miles, selections from the Song-bag startle the natives.

Then, --'Say, Boots. How about some food?'

'Suits me. Can it be hot dawgs?'

'No, not hot dawgs! I don't eat 'em.'

'Wh--a--at? How can you be the Great American Poet then, if you don't know your hot dawgs?'

'Oh, I know 'em all right. But we just don't get along. What do you say we try waffles instead?'

Lapse of many minutes.

More selections from Songbag. Then, 'Well, here's dear, old Tampa, Mr. Sandburg. But before we part, is there any more dope on the writing game?'

'Just one more thing, youngsters. If you make up your minds to become writers, you've also got to make them up to be lonely.'

'I should think any famous person would be lonely, Mr. Sandburg. You see, other people would be so in awe of 'em, that they would never act natural with 'em.'

'That's all too true, Boots. Birds in glass houses gather no moss. And that's why I've had such a fine old Rootabaga time today. G--o--sh! Well, thanks for the buggy ride and--(a trifle wistfully) so--long, kids! S--o--l--ong.'

In her manuscript, Stella did not record, as she did in 1970: "The car had a flat tire. Sandburg sat there in his workman's shirt while we arranged to get it fixed." She thought of herself as amused at his sitting there while she "scurried around in the heat trying to find some one to fix the puncture." The reference to "wildly wandering wobbly Willy," she recalled, was a direct quote concerning her car, a Willys Knight. During lunch, which they had in Plant City, she asked him why he wore his hair hanging down in his eyes. He replied, "My great American public likes me this way."

Dorothy could not remember anything of the parting, but Stella recalled they left him standing on the curb in Tampa, "looking (I thought) rather wistfully after us. We did not leave him at a hotel or any one's home. He had obviously had a great time with us possibly because we were so used to having celebrities at Rollins that we were un-awed, even by someone of his stature. It was just a mu-tually delightful adventure."

Neither Dorothy nor Stella knew why Carl was going to Tampa. They assumed he was on his way to his next appearance. Stella thought he might have been going to sing somewhere. "He was promoting his Songbag at that time and had a guitar with him." She had recorded they did a lot of singing on the trip.

Stella had been charged with bringing back the sweater Carl had borrowed. She remembers: "I did everything but tear it off Carl's back. I insisted on his giving it to me to return to Mr. Wattles and he kept insisting that he would mail it back." After she returned to the Rollins campus, she would ask Professor Wattles if Sandburg had returned his sweater. Each time Wattles replied he had not. Dorothy presumed he never did.

However, Sandburg did not forget his new friends. A few weeks after the ride to Tampa, he sent each of them an inscribed copy of The Prairie Years. When Sandburg was editor of the year book at Lombard College, he had referred to himself as the editing manager and his close colleague as managing editor. He used the same reversal game in inscribing for his two new friends, who were addressed "To Stella, dreamer and child" and "To Dorothy, child and dreamer."

On March 15, 1929, Sandburg sent Dorothy a clipping from his "From the Note Book of Carl Sandburg" in the Chicago Daily News, referring to her. He had written that at first glance he thought she had a sweet face. Then he saw it was not sweet but rather something "better and bitter." He thought it had something of the "droll finality" of her five-line poem:

The end of the world had come,
And no one said anything about it,
And no one thought anything about it,
For the end of the world had come,
And there was no one to know anything about it.

(Dorothy Emerson had gone to Rollins College on a scholarship as the result of winning the Witter Bynner Poetry Contest for 1927, conducted by Scholastic Magazine.)

Dorothy wrote in 1970 that she stopped short in the
doorway of her room when she read the words "better and
bitter. " She "felt that Sandburg apprehended with quick insight a major part of myself that I had tried to put aside
during those days at Rollins. " Though she found herself
given as an example that "poets are just like other people, "
she knew that "in truth I hid great anxieties beneath my
young prettiness. Even today I feel that Sandburg had unusual perception. "

On April 26, 1929, Carl wrote to Stella, who retained only the envelope in which it was delivered. However, she remembered what he wrote. "I had sent Carl
some poems by a boy I was dating, and he replied: 'You
or Dorothy, either or both, have a better batting average
than this young man. But no matter what I say, if he is
going to be a writer, he will be one--in spite of hell or
high water. '"

The last time either of the students saw Sandburg
was in February, 1940, when Sandburg made his second and
last visit to Rollins. Stella recalls:

> I was doing stenographic work in [the president's]
> office at the time and overheard Carl asking Dr.
> [Hamilton] Holt's secretary to reserve a drawing
> room for him on the train for the next day. This
> was about the time when he had completed his
> biography on Lincoln. I recall that I told him I
> was amazed to find a poor poet travelling around
> in a drawing room, and he replied, 'This trip
> I'm not travelling as a poet but as an eminent
> biographer!' It was said with no conceit at all,
> but with warm humor.

To fully realize the significance of the time Sandburg
spent with the two students, one needs to know what Mrs.
Wattles told the writer in an interview. Mrs. Hamilton
Holt [wife of the president of the college] had invited Sandburg to a dinner in his honor. Unknowingly, she had planned
it for a time when he rarely ate, just before his evening
performance, a time when he felt tense.

He arrived at the Wattles home in the afternoon and

said he would take a nap.   He slept so soundly that Mrs.
Wattles finally woke him so that he could go to the Holt dinner at 7 p. m.   He said, with finality, "I'm not going."
Mrs. Wattles went next door to telephone Mrs. Holt, who
was, naturally, very upset.   He did eat "pot luck," which
happened to be stewed tomatoes, with the Wattleses.   "This
is just fine," he said.   [Most other accounts call for his
waiting till after his performance to eat.]

Cyril Clemens Meets Carl*

Just outside the hamlet of Harbert, Michigan, lives
the poet and biographer, Carl Sandburg, in a white stucco
house atop a steepish hill commanding an unparalleled view
of Lake Michigan.   Touring through the vicinity I stopped
by one evening.   The poet himself answered my ring and
shook hands most cordially.   He is a strong virile man of
something above middle height with a tanned, boyish looking
face, straight brown hair parted at the side (now almost
grey) and deep humorous kindly grey eyes.   The frank boy-
ishness of the face made me feel that I knew exactly how
Sandburg looked as a lad of ten or twelve.

"I have been working on the final volume of my Lincoln," began Sandburg as we took seats on the porch facing
the lake, "dealing with the assassination and the numerous
and complicated events that led up to it.   I have now finished
writing an exhaustive account of the character and origin of
Wilkes Booth.   Not a very pleasant task--but one that had
to be done."

"What do you think, Mr. Sandburg, of that theory
which contends that Booth was not killed a few days after
he murdered Lincoln, but that he escaped the country, and
finally died in China some thirty years later?"

"I think no more of it," returned the biographer,
"than I do of the theory that Judas Iscariot did not hang
himself, but went to Gaul where he became a prominent
citizen.   No, every inch of the way that Booth covered after
the assassination until his death, is accounted for.   We are
as certain of the time and place of his death as we are of
the death of anybody in history."

---

*Cyril Clemens, "A Call Upon Carl Sandburg," Hobbies,
February, 1947.   pp. 126-8.   By permission of the publisher.

After letting his eyes wander over the broad expanse
of Lake Michigan for a few moments, Mr. Sandburg continued,

"I have pondered much on what made the man do that
heinous deed, and I finally come to the conclusion that he
was insane, as his father Julius Booth had been before him.
He was that type of man who broods and broods upon fancied
wrongs until, bereft of any modicum of sense that he ever
did have, he attempts to strike down the man he feels is
responsible for his misfortune."

For a while we discussed different points in connection
with Lincoln's life until I stated that a recent biographer had
declared that Lincoln never gave his law-partner, William
Henry Herndon, an appointment in Washington because Mrs.
Lincoln had acquired a violent dislike for him. It seems
that after dancing once with Mary Lincoln, Herndon had told
her that she danced as gracefully as a snake glided through
the grass--really meaning a compliment in his blunt, male
way. But as most women would have done, Mary took it as
an insult and never forgave him.

"I do not think that was the reason why Herndon
never received any Washington appointment," returned Sandburg. "After all, he always remained Lincoln's law-partner,
and while in Washington, Lincoln often remarked that after
his retirement he would again become associated with Herndon in the practice of law. That shows the high esteem in
which Lincoln held the man. But if any reason existed for
not inviting him to Washington it lay in the fact that Herndon
loved the bottle too much. That fact alone would have made
it impossible for Lincoln to have appointed him to high office.
As you doubtless know Lincoln was exceedingly particular in
making his appointments."

"Have you been to St. Louis lately, Mr. Sandburg?"

"No, it has been sometime since I was there. I was
a great admirer and friend of the late Marion Reedy. He
was one of the very first to give my writings encouragement
by publishing them in his Mirror. Whenever I went through
St. Louis I always looked him up for a chat on literature.
His untimely death in 1920 was a grievous loss to American
letters. It has long been my feeling that his life should be
written by a competent hand."

"Our mutual friend, Edgar Lee Masters, has been

talking about writing his life for some years now," I remarked. "In the old Chelsea Hotel where he lives, he has--
so he tells me--a whole trunkload of letters which Reedy
wrote him."

"Another man I used always to see when I went to
St. Louis," continued Sandburg, "was Robertus Love. For
many years he served as literary critic of the Globe Democrat, and impressed me as a man full of life and animation.
His biography of Jesse James was an excellent piece of work,
and especially interested me because I have sometimes thought
of writing a poem on the colorful outlaw: the best representative that we have of the lawlessness which prevailed in
many of the border states directly after the Civil War."

"Frank James, Jesse's brother," I remarked, "was
never convicted for any of the murders or robberies in
which he and his brother had participated, and he lived the
quiet life of a farmer until his passing in 1915. On account
of their spectacularity and extraordinary daring these men
have always fired the popular imagination."

"Another St. Louisan whom I much admired," continued Sandburg, "is Charles H. Compton, the head of the
St. Louis Public Library. His book Who Reads What certainly does American literature a yeoman service. How
fascinating to know just what class of people read our well
known writers such as Sinclair Louis, Booth Tarkington, and
the inimitable Mark Twain. When I visit St. Louis, Compton and I always foregather. America needs more librarians
of his sterling style."

"What did you think of Masters' recent Life of Vachel
Lindsay," I next asked Sandburg.

"I found it a stimulating work," returned Sandburg,
"but I did feel that he drew far too dramatic a contrast between the Northern Yankee and the full blooded Southern
gentleman. Such a contrast is not entirely warranted by the
facts. And then again he lambasts the American public for
not taking Lindsay more seriously as a lecturer, when as a
matter of fact it must be admitted that Lindsay did not take
much pains in improving his method of delivery as time
went on. With the result that at the end of his career he
was about the same as he had been at the beginning. For
one thing he did not seem to know how to save his voice
which because of his shouting on the platform usually gave

out long before his program had finished. Naturally this
must have been annoying to his audiences.

"Then again I do not think Masters should have been
so dogmatic about his suicide. I still feel that it may well
have been an accident. When a man is half crazed from
worry and cannot sleep at night, it is the easiest thing in
the world for him by accident to take an excess of sleeping
powders."

When Sandburg asked me what I had been doing lately,
I spoke of my work on the lives of the old humorists Shilla-
ber and Marietta Holley.

"One of my own favorites among the elder humorists," he remarked, "was 'Orpheus C. Kerr'--a quaint way
of spelling office seeker. He took off in a superb manner
that terrible pest the sinecure-seeker who drove Lincoln to
distraction, and was responsible for the death of poor Gar-
field. Some of Robert Newell's (Kerr's real name) humorous descriptions are exceedingly poetical. One of the best
things he ever did was that inimitable piece, 'The Outrage
at Utica,' a prime favorite with Abraham Lincoln. It is,
indeed, interesting to note how exceedingly fond Lincoln
was of all our humorists. If he had lived. I have no doubt
but that humor would have flourished much more during the
post-war period."

"This is a wholly delightful house," I told Sandburg.
"Do you come out here every summer?"

"No indeed," he replied, "this is where we live all
year round--rain or sun, fair or foul. I have gotten so
now that I must have peace and quiet before I can do my
writing. In my younger days I was able to write anywhere.
As a lad I traveled a good deal by freight train. I well
remember how I used to compose poetry as the train rumbled
along. The noise sort of beat out the rhythm of my lines.
I well remember that one June night in the year, 1897, I
arrived in Hannibal traveling by freight--my face and hands
black from the train dust and soot. I wanted so much to
see the boyhood home of my favorite author and that was my
only chance of doing so because I was entirely on my own
and lacked all funds. I never regretted the effort and
trouble that it cost me. I say without hesitation that Mark
Twain has had a very great influence upon my style."

A few minutes later Sandburg mentioned having just

returned from attending the University of Colorado Writers' Conference under the general direction of the poet Edward Davison.

"Those Writers' Conferences are splendid things, and certainly enable many a young struggling author to get just the encouragement that he needs to carry on. It won't be denied that the writing game has a longer apprenticeship than almost any other profession. And many a promising young writer has fallen by the wayside for lack of just that modicum of encouragement. Many incipient Chattertons have been quite as effectively silenced by entering the oil, grocery, or insurance business as he was by the more speedy method of poison."

"What did you do at the Conference, Mr. Sandburg?"

"I gave several lectures on poetry in general and conducted a sort of class of poetic writing. But most of our worthwhile results were obtained through informal discussions in the evenings. I am a strong believer in the form of conversational teaching, where both students and teacher feel perfectly at ease. As a rule students are so uncomfortable in the average classroom, that they do not derive much benefit from the instruction that is handed out."

Sandburg was soon telling me about his early years.

"My parents were Swedish immigrants with barely six months formal education between them. My father, born August Johnson, had his name changed to Sandburg, because there were several other August Johnsons in his railroad construction gang and the pay envelopes sometimes got mixed. During my youth father worked in the railroad blacksmith shops at Galesburg.

"As a boy I worked hard at all sorts of jobs, with practically no opportunity for regular schooling. From thirteen to seventeen I successively drove a milk wagon, served as porter in a barbershop, scene-shifter in a theatre, and truck-driver for a brick-kiln. At seventeen I went West, riding freight and blind baggage cars. I served as a farm-hand in the Kansas wheatfields, washed dishes in hotels in Kansas City, Omaha, and Denver, and worked under a carpenter in Kansas. Once I even went from door to door, offering to do a neat painting job for a meal."

"Is it correct that you served in the Spanish American War?"

"As soon as the conflict broke out I enlisted in the Sixth Illinois Infantry and went to Porto Rico, where I served for eight months.   Down there I met a young man from Lombard College, Galesburg, who induced me to enter at his college when the war terminated.   There I stayed from 1898 to 1902, earning my expenses as tutor, bell-ringer, and janitor of the gymnasium, I had the honor of being the editor of both the college monthly magazine and annual.   I joined the Poor Writers' Club, the purpose of which was for the members to criticize each other's work savagely.

"After doing various things about the country and marrying in 1908, I joined the staff of the Chicago Daily News in 1917, and the next year I visited Norway and Sweden, as correspondent for the Newspaper Enterprise Association. Although my first full volume of poetry was not published until 1916, Chicago Poems, I had been dabbling in verse writing for fully twenty years before."

To my query about his inspirations he answered:

"Poems are the results of moods.   I don't approach a subject in the same mood every day.   Maybe some days I am in the mood for the prairie, the skies, the trees.   On other days I can feel the noise, the jumble, and the confusion of the city.   There have been days when I could not have written or even tolerated the idea expressed in my Smoke and Steel."

"I found very stimulating your article of a few years ago in which you gave the astounding number of forty different definitions of poetry.   Which one was your favorite?"

"I think this one was my favorite, 'Poetry is a sliver of the moon lost in the belly of a golden frog' and if I had to choose a second best I think it would be, 'Poetry is a phantom script telling how rainbows are made and why they go away.'"

When I told Sandburg that I felt his greatest contribution to American poetry had been his indication that a vast modern city like Chicago could be the subject for genuine poetry, he answered:

"Well, you may be right.   The opening line in my

first book of poetry, 'Hog Butcher for the World,' stirred
up the hue and cry that I had anticipated. The critics declared that I had struck out a new path for American poetry,
and most of them were kind enough to say that my words
usually fitted my theme."

A little later Sandburg made the significant statement: "The kind of poem most congenial to me is neither
the etching nor the symbolic poem of industrialism, but a
kind of condensed fable, a snapshot of some scene or action,
so written as to set in motion in my reader's mind some
train of reflection; I like very much to invest the single incident with cosmic significance. My poem, 'Buttons,' a
picture of a newspaper man adjusting a war map, drives
home the horrible cost of war. 'Soup,' a snapshot of a
famous man in a restaurant, is not intended to present any
lesson at all, but simply to give us humorous reflections
on the inescapable commonplaces of the great. 'Limited'
endeavors to point out what an obviously long journey each
man must travel, but yet how seldom we look ahead."

The last author we discussed was Mark Twain of
whom Sandburg said, "In the range of his work Mark means
America making an art of its own, means laughter and
story-telling pointed up with American accent and lingo,
means philosophy running a gamut between optimism and
pessimism. He was in Innocents Abroad a showman and a
laughmaker whose clowning lives on as a significant register.
His tolerance ran far and had its main difficulty with hypocrites. As an American index he is a towering portent with
a vast audience."

I left Sandburg refreshed and inspired, feeling that
I had been fortunate in having met one of the most vibrant
and stimulating persons in contemporary American letters....

Carl Sandburg Program*

[A note by Wilson O. Clough, professor emeritus of
English at The University of Wyoming and the author of
these lines, says that Sandburg appeared at the University
of Wyoming in February, 1929.]

*Reprinted by permission of the author, from his Past's
Persisting.

Then he came,
With a quick, lithe tread
Of a man who could stir his stumps,
And a frugal, pithy frame
Trim for bouts with old flint-heart Time.
Under his lancer's pennon drooping iron grey,
Grey eyes held steady
As the sun's grave gaze through morning mists.
Swaying to some inner rhythm,
His comments came, in a casual, mellow key,
On will-o-the-wisps and hard tack,
On tough guys and rainbows,
On cabooses, and swamps that lie
Lonely and lovely under the stars.

He chanted low-down songs,
Beach-comber tunes and negro songs,
Touching soft chords on his handy guitar,
Mm-plinkety-plank-plank, mm-plunk, plunk;
Till you saw him squatting by a hobo fire
Serenading the moon,
Not giving a damn for proper folk.

Butter-and-egg men were trapped in a chuckle
In the Village of Liver-and-Onions.
Flapper folly knew a strange moment of wonder
At this mad, sad, fair world of ours.
In some dreamland a shadow dancer gestured free,
Strewing--was it biscuits or hyacinths?

John Doe, citizen, standard U. S. A.
(Cash register tinkle was music enough),
Cleared his throat and stirred at the lure and
          insistent beat
Of an outcast rhyme from the tattered fringes of
          money-folk.

But hard eyes stared at the platform singer
From here and there
Like hawks to pounce on a light-pink rat,
Any unguarded yawp at the status-quo;
Scowling, growling, "Say, who does he think he is?"
Say, Carl Sandburg,
Loafer, Swede, toiler, poet, melter of frozen words,
Who the hell do you think you are?

A Writer's Admiration*

[These two articles by Nelson Antrim Crawford in
successive years in Manhattan, Kansas, demonstrate the enthusiasm of another writer for Sandburg's work:]

"The new poetry movement, " Carl Sandburg believes,
is not altogether a happy term. The word "phenomenon"
would be better.

So Mr. Sandburg himself is not merely a poet--there
are several scores of authentic living poets--but a phenomenon, as much a phenomenon as the sea, a group of grave
rocks, a great earthquake, or a caressing wind. And he is
maybe the only living poet to whom the term may be applied.
Other poets have fanned a spark of talent--many of them
with the leaves of books as a fan. One feels, on the other
hand, that Mr. Sandburg is inevitable. He is essentially
and throughout an artist--not an artist made by any external
influence. This is obvious in his poems, in his reading, in
his talk, in his personality.

Mr. Sandburg was the principal speaker at the spring
meeting of the Kansas Authors' club here Monday. At each
of the two sessions--afternoon and evening--he gave a lecture-
recital, reading his poems, singing American folk songs,
and discussing artistic principles. No speaker at the college
in many years has provoked more enthusiasm and at the
same time more distinct reactions on the part of members
of the audience.

Pointing out that there is no definition of art or of
poetry that has lasted, Mr. Sandburg showed the importance
of implication, overtones, mystery, to art. He quoted
Millet's definition of the beautiful as "that which is in place."
Reverence, leisure, and humility, he said, are character-
istics of the artist. He illustrated the last mentioned quality
by the incident of Hokusai, probably the greatest Japanese
artist, who after producing 30,000 paintings said on his
deathbed, "If God had let me live five years longer, I should
be a great painter. "

In his reading of his own poems, Mr. Sandburg ex-

---

*Nelson Antrim Crawford, The Industrialist (Kansas State
Agricultural College), May 16, 1921 and March 8, 1922.

emplified the qualities which he ascribed to the artist. His
poems are more articulate and living, they have more grave,
god-like humor, they have more of the uninhibited, uncare-
ful freedom of great natural phenomena, than those of probably any other poet now writing. Their now powerful, now
delicate beauty is tremendously enhanced by the voice of the
author, which brings out every cadence, every nuance of
music or conception.

The localization of the poems, their gloriously un-
generalized character, reminds one of the recent work of
Maurice Vlaminck, the French painter, "Intelligence is international, stupidity is national, art is local."

From this point of view, as from others, Mr. Sandburg's work is outstanding art. A great reporter, he sees
even very slight things precisely as they are. A great
artist, he gets at their elemental significance, which he presents subtly and with quiet overtones. In his work, there
is the stuff of life, understood.

The American folk songs given by Mr. Sandburg to
the accompaniment of his guitar were both interesting and
revealing. Among them were "Stackeriee" and "The Boll
Weevil Song."

"If we ever have any honest-to-God grand opera in
the United States," he commented, "it must take into consideration the folk songs."

* * *

A mark of great literature and of a great personality
is that they improve on acquaintance. By reason of this
fact the recital and addresses of Carl Sandburg at the college Monday and Tuesday made an even more powerful impression than did his appearance last year. Mr. Sandburg's
poetry is great, yet he himself is greater than his work--
an indication that he is far from having finished his contribution to American art.

The audience which heard Mr. Sandburg in recital
Monday afternoon was stimulated by the power, vigor, and
compression of his thought and thrilled by his mingling of
powerful and delicate cadences. The two long poems which
he read, "And So Today" and "Slabs of the Sunburnt West,"
particularly impressed his hearers. The poems themselves

are among the most effective that he has produced, and their power and subtle beauty were made manifest in his reading. He is not improbably the best vocal interpreter of poetry in the United States.

Mr. Sandburg also sang several American folk songs, accompanying them on the guitar. These made a strong appeal. "The Boll Weevil Song" was perhaps most popular with the audience.

In both his poetry and the music, Mr. Sandburg's hearers felt that they were listening to authentic America. His voice, they were convinced, is from the soul of the country, however many may be unconscious of the existence of such a soul.

Mr. Sandburg's recital was under the auspices of the College Social club.

The motion picture as an industry and as an art was discussed by Mr. Sandburg in his address at assembly Tuesday morning. Mr. Sandburg is motion picture critic for the Chicago Daily News.

Characterizing the motion picture as a greater potential force than the stage, Mr. Sandburg pointed out that the daily audience of the pictures in the United States is 20,000,000 and that this number will soon increase to between 40,000,000 and 50,000,000. There is now, he said, a larger number of projection machines outside theaters-- that is, in schools, clubhouses, and similar places--than in the movie houses. The number and use of the machines, he predicted, will grow.

Mr. Sandburg looks forward to great development in the art of the motion picture, which he holds can produce effects impossible to the spoken drama. He makes a plea for more intelligent criticism of motion pictures, both in newspapers and magazines and in the talk of educated people.

Mr. Sandburg talked to the class in the ethics of journalism, discussing various human elements involved in editing a newspaper. These elements, he pointed out, are often over-looked by critics of the newspaper. He answered a number of specific questions from members of the class.

Meeting a First Major Poet*

     Carl Sandburg was the first major poet I had met,
and the experience was pretty overwhelming. He spoke during our chapel hour that morning and, as I recall, his program was characteristically informal, the major part of it
being folk songs rather than the reading of his own poems.
This disappointed me in a way.

     I remember that he seemed a lonely figure on the
bare platform, a sense of isolation about him, somehow as
if he and the music were alone. His speaking voice was
quite remarkable, with a quiet rolling resonance--very com-
pelling. Even after so many years, I can still feel the
timbre of that voice.

     In the afternoon he met with the English majors in-
formally, and I remember his manner as being easy but
rather remote. Of course, I was painfully shy, and sat
wordless in the aura of just being in the same room with
him. I think he may have been tired, though I don't know
this. He was patient and polite, but I didn't feel as though
any one really connected with him, which is much more un-
derstandable to me now than it was then.

     [After the experience recalled in the foregoing com-
ment, written in 1970, Marden Armstrong wrote the following lines for The Arrow of the Pennsylvania College for
Women (November 12, 1941):]

Carl Sandburg Speaks
(October, 1941)

"Follow your heart," he says
As he stands on the chapel platform,
Wearing a dark blue suit, his straight white hair
    gleaming above his tanned face.
He leans on the golden oak desk,
And then his words roll on again
Like wheat on the prairie
Rippled by the wind;
Strong words that cry out freedom,
Something of Lincoln in them--

---

*Letter from Marden Armstrong Dahlstedt, Beach Haven
Gardens, N. J. , 1970. By permission.

But the words mean less than his voice,
He bows his head quite humbly.
"Your faces have been kind to me, " he says.
And then--a moment of deep silence
Before the applause.

Poetry's Medicine Man*

Carl Sandburg is more than an American poet; he is
America's troubadour. For 15 years he has trouped up and
down America, telling all manner of people in all manner of
places what is poetry; interpreting America to them in his
own poetry; singing them the songs of the American folk.

Last night he talked in the John Hay High School auditorium jammed full of delegates--high school students and
teachers of journalism--before the convention of the National
Scholastic Press Association.

Sandburg was a liberal agitator in his youth, when he
thought that liberal meant just labor. He is still a liberal
agitator. Now he knows it means poetry. Poetry is the
ultimate realism. A people's folk songs are their most
realistic literature. They are elemental as the earth. Is
there something in poetry which baffles?

"There is something important in the fact that one of
the most important scientific books of our times is called
by its eminent scientist author, 'This Mysterious Universe,'"
he says.

"Some people say that all about a tree that they believe is what they can see with their eyes and smell with
their noses and feel with their hands. Do they forget how
much of a tree they can't see, can't smell, can't feel? Do
they forget the chemistry of the leaves; all of the tree that
is underground; the maze of roots driving thru the earth
practicing the mysterious economy of life?"

Thus he makes poetry and song homely and familiar
to folks many of whom have never known it was homely and
familiar at all.

*Elrick B. Davis, "Troubador of U.S., " The Cleveland
Press, Dec. 5, 1930. By permission.

Once I called him poetry's medicine man. I shall do it again.

Concerning the Matter of Justice*

The Chicago dinner mentioned by Mr. Mearns was a dinner honoring some centennial of Peter Altgeld, famous governor of Illinois. I read a paper, as did others, including I believe, Harold Ickes.

It was Carl Sandburg's turn and he stepped to the radio microphone to speak. After a few sentences his voice broke and he had difficulty regaining his composure. But he did recover and ended in his usual strong voice.

Afterwards I was teasing him about it--how he, an old troubador, cracked up on the air. And then he told me a story.

As a boy in Galesburg, he sold papers; and one night a bundle was dropped at his stand where the headline read "Haymarket murderers executed."

He told me how good he felt, how safe, how secure now that the bad men had been put away.

Years later when Altgeld pardoned a remaining member of the "anarchist" gang, it suddenly dawned on Carl that as a boy he had been elated at the execution of innocent men.

It was this experience that he relived in a few seconds on the radio at this Altgeld centennial and which almost laid him low.

Collecting Folk Songs†

One night Keith Preston, a columnist on the <u>Chicago</u>

---

*Letter from Justice William O. Douglas, August 22, 1968. By permission.
†Based on an interview with Alfred Frankenstein, San Francisco, February, 1970.

<u>Daily News</u>, met Alfred Frankenstein at a concert and told
him, "Carl Sandburg wants to see you. He's given me a
message that he wants you to get in touch with him." (This
was a typical Sandburg procedure. Instead of using letters
or telephone calls, he would depend on an oral message and
an accidental meeting.)

Sandburg wanted Frankenstein to write down the music
for the songs in his collection. Many meetings in his office
and at Elmhurst followed. Usually they met on Monday
afternoon and went out to Elmhurst. "Paula would give me
dinner."

All that winter of 1925, approximately once a month,
Sandburg and Frankenstein had these encounters, mostly at
his home.

"He had private hideaways all over town. He had
friends who would take him in. They were never sure when
he would appear and hole up for a couple of days. There
was a vagabondage in his work. Once we spent the evening
in the reception room of a Polish dentist."

It was very difficult to write the songs down. Sandburg never sang a song the same way twice. Frankenstein
would say, "Carl, do it again." He would do it in a
totally different way. Frankenstein found himself writing
the lowest common denominator of four or five versions.
He tried to find the skeleton of the tune.

Sandburg had a quick ear but only a vague idea of
how to write music. Very often he would take paper and
write note heads to show the relationship. He invariably
started on the second space. As the result, the book is
all in A major.

In the course of this work, Frankenstein, who knew
little about American folk songs, saw what Sandburg was
giving him as separate songs were really different versions
of the same songs.

"When this was mentioned, I always got the same
reply: 'Philology! Philology!' said sneeringly. He had no
idea of scholarship in folklore. He not only knew nothing
about it but also had nothing but contempt for it."

In the middle of that winter (1925-26) he met Robert

Winslow Gordon, "one of the most brilliant of American folklore scholars." He was of the Kittredge school, though he
had no academic job. He was running a section of <u>Adventure</u>
magazine called "Songs Men Have Sung."

Bob and Carl got together and Gordon opened his eyes
to scholarship in that area. Carl tried to swallow the whole
thing too fast. It became a large, indigestible mass. Gordon, who established the folklore archive in the Library of
Congress, cured, for better or worse, Sandburg of his dis-
respect for scholarship in folklore. Then Sandburg tried to
bite off too much.

The original <u>American Songbag</u> consisted of sixty
songs. Frankenstein went to Europe in May, 1926, and
handed over to Harrison Smith the original manuscript of
the book. It had exactly sixty songs. These had been collected by Sandburg alone. In many cases there were entire
songs which no one had ever collected. It had melodies
only and was a very personal book. It had simple tunes
and texts with little or no headnotes. There was a preface
with notes about sources. Frankenstein also contributed a
brief preface about the problems of transcribing Sandburg.

Frankenstein was in Europe for four months. "I had
a promise that proofs would be sent to Paris. But I had
no proofs and no word. I went back to New York and called
on Harrison Smith, who told me the salesmen had decided
the book would sell better with piano accompaniment. This
would tend to make the book a family song book."

Frankenstein objected to this abandonment of the folk
character of the book.

After Sandburg met Robert Winslow Gordon, he decided to make it a general anthology. It was no longer to
be his personal book. In order to make room for some of
the new material, he threw out some of the best things he
had collected.

He also farmed out the job of preparing piano accompaniments to people who had no sense of folk music. One
of these was Hazel Feldman Buchbinder, a commercial
arranger. The result of miscellaneous farming out of accompaniments was a two-fold disaster: 1) Accompaniments
were too complicated for a book to be used at home by
amateurs. It contained very difficult materials, suitable

only for professional pianists. Buchbinder and others changed
texts to accord with music; 2) Material was selected from a
series of already-published and not-very-profound anthologies
(Shea: Pious Friends and Drunken Companions; Rickaby:
Ballads and Songs of the Shanty Boys). As a general anthology it was not a success. It had bad transcriptions
and overloaded accompaniments. Frankenstein was bitterly
disappointed and had little contact with Sandburg thereafter.

Sandburg's interest in folk songs and Lincoln were
tied together. They were part of a great American vernacular movement. All the opposition to and derision of Sandburg came from those who did not understand this. He
wanted to rescue the Lincoln of Galesburg, wanted to see
him on the prairie. There was a vernacular scenery, too.

He had a broad humanitarian interest. The esthetic
was much less important than the vernacular atmosphere.
He had a great mystical feeling about the Middle West. It
shows up in everything he does, even the children's stories.
It involves the effort of the immigrant to prove that he belonged in America.

There is a relationship between Sandburg and the political Left. He was mixed up with a lot of left-wing characters. There was always in those days (20's) a certain uneasiness about this, but for Sandburg, strike and union
leaders had vernacular character.

Two Sandburg Encounters*

In the forties Mrs. Reuben Robertson came to me
for help with her songs. The wife of the chairman of the
board of Champion Papers, she had attended the Cincinnati
Conservatory when it was presided over by the Bauer sis-
ters. She and her husband lived outside Flat Rock and
when Carl Sandburg left Harbert, Michigan for North Carolina, he bought the estate adjoining theirs. It was at their
home that I first met the poet, among guests invited in one
evening to hear a program of Mrs. Robertson's works and
mine.

*Excerpt by Edwin Gerschefski, taken from his forthcoming
autobiography, tentatively entitled, "At Random." By permission.

I often wonder whether Sandburg ever got around to putting down the idea for a children's story which he related to me that evening.   We had just listened to my folk-ballad, 'Half Moon Mountain, ' a word-for-word setting of a news article from Time magazine.   After discussing the piece at length (even including the headache of producing photostats of the parts, a comment on which naturally ended up later in the evening with Sandburg improvising a whole song on "Gerschefski has those photostatic blues" while he strummed away on the guitar), he told me he would like to have me set to music a story about three young boys which went something like this:

> Many years ago three youngsters were sitting on the side of the road playing with mud.   It was obvious that two of them were more gifted than the third when it came to making objects out of mud.   First they built castles, then carved figures, and finally tried their hands at molding birds.   By now the third boy seemed hopelessly behind as the three engaged themselves in creating pigeons; so much so that the first two stopped their play to come over and sympathize with their friend.   'Don't feel too badly, ' they said.   'After all not everyone can be talented. '
> 'It's true, yours are much prettier than mine, ' the third boy mused wistfully.   Then, after a pause he went on, 'but mine flies. '   And with that he brushed the tail of his pigeon with his hand and it soared into the sky--for that boy was Jesus.

My second meeting with Carl Sandburg was something else.   I was to have a one hour appointment with him at 3:30 on a Sunday afternoon to talk about setting some of his poems to music.   When I arrived he was resting upstairs so his wife showed me to the drawing room and suggested that I make myself at home.   I did, by playing on their excellent Steinway B grand piano (I remember noticing choral works by prominent Americans strewn on the piano, evidently gifts from the composers to Sandburg).   I started with Beethoven sonatas, then proceeded to Chopin Etudes and Cesar Franck's Prelude, Chorale, and Fugue.   About this moment I was aware that Sandburg had slipped into the room and was sitting in the corner quietly listening.

My first impression was a figure slumped in a chair, completely relaxed physically, with an enormous scarf wound around his neck.

Now we talked between numbers and the music began
to reflect my experiments. I played Bach "back-wards, "
classics "expanded, " and popular tunes upside-down.

We enjoyed whisky, brought in by his daughter. Suddenly he jumped up and exclaimed, "Gerschefski, we've got
to adopt you. " I was all for it.

I started on some of my own things. Everything was
calm until I played my setting of "A Man on the Cross" by
Elizabeth Cheney. He hit the ceiling. The music was "fine"
but those sickishly-sweet words. "Didn't the woman realize,"
he shouted, "that was a LYNCHING!"

It took time, but finally things quieted down. Along
the way Sandburg allowed that Time style might also be improved upon for musical settings and with that he disappeared
and returned moments later carrying a sheaf of neatly type-
written pages. These he described as unpublished poems
and stories for children which I should have to set to music.

All was good cheer again. Mrs. Sandburg appeared
and invited me to stay for supper. I shall always remember the goat's milk cheese.

Then we went down to the basement and looked at
the new kid that had just been born. And from there we
went outside and looked over the rest of the goat herd.
(I was in my element. As an old goat man I even took a
turn at milking.)

It was time to leave--10:00 p. m. ! My last recollection was being accompanied to my car by a personable young
man who apparently was assisting Sandburg in his literary
activity. He seemed to feel it his responsibility to assure
me that I should not take personally the out-burst Sandburg
had delivered about Mrs. Cheney's poem. After all, he
said, the man had gone through and done so much in his
lifetime that his touchiness when riled up should be accepted
with understanding and sympathy.

I couldn't agree more.

Harry Golden Visits Carl Sandburg*

I spent eight hours with Carl Sandburg. Except for
a short walk around his Connemara Farm at Flat Rock,
North Carolina, we sat on his porch side by side and exchanged stories. But mostly we laughed just as the poet
Blake had imagined it--". . . we laughed and the hills echoed."

Carl Sandburg and I spent eight hours together and we
talked and we laughed and the sapphire mountains of North
Carolina cast echo and shadow of Lincoln; of Swedish immigrant farmers to the broad plains of the American midwest,
of pushcarts on the lower East Side of New York, and of a
long-ago place in the province of Galicia of Austrian Poland--
and this can happen only in America.

And when we rested from our labors, Margaret, the
charming daughter of the Sandburgs, read to us out of
George Ade, a household favorite.

Nor did even the dinner bell intrude upon us. "Bring
it out here on the porch," said Mr. Sandburg; and I re-
flected later, with considerable chagrin, how I had not offered to help Mrs. Sandburg and Miss Margaret when they
lugged the side tables to us; and they tried hard not to disturb us.

And when it was all over Sandburg said, "Harry, it's
been about fifty-fifty, you talked half and I talked half."

I am certain that Carl Sandburg had thought of this
appointment as just another "interview." Just another newspaper fellow, standing first on one foot and then on the
other, asking how do I like North Carolina; what am I writing now; a question maybe about Lincoln, or Nancy Hanks,
or Mary Todd; who is my favorite novelist; what do I think
of Andersonville, etc.

I shuddered at the thought that he may associate me
with such nonsense.

Nor did I carry a book for him to autograph, or a
camera to snap his picture, or a manuscript for him to

---

*Harry Golden, "A Day with Carl Sandburg," The Carolina
Israelite, March-April, 1956. By permission of the author.

read in his "spare time. "   All I brought was a bottle of
whiskey.   Whiskey?   Who ever heard of bringing a bottle of
whiskey to Carl Sandburg?   Well, I figured that even if he
doesn't drink he probably would not think it in bad taste if
I drank a few toasts to him--right on the spot.   Margaret
Sandburg kept us supplied with fresh North Carolina branch
water, but first we had to agree not to do any talking during her short absences.

I had planned the appointment for a long time.
Several years ago Don Shoemaker, the Asheville Citizen-
Times editor, had introduced Mr. Sandburg to the Carolina
Israelite and we exchanged a few letters during the past five
years.   Several months ago I wrote him for an appointment,
and received a note:

> Brudder Golden: All signs say I'll be here April
> 3 and if you're here we won't expect to save the
> country but we can have fellowship.   Carl Sand-
> burg.

I arrived about noon and as I got out of the car I
heard Sandburg's voice through the screen door of his
porch: "That must be Harry Golden, I want to see what
he looks like. "   There are about ten steps leading up to
the porch of the old plantation home and when I reached
the top Mr. Sandburg was already outside to greet me.
He wore a Korean army cap low over his eyes, a khaki
shirt and work pants.   I turned from him to take a long
look at that breath-taking scene, the acres and acres of
"lawn" in front of the house as clean as a golf course, the
heavily wooded areas to the right, the majestic North Carolina Rockies in front--the whole thing like a Christmas card
without snow, and I greeted Sandburg with the first thought
that came into my head: "Well, I wonder what old Victor
Berger would have said if he had seen this place. "   (Victor Berger, the first Socialist ever elected to Congress,
was publisher of the Socialist paper The Leader on which
Sandburg had worked in his early newspaper days.)   Sandburg threw his head back and roared; called back into the
house to Mrs. Sandburg, "He wants to know what Victor
Berger would have said if he had seen this place, " but then
he motioned me to a chair on the porch and began to "apolo-
gize" in all seriousness about how come a poletariat has an
old Southern plantation.   "When did I get this place, --1945,
right?   And how old was I in 1945, --seventy years old,
right?", but I told him he had nothing to worry about; that

from some parapet in heaven Victor Berger and Eugene V.
Debs look down upon Carl Sandburg with love and devotion
and by now even the writer of Psalms has memorized a bit
of Carl Sandburg:

> There is only one man in the world
> And his name is All Men.

We discussed Socialism of course, the American Socialist movement and the tragedy of so many, many unedu-
cated editorial writers who speak of "Communism, socialism, etc. , " as though they were the same; and this, the
supreme irony: wherever the Communists have conquered,
the Socialists, the Social-Democrats were always the first
ones they killed. We spoke of the days when the movement
was at its height, when Walter Lippman was secretary to
Socialist Mayor George Lunn of Schenectady, New York; and
the Party stalwarts included Margaret Sanger, Heywood
Broun, Morris Hillquit, Algernon Lee, Alan Benson, August
Claessens, and Charles P. Steinmetz, the electrical wizard.

We swapped tales of the lower East Side of New York,
the Jewish Daily Forward, and Morris Hillquit, who I believe, foreign accent and all, was the best orator I have
ever heard. And Sandburg brought out a volume of his poetry, Smoke and Steel (Harcourt, Brace and Co. , N. Y.) and
read to me of the East Side:

Home Fires

In a Yiddish eating place on Rivington Street
faces ... coffee spots ... children kicking at the
Night stars with bare toes from bare buttocks,
They know it is September on Rivington Street
When the red tomatoes cram the pushcarts,
Here the children snozzle at milk bottles, children
    who have never seen a cow
Here the stranger wonders how so many people remember
    where they keep home fires.

We talked of the poor immigrants and how much more
it cost them to live than the rich. They bought a scuttle of
coal for ten cents; a bushel was a quarter. This in the
days of $5-a-ton coal, and they were paying $35-a-ton in
dribs and drabs the way poor people have to buy. I told
about how the Germans paid no attention to bare floors, con-
centrating on overstuffed beds; but that the Irish were nuts

about carpets and curtains even if they had no other furniture; and how the Jews paid little attention to either carpets or beds, and concentrated their all on FOOD on the table, the carry-over from centuries in the ghetto and the will to survive, to survive at all costs.

Sandburg brought me a little volume by the late August Claessens, Didn't We Have Fun. Claessens was one of the most famous Socialists on the East Side, a man with a brilliant mind and a wonderful sense of humor. This little book is a humorous record of thirty years on a soapbox. Mr. Sandburg inscribed the book: "For Harry Golden whose heart is not alien to agitators." Interestingly, I had once carried the American Flag for August Claessens at one of his street-corner meetings.

This charming Claessens had represented his all-Jewish district in the New York Legislature and eventually joined the Arbeiter Ring, "Workman's Circle." A Roman Catholic, Claessens said that he joined the Jewish fraternity because of its cemetery benefits: "The last place in this world the devil will look for a Gentile is in a Jewish Cemetery."

And of course Sandburg and I exchanged anecdotes about Emanuel Haldeman-Julius, the Little Blue Book fellow. Haldeman-Julius was a feature writer on Victor Berger's Socialist paper at the same time that Sandburg was a reporter. Later, Haldeman-Julius went to California, Sandburg went to the Chicago News, and thereafter wrote his "Chicago, Hog-butcher of the World," which started him on his way into the mind and heart of America, --our national poet. We swapped a dozen stories about this interesting Emanuel who published and sold three hundred million books in his lifetime and really invented the "paper-back" book industry. Emanuel would watch the sales of his Little Blue Books carefully. If a book sold less than 10,000 a year he gave it one more chance. For instance, Gautler's Fleece of Gold, sold less than 10,000. The following year he changed the title: The Quest of a Blonde Mistress, exactly the type of story it is; sales jumped to 80,000.

Late in the afternoon a car drove up with Florida license plates and Mr. Sandburg went down the porch steps to greet the visitor. I followed a step or two behind. The fellow wanted to know something about Lincoln's "money-policy." Mr. Sandburg was gracious in his greeting, but

told the visitor, "It's all in my books, look in the index."
An hour later a phone call for Mr. Sandburg, and through
the open window I heard: "It's all in my books, look in
the index." And after another phone call: "That was Senator Johnston of South Carolina, his daughter is writing a
term paper on me and wants to come out. I told him to
call me sometime after May fifth."

We discussed Oscar Ameringer, Herbert Hoover,
Richard Nixon, Clarence Darrow and the famous trial of the
McNamaras, and Mr. Sandburg had a few new facts about
Darrow's trouble with Labor after the Los Angeles tragedy.

I was happy when he agreed that Anzia Yezierska and
Abe Cahan were among the best "Jewish" writers of modern
American literature. We discussed Chapel Hill and Sandburg told me that he has known Phillips Russell for over
forty years. I told him that a literary columnist had included his name among a list of "North Carolina Writers,"
and how someone disputed it as a bit of provincialism. Sandburg was indignant. I pay my taxes here; I write here; and
I shall die here; indeed I am a North Carolina writer. He
was genuinely sorry that he had not met Jimmie Street after
I had told him all about the late novelist. "He was over
here in Asheville, speaking one night and if I had known
about him then, I would have gone over." Street was a
much greater writer than his books indicated, and we discussed how completely true that has been of others; and of
course how it happens in reverse too.

When Margaret Sandburg excused herself, she shook
my hand with the best "goodbye" I have ever heard--"I wish
we had put this day on a tape recorder. I would have loved
to have a playback of your conversation with my father."
And "my father" in this case, my friends, is CARL SAND-
BURG.

But it was hard to break away, and finally after the
second "goodbye" Sandburg brought me another book, Home
Front Memo (Harcourt & Brace, 1942), being a hundred or
more newspaper columns Mr. Sandburg had written during
the "America First" and "phony war" period and right up
to Pearl Harbor. And Mr. Sandburg inscribed this book
too: "For Harry Golden who is also slightly leftish, and
out of jail, and loves the Family of Man."

At home the next day I thumbed through the volume

and came across a paragraph in which Mr. Sandburg describes a parting with a close friend and how he had put his arms around him and kissed him on both cheeks, "the second time in my life I have done this."

I closed the book. I did not need to read anymore for a little while. I recalled how the night before, as I was leaving, Carl Sandburg had put his arms around me and kissed me on both cheeks.

The Students Were Disappointed*

Students are uncertain but inclined to be a bit disappointed after Carl Sandburg's highly advertised visit here last Sunday (February 1, 1951). America's Elder Poet had much to say in his disconnected, off-the-cuff fashion, but we wish his whole program could have been more carefully organized.

As it was, he struck us as serious, interesting but a bit aloof from his audience. He was good, no doubt, but we had been led to expect more.

Perhaps his most outstanding characteristic was the fact that for the first time in a long time we had the feeling of being addressed by a normal human being. After the endless high-strung political harangues which all of us are subjected to via radio every day, his earthy, earnest analysis of our times was refreshing in spite of its disconnectedness.

First part of his program was by far the most impressive. The parallel which he drew between Lincoln's time and our own was well executed, and his points well taken. Many of his statements might well be taken to heart by our Washington administrators.

"In times like the present, we should not utter anything for which we would not willingly be responsible in time and eternity. The question is not: can any of us imagine better, but: can any of us do better.... We must disenthrall ourselves if we would save our world."

*Claude Grelling, The Wartburg Trumpet, Feb. 24, 1951. By permission.

He dwelt at length on this point--the danger of being
made slaves of tradition. When circumstances require it,
we should be willing to throw our habits and established
ways out of the window.

He gave a little known quotation of Lincoln's, which
applies surprisingly well to the present: "Fellow citizens--
we cannot escape history; we will be remembered in spite of
us. "

"When we look back to those times, we feel sorry
for the little men who did not know that history was in the
making, " he added.

He went on to quote from a letter by the famous
British surgeon McIntosh, written to a Viennese colleague:
"The race of man may reach the promised land, but there
is no assurance that the present generation will not perish
in the wilderness. "

Remainder of his program consisted of the reading
of his own poetry and some popular ballads which he sang
to the accompaniment of his own guitar.

It was here that he gave the impression of aloofness
more than anywhere else. His poetry seemed chosen at
random, some of it coming from among his worst. If he
attempted at all to key it to his audience, we failed to notice
it.

Furthermore, he arrived 45 minutes late. That, however, was not his fault. But he might have cut his singing
program a bit short. Toward the end, his audience responded with applause only when he made it obviously desirable by stopping after several numbers. Many of his
listeners, however appreciative in the beginning, left the
Knights gym with a definite feeling of relief. It was too
long.

Informality and Modesty*

We were guests at the house of Pres. and Mrs. C.

---

*Letter from Mrs. Esther M. Haefner, Waverly, Iowa,
May 18, 1976. By permission.

H. Becker on Carl Sandburg's first visit [1951] to Wartburg
College. I was struck by his informality and modesty--the
absolute absence of any feeling of superiority in the presence of the rest of us ordinary mortals. In fact, when I
began conversing in Norwegian (which I had learned from
childhood), his eyes sparkled as he remarked, "We have
some very intelligent people here." His searching eyes, I
felt, took in the minutest details at the dinner table and
among the company assembled. He didn't talk too much,
but listened. On the other hand, he was always ready when
comment or response was expected of him.

The same informality I remember on stage at the
time of his second visit. He was delayed for half an hour
because of the weather--had to put on Wendell Liemohn's
boots to wade through the slush. But this didn't bother him.
He came on just as casual with his guitar, took his seat on
the stool provided, and began pulling one song after the
other out of his "songbag." We forgot we had been waiting
thirty minutes for him--sat back as though we were around
a fireside listening to an old balladeer. I forget the number of encores called for; somehow he had an uncanny way
of identifying with the people. The people felt it; felt that
he understood their joys and sorrows--the little significant
things in life which the career men pass and miss entirely.

Carl Sandburg had grown up with America.

Umpiring at French Lick*

When the writer told Col. William Herzog that he
knew of Sandburg's intense interest in baseball, he related
the following anecdote.

Though he could not recall why Sandburg was there,
Herzog encountered him at French Lick, Indiana, where
Herzog was attending a meeting of the American Hospital
Association (evidently in 1923). A group of conventioneers
agreed to play a team from French Lick. Herzog, whose
athletic endeavors Sandburg had known in Chicago, asked
Carl to umpire.

One man, whom Herzog did not know, he assigned

*Based on letter from William Herzog, Santa Barbara,
Calif., March 25, 1970.

to right field, which Herzog considered the least significant
role on the roster. The man he chose as pitcher soon
tired. As the third inning approached, Sandburg whispered
that the man who was in right field was a pitcher in the
major leagues. When the man was questioned, he admitted
he was Douglas McWeeney, then very well known as a pitcher
for the White Sox. He was not playing then because of an
attack of boils, which he displayed on his neck; he was at
the spa at French Lick, seeking a cure for them. It took
only a few throws to prove that it was indeed McWeeney
(who, the records show, played for the White Sox in 1921,
1922, and 1924).

The Lincoln Mission*

Carl Sandburg lived from 1932 to 1945 at Harbert,
Michigan, near St. Joseph, where Arthur Hoffman lived.
Hoffman met Sandburg about a dozen times, twice at a barber shop and otherwise when Sandburg came into the large
town, it being the nearest to his house (which was on a sand
dune overlooking Lake Michigan).

When Hoffman encountered Sandburg the first time in the
shop of Benny Simms, one of a handful of blacks in St.
Joseph, he asked him if he were the writer. After the
white-haired Sandburg said he thought so, Hoffman told him
he found "Grass" appealing as an attack on futile killing in
war. Sandburg replied he was doubtful that Hoffman had
truly understood the poem. Hoffman, a fervent pacifist,
recited the poem, thus mollifying Sandburg. Hoffman went
on to ask if the poet knew that a million men, including
some of Hoffman's German relatives, had been killed at
Verdun. Sandburg replied he knew the toll was great but
had not known it was that large a number when he chose it
as one of the battlefields mentioned. At the end of that encounter, Hoffman asked Sandburg when he was going to get
his next haircut and successfully arranged to be in the shop
on his next visit.

Hoffman, as suggested by the foregoing, found Sandburg always friendly and as approachable as any well-known
figure could be. Sandburg said something to that effect,
enunciating a point he repeated when Hoffman visited his

---

*Based on a letter from Arthur Hoffman, Indianapolis, Ind.

home: he thought of himself not so much as a great writer
but rather as one with something to say.   Knowing that Sandburg was deeply involved in his study of Lincoln and the
Civil War, Hoffman expressed his idea that young American
men, involuntarily caught up in war, thought the Civil War
was one of the nation's greatest catastrophes.   Sandburg
vigorously responded that Lincoln risked being called a
traitor to arrange for peace.   Sandburg documented his case
so well that it changed Hoffman's view of Lincoln.

When Hoffman asked Sandburg if he could visit his
home, Sandburg agreed, making the definite stipulation that
he should make an appointment. Ignoring that provision,
Hoffman led a group of students at Anderson College (located a hundred or so miles to the south, in Indiana) to the
Sandburg home one Sunday afternoon in the spring of 1941.
The daughter who came to the door advised him that her
father was too absorbed in his writing to see them.   When
Hoffman persisted, Sandburg appeared on an upstairs porch,
pointing out that an appointment was required and that he
was racing with time in writing of Lincoln.   He added he
did not think college students would understand his problem
of meeting a writing target.   When Hoffman acknowledged
his error in the matter, another of the students objected to
the suggestion of frivolity or insensitivity on the part of all
college students and pointed out that all of the group were
working for their education, many working at night while
attending classes during the day.   Sandburg liked the coura-
geous reply and invited the group to return when he had more
time.

Hoffman recalled Sandburg explained to the students
that he felt his telling the story of Lincoln was a mission
assigned to him by fate.   His losing himself in the Lincoln
task had cost him much time he might have liked to devote
to other endeavors.   He told the students they would come
to understand "old Mr. Sandburg" if and when they got their
own obsessions.

After that meeting at the barber shop when he recited "Grass," Hoffman was surprised when asked during a
casual meeting on the street, "Do you think that I'm doing
anything for generations to come, the young ones?"   Though
Hoffman had thought Sandburg was hardly one to worry about
the judgments of others, Hoffman found Sandburg was pleased
to hear him say that he placed him next to Whitman in the
power of his impact on youth in many countries.

Another major impression was that Sandburg was
what Hoffman called "a preacher." As he sat in the barber
chair, he gave forth readily with ideas on a variety of subjects, including how youth could improve their ways. Hoffman could see the white-haired, driven, opinionated, old
man in a country pulpit guiding the members of his congre-
gation in how they should live.

The First Prominent Speaker*

He was the first prominent speaker, as the Poetry
Society of South Carolina had just been organized and we
chose him because we thought he would really make Charleston come awake to the New Poetry.

At that time (February, 1921), in spite of my rather
extreme youth, I was Curator of Public Instruction at the
Charleston Museum, and he appeared there on the afternoon
before his performance. We saw a tall, rugged, graying
man wearing a black railroad engineer's cap and entering
the hall in the slow, casual, unexcited manner which proved
to be his natural demeanor at just about all times. I do
not recall how he was dressed; I was fascinated by the engineer's black cap. After we greeted him as cordially as
we knew how, he looked around in a vague sort of manner
and asked, "Can you find me a banjo? I need a banjo for
tonight." We assured him that we could provide one and
then tried to take him on a short tour of our museum. He
apparently was not interested by anything until we came to
a case which exhibited primitive African artifacts and the
lifelike statue of an African tribesman. Here he became
quite voluble, disregarding our more highly-prized Poly-
nesian, Egyptian and Greek exhibits. After this he remarked that he was tired and would like to leave and prepare for the evening. In this first encounter he seemed
colorless and we wondered apprehensively what his stage
presence would be like.

The meeting was held at the South Carolina Society
Hall, and it looked as if every member of this very new
Society was present. The hall holds about 200 people, and
they were even sitting on the windows. Prominent on the

---

*Letter from Mrs. Helen von Kolnitz Hyer, Charleston,
S. C. , September 28, 1969. By permission of the author.

first row was a choleric old lawyer who as President of the
Saint Cecelia Society was the current social arbiter of the
town.   Only, nobody had thought he liked poetry and there-
fore he had not been sent an invitation to join the Society
when it was being organized.   His indignation at this over-
sight had been voiced indignantly to the whole town.   Ac-
cordingly an invitation accompanied by profuse apologies had
been hurriedly produced, and, upon his appearance at the
meeting, the ushers had put him as close to the poet as
was possible.

Our President, Mr. Frank Frost, also a well-known
and immensely popular and revered gentleman, made his
gracious introduction of the poet, and the entire audience
leaned forward to hear the magic words which would introduce The New Poetry.   Mr. Sandburg stepped forward,
cleared his throat, made a slight bow, and declaimed in
ringing tones: "Why does the Hearse Horse snicker when it
drags away a lawyer's bones?"

There was a communal gasp from the audience and
then such thunderous applause as had never before stirred
the sacred halls of The South Carolina Society.   I am sure
Mr. Sandburg never realized what had set us off.

Amidst half-smothered chuckles, we all settled
down to hear what this strange person had to say next.   He
promptly set out to enchant his audience, and marvel of
the marvels he succeeded.   I am sure that at some early
time in history Sandburg must have been a Troubadour.
His voice was magic.   I wish I could remember more about
the actual poems he read; time has erased that memory.
He held his listeners spellbound.   I recall the exquisite
pleasure with which I listened to "The fog comes on little
cat feet-" and how the lines to "A Deserted Brick Yard,"
"made a wide, dreaming pansy of an old pool at night."
(And if I have misquoted some of the words, I still feel the
enchantment with which he presented them.)

For the second part of his program he produced the
banjo. Never before, I am sure, had a Charleston audience
listened enthralled to such songs.   They were wholly strange,
but the intonations of that marvellous voice, the always
slightly-muted harmonies of the banjo, and the attitude of
the singer, who sat, relaxed, as if listening to distant music and then passing it on to us, made an unforgettable impression upon all who heard him.   Most plaintive of all, to

that group, who were unhappily witnessing the passing of
their greatest agricultural crop by the arrival of the small
creature in their midst, was his plaint of the Cotton Boll
Weevil who, "ain't got no home, ain't got no home."

This, I think, is about all I can recover from that
far distant year when the midwest came to Charleston and
shook its people and opened their hearts to a new, young
and vigorous concept of what poetry could mean.

Sandburg and a Photographer*

My newspaper, The Christian Science Monitor,
wanted an exclusive photograph of him and asked me to
arrange for it. I made a date with a popular photographer
of men and Mr. Sandburg obligingly went with me at the
appointed time.

As we walked to the studio from the Monitor office,
we had a little conversation. I was in awe of him, of
course, but the big man with the shaggy hair put me at
ease. He plied me with sensible questions about my newspaper, talking as one pro to another. I forgot my timidity.

At the photographer's he behaved like a naughty boy,
and I didn't blame him in the least. The photographer put
him under studio lights, asked him to hold his head a little
this way and that, and fussed over him until he struck. No
more posing. I'm sure he would have been cooperative if
the photographer had been an artist, but this man took pictures so they flattered the subject, and Sandburg would
have none of it. He got up and we left.

Walking back from the studio, Mr. Sandburg was
his usual friendly self, asking about my work and making
me feel he took a real interest in a young reporter. I
was thrilled.

*Letter from Dorothea Jaffe, Cambridge, Mass., Sept. 17,
1969. By permission of the author.

The Most Disheveled Guest*

Mrs. Paul Keck, president of the Union City High
School Mothers' Club, wrote to Sandburg and arranged for
him to appear for them on November 10, 1943, for a fee of
$600. Apparently the matter was handled through him rather
than an agent.

He informed Mrs. Keck, at whose home he was invited to stay, that he would arrive in Fort Wayne about ten
o'clock the preceding night. He was to have in his room a
typewriter, a guitar, and a table. He told her that he would
be going from there to Yale to lecture.

Mr. and Mrs. Keck went to Fort Wayne in great an-
ticipation. Sandburg got off the train and appeared carrying
"a little valise." Mr. Keck said, "We will wait for your
luggage." ... "This is my luggage," he replied, indicating
the small hand bag.

On the trip from Fort Wayne to Union City by car,
Sandburg sat in the front seat beside Mr. Keck. Mrs. Keck
noticed Sandburg's hair was tousled and very unkempt.

When they arrived at the Keck home, then 326 W.
Division St., he requested, "I would like you to put my
goat's milk in the ice box." He had a dozen half-pint (like
medicine) bottles of goat's milk in his small bag. After the
milk was put in the refrigerator, the three sat in the kitchen
and had a snack at the table. Sandburg talked very freely
on a variety of subjects, including his brother-in-law,
Steichen, and delphiniums, also an interest of Mrs. Keck.

When Mrs. Keck showed him upstairs to his room,
she asked, "Would you like to have your breakfast in bed or
downstairs or when would you like to eat?" His reply was,
"I believe I would like to have it in the bedroom about nine
o'clock."

The next morning Mrs. Keck's daughter, a student at
Indiana University, and her roommate arrived and were
eagerly anticipating meeting the famous author. When the
breakfast tray was taken up, the two students followed closely

*Based on an interview with Mrs. Paul Keck, Union City,
Ind., Sept. 22, 1969.

on Mrs. Keck's heels. In response to the knock on his door,
Sandburg said, "Come in." He was sitting up in bed, wearing a white knit sweater, "shot full of holes. If there was
one hole, there were a hundred." His hair was tousled.

Mrs. Keck introduced him to her daughter, Margaret,
and to her roommate, Majie Alford. He engaged them in
conversation for a few minutes.

Mrs. Keck asked, "Mr. Sandburg, when would you
like to have your lunch? I have asked in a few friends who
are very interested in your work." "One o'clock," he replied, accepting the visitors without comment.

The conversation at lunch was very interesting. One
particular person recalled things he had forgotten. She
would quote lines and cause him to say, "Yes, I did write
that." Or he sometimes said, "No, I don't think I wrote
that." The person would then quote further and get him to
recall that it was indeed his own work.

After lunch he walked around the house and went back
to his room. He was quite pleasant, responding when spoken
to, and told Mrs. Keck he liked her home. He stayed in
his room most of the time. He was working on his newspaper column.

Mrs. Keck introduced the subject of his next meal:
"About your evening meal...." "Oh," he replied, "I don't
want anything to eat, nothing. I just want some goat's milk."
As the time for the performance approached, Mrs. Keck took
to his room a glass of goat's milk, which had also been
served at lunch.

During the day a search for a guitar, an instrument
not very common in those days, was made. Eventually one
was found in the possession of some one out in the country.

He was asked to be downstairs and ready to go at
7:00 for the 8 p.m. performance. A large audience had
been attracted to the performance: "People were coming
from everywhere."

He appeared, ready to go, in the one suit, a blue
one, in which he was traveling. "It was covered with dan-
druff and hair and everything." Mrs. Keck asked her husband, "Do you suppose I could offer to brush his suit off?"

Mr. Keck thought it was worth a try.   The approach she
used was, "I have just brushed my husband's suit off.   Could
I brush yours?"   He accepted with, "Very, very fine."

Taking the borrowed guitar, Sandburg accompanied the
Kecks to the school building, where they discovered he had
no program planned.   Mrs. Keck introduced Sandburg, and
he started by reciting his "Chicago" poem.   Then he did a
couple more poems and sang a few songs.   "The program
lasted twenty-five minutes.   No encore.   He was through."
So many people had come to hear Sandburg that, "they were
standing in the streets.   They could not get in."   The abbre-
viated performance was quite embarrassing.   Admission was
a dollar for adults and fifty cents for students.

Sandburg had told the Kecks that he would be leaving
for Yale on the midnight train from Richmond, Indiana, to
New York.   That evening, before starting for the performance, Mr. Keck offered to check Sandburg's train reservation.   "I have no reservation," was the response.   "I just
get on the train and ride."   Seeing he seemed quite hungry
after the performance, Mrs. Keck packed a lunch for him,
containing sandwiches and cookies, which he carried on the
train in a paper sack.

The Kecks had friends in after the performance.   He
mingled.   "We had sandwiches and coffee.   He had goat's
milk."   Everybody visited and talked for about an hour.
About eleven the Kecks started out for Richmond with their
guest.   They waited and put him on the train.   Being concerned about his traveling by day coach, especially in view
of his being scheduled to lecture the next afternoon at Yale,
Mrs. Keck asked, "Won't you be tired?"   He replied, "I
ride this way all the time."   He took his remaining bottles
of goat's milk and the empty bottles with him.

The roommate, from Indianapolis, wrote for English
class a "short story" about her experience in encountering
Sandburg, calling it, "I Met Him in Bed."   She wrote to
him and asked if she could do that.   And he agreed.   This
paper was published at Indiana University.

Mrs. Keck recalled Sandburg as "the most disheveled
man I have ever entertained."   She recalled that he stuck a
pin in the short cigar segment he smoked.   Mrs. Keck's
father, a contemporary of Sandburg, a self-educated indi-
vidualist and investor, had read Sandburg's Lincoln and got
along very well with him.

He wrote Mrs. Keck a note, not saved, thanking her
for treating him like a member of the family and making
him comfortable.

The Leiserson Friendship*

[When William M. Leiserson, who was the deputy industrial commissioner of Wisconsin, wrote his wife-to-be,
Emily, from Milwaukee on March 18, 1911, he told her of
his experiences with Carl Sandburg, city editor of the Social
Democratic Herald, who had interviewed him in the City Library on unemployment:]

I talked to him on unemployment until 11 o'clock.
He thought he was getting great dope. He will write a series
of short articles covering the whole question and get his information from me. I don't want my name to appear on
them, and he will merely state in a foot-note, "Prepared
from materials gathered by the Municipal Reference Library."

After eleven I went with Sandburg to Brisbane Hall,
the socialist trade union headquarters which was recently
built. He showed me around the building and I met a number of new people, among them Miss E. H. Thomas, state
secretary of the S. D. Party.

Then Sandburg and I went to lunch. He wanted to
take me to a "Baltimore Lunch" Place to eat--and he was
hungry too. I said, "Look here. I haven't paid for a meal
in three days. People have been taking me out all the time.
You come with me to the Gargoyle (the restaurant McLenegan
took me to) and let's have a square meal." He agreed and
said, "All right, and some day you can come to my house
and have a home meal."

Sandburg is a bulky fellow. He began as a boy driving a milk wagon and he has knocked around all his life and
educated himself. He entered some dinky college in Illinois
and stayed there three years struggling along. Then he had
to quit. [Sandburg had evidently presented a variation of
his Lombard College career, which lasted from 1898-1902,
taking both high school and college courses and getting valuable athletic and writing experience.] He took up newspaper

---

*Letter of William M. Leiserson. By permission.

work and has knocked around reporting on papers in almost
every city in the country.   [Certainly a gross exaggeration.]
Also he has lectured for lyceum bureaus, written ads for
stores and washed dishes in a restaurant when he was dead
broke.   Now he shows in his looks the experience he has
gone through.   He is broken down in health and his eyes
have gone back on him.   He can hardly keep them open.
[This problem is not otherwise thus far documented.]

I feel awfully sorry for him.   He seems to be very
poor, too.   He is now receiving $1, 200 a year as City Editor
of the Herald.   He is married but has no children.   Before
he took up the Herald work he was secretary to the Mayor
[of Milwaukee] and before that he had knocked around reporting and writing special articles for all the Milwaukee newspapers.

Sandburg is just full of enthusiasm and idealism.   It
is an inspiration to talk to him and to see how thoro'ly devoted he is to the cause and how completely he forgets himself.   I am afraid he overdoes this, however, and I feel so
strongly that he is neglecting to take care of himself and
his health that I am going to try to teach him little by little
to take more care of himself.   He's too good a man to lose
and he would accomplish wonders if he just looked out for
himself a little more.   I asked him to come for a good long
tramp with Fred King and me tomorrow and he will try to
come.   He thinks he has got to work all the time.

We had a good long talk at the lunch and I gave him
a good feed, a beer, and a cigar.   The treat cost me $2. 05
and I was left with 25 cents in my pocket, but I didn't care.
He seemed to need a feed.

* * *

[The friendship with Leiserson and his family continued for many years, as the following items show.   Mrs.
Leiserson has supplied these observations of Carl:]*

If I remember rightly, Carl Sandburg and Bill Leiserson's friendship began when Carl was working on a Chicago
newspaper and Bill had a summer job as a bill-clerk at
Sears Roebuck & Company in Chicago, 1906-7?   They would

*Letter from Emily Leiserson.   By permission.

sit beside the drainage canal and discuss philosophical subjects.

My husband invited Carl, on one of his lecture tours, to spend a week with us at our home in Yellow Springs, Ohio. Carl came, but when dinner time arrived he said he was "off his feed" and couldn't eat. "What else do you have?" he asked. "Anything in the garden?" I replied, "We have lots of tomatoes." He answered that tomatoes would just hit the spot. So I peeled and sliced a big bowl of tomatoes for him. Next day I did the same, and the next, and the next. He avidly ate them. His appetite improved. He went next to the Arthur Morgans, as their guest.

Lucy and I had a good laugh because when she asked him what he could eat he replied, "Anything BUT tomatoes!"

When Carl came to visit in Yellow Springs, Ohio, one time as a guest of Antioch College, he slept at the Arthur Morgan House. One night after one of his long sessions of discussion, about 2:00 A.M. he came over to our house near the Morgans to ask if he could borrow a blanket because he was "freezing." So I gave him a pair of pink woolen blankets. But I said, "Mrs. Morgan has plenty of blankets; just ask her for some next time you sleep cold." He replied, "I wouldn't like to hurt her feelings. It is one of the students who makes up the beds." The next night about 3 o'clock in the morning there was a hard knock at our door. It was Carl bringing back my pink wool blankets, thanking me sincerely for lending them. I couldn't help but wonder what anyone would think who might have seen him stealing out of the Morgan House with those pink blankets in the wee hours of night!

During World War II we had "drives." There were paper drives, and metal drives. If we had something to contribute we phoned a certain number and a truck was sent to pick up our contribution. I had a brass bed to contribute-- it was a "beauty," in our guest room on the third floor, "in the tree tops," at our house at 3210 34th Street, N.W., Washington, D. C. I contributed it. The truck came and took it away.

The next time Carl came to talk with my husband until two or three o'clock in the morning, I was awakened by a sonorous roar at the top of the "garret stairs" (Carl always referred to the top floor as the garret), WHERE'S MY BIG BRASS BED?

The big brass bed had been replaced by a green iron
bed which Horace Mann MIGHT have slept in because we had
bought it when we were at Antioch College, but Carl wasn't
impressed. He wanted the ornate big brass bed which he
thought of as "his. " It really was a splendiferous monster.

One of my grandchildren had imaginary playmates.
After World War II he, Carl, was visiting us, or maybe it
was during the war, Carl came and was about to sit down
on the davenport, when little Christopher Sims screamed,
"Don't sit on that side or you'll sit on my Blue Goose!"
Carl understood; said he'd chase the Blue Goose off. So he
did and they had a high time chasing the Blue Goose all over
the house. (Christopher now has a Ph. D. degree and is a
university professor at Harvard.)

When Carl Sandburg got his first big check (royalties)
for The War Years he stopped off in Washington, D. C. , on
his way home, to see us. He showed me the check and
asked, "What would you do if you had a check like this?"
I replied, "I'd go down town and buy myself a good new suit."
He said, "I'll do just that if you'll go with me. " He added,
"Price no object. "

Rain was pouring down. I donned a raincoat and took
him down town in my car. Since he had said that price was
no object, I took him first to Garfinckels. Nothing suited
him. The next store we went to was Raleigh's because that
was where my husband bought his suits. Carl found nothing
there that he liked. We then went to every men's clothing
store on F Street but he found nothing he liked. At last,
at Woodward and Lothrop's he found just what he wanted and
bought it.

When it came to paying for it, Carl had no money--
just the large check from his publishers, $60, 000, $70, 000,
$80, 000? He told the clerk he'd pay for the suit by check.
The salesman asked, "What's your identification?" ... Carl
replied, "I am Carl Sandburg. " ... The clerk said, "Don't
you have an identification card?" ... I said, "Charge it to
my account. You can reimburse me later. " ... Carl re-
iterated, "I want to pay for it myself right now. " So there
was a lot of scurrying around in the Men's Clothing Department until a clerk was found who said he recognized Carl.
So Carl's personal check was accepted.

The very large check was flashed around so much I

was worried for fear it might disappear! But Carl enjoyed
the rumpus.

* * *

[The Leiserson's son, Mark, also remembers Sandburg:]*

My most real and lasting impression from those childhood years is of a white haired man with twinkling blue eyes
who filled our house with good talk, good jokes and high-
pitched hoots of laughter. It was not until my last meeting
with him (shortly after my discharge from the army in 1946)
that I had a glimpse of his loneliness and melancholy. Carl
asked me to stay up and talk with him, when, after midnight, my parents indicated it was time to go to bed. Our
conversation, which lasted another two or three hours, was
rather strained. Carl's mind was obviously on other things--
I think mostly the war and its aftermath--and he simply
wanted company while he smoked his cigar halves and sipped
his drink. The only specific subject I can remember discussing was the totalitarian and conspiratorial character of
Communism; the "cold war" was hardly beginning and the
optimistic attitude toward Stalin's Russia which I must have
conveyed, undoubtedly struck an old socialist and veteran observer of the political left as sadly naive. He promised to
send me a book--Jan Valtin's Out of the Night--which he
thought would be useful for my education. I was pleased
but somewhat surprised when it arrived since his preoccupied
manner led me to doubt that he would remember. Sometime later, I wrote thanking him for the book and explaining
in some detail how it had led me to other books in pursuit
of some resolution of the issues he had raised in our conversation. I did not expect a reply and our paths did not
cross again although he did, I believe, stay at our house in
Washington a few more times prior to my father's death.

What intrigued me most was the obviously deep and
abiding affection my father and Carl had for one another
which was rooted in the shared experiences of past years
about which I knew little or nothing. This was my first ink-
ling of the kind of love that could exist between mature men
(I can remember my surprise at seeing them holding hands

---

*Letter from Mark W. Leiserson, New Haven, Conn., July
16, 1970. By permission.

briefly as they sat down on the sofa after Carl's arrival)--
a love that could persist despite the fact that they saw each
other only every year or two and as far as I knew, did not
correspond. Piquancy was added by my mother's mild disapproval not of Carl but of his "lifestyle. " Pre-occupied
as she was with the proper upbringing of her family she
tended to be sensitive to what she viewed as improprieties
or irresponsibility in Carl's behavior. Although I know that
she thoroughly enjoyed his visits she could not help but be
irritated that most often they were unannounced and of in-
definite duration (though never more than a few days). His
use of expletives, though mostly confined to "goddamn" and
"hell, " was more liberal than she permitted in front of her
children. She worried about the example he set by his
obvious enjoyment of talking, smoking and especially drink-
ing late into the evening. Although by no means tee-totalers
my parents rarely offered their guests hard liquor; but it
was an inviolable tradition that there always be a bottle of
whiskey in the dish cupboard of our house in Washington in
case Carl Sandburg phoned from the station that he was
coming to visit.

I suppose that my mother's uneasiness with certain
aspects of Carl's behavior was connected with her determined effort to bridge certain ambiguities in her own position. Having chosen a more or less emancipated role for
herself in her early years as an independent "working girl"
and then by marrying a "leftist" Jewish immigrant from the
slums of New York, she was determined to demonstrate that
enlightened intellectual, social and political views were
wholly consistent with the family-centered traditions and
strict personal morality of her New England family background. The importance of "family" tended to color all of
her attitudes. I can remember, for example, being taken
aback by her reaction, after the publication of The War Years,
to a newspaper story in which Carl was pictured as a kind of
gentleman farmer raising prize goats as an avocation. According to her the fact [was] that Carl had nothing to do with
the goats, that his wife had been forced to start raising
goats to support the family while Carl was writing. And
there always was the slightest tinge of resentment at the
family joking that the only notice of her wedding (carefully
preserved in the "guest book" of our house in Salem, Connecticut) appeared in a Chicago paper not as a society item
but as a news column written by Carl under the headline (to
make matters worse) W. M. LEISERSON MARRIED TODAY.

It was, of course, true that the relationship between

Carl and my father rested on things other than "family"
matters and to this extent excluded her. As I recall, the
conversations I was privileged to listen to (or to eavesdrop
on from the top of the stairs) were almost exclusively concerned with social and political affairs--philosophizing, gossip, story-telling, jokes and general discussion.   There was
much of Civil War history and Lincoln but neither poetry,
folk music or family ever entered, or if it did, it made no
impression on me.   I can remember being surprised to learn
that Carl had a wife and family.   And part of the delight of
first attending a performance by Carl with his guitar (I could
not have been more than 10) was to discover a whole new
aspect of him which he had never revealed in our living
room.   But though I cannot recall him talking about or reciting poetry in our home, I had little difficulty in identifying him as a poet (and later when I came to read it) with
his poetry because of the accents and rhythms which marked
his ordinary speech and the transparent satisfaction which
he derived from the sounds and shapes of words and phrases.

[I enjoyed] recalling how a great and good human
being, in ways unknown and unknowable to him, was a source
of such brilliant illumination for a young boy's adolescent
awakening to the human condition.

From Lincoln to the Atomic Age*

(The following is the word-for-word account of a
press conference held Jan. 6, 1953, when members of the
Chicago press interviewed Carl Sandburg, the poet, Lincoln
biographer, and author, on the occasion of his 75th birthday
celebration.   We are indebted to Columbia Broadcasting System for a complete tape of the conference, which I have
edited slightly for clarification and continuity.)

The scene is not Mt. Olympus, but a room on the
third floor of the Blackstone hotel.   Sandburg, sitting on a
throne-like chair with his white, square-cut mop shining
under the lights, looks eternal.   His wife, Lillian [known
as Paula], quite properly sits in a smaller throne-like chair

---

*Leo A. Lerner, "From Abe Lincoln to Pogo and the Atomic
Age: A Press Interview with Carl Sandburg," North Side
Sunday Star (Chicago), Feb. 1, 1953.   Reprinted by per-
mission.

on his right. The press, radio, television and movie
people, 20 to 30 in all, are seated around in a semi-circle,
with the technical equipment in back.

Sandburg is wearing a new black double-breasted suit,
an incongruous blue tie with shiny golden triangles on it,
and there are a few cigars sticking out of his breast pocket.
He looks somewhat embarrassed by all this concentration on
him, but he feels better as he looks out through the smoke
haze and movie lights and sees some of his old friends in
the group. He speaks quite slowly and deliberately, and
carefully thinks out the answers to the questions. There is
an ever-so-slight touch of Swedish accent.

Sandburg: Well, here's Gene Reynal, vice-president
of Harcourt Brace. He's responsible for some of this. If
it hadn't been for their saying the book (Always the Young
Strangers) would be published on my seventy-fifth birthday,
I wouldn't have made haste and finished the book. And if
we had gone longer it would have run into two hundred
thousand words. But at last I've got a book that people can
read in a day or two.

Question: What do you think of Always the Young
Strangers? Does it compare favorably with your other
works?

S.: I wrote it just like I wrote all my other books.
I wrote a book that I wished I could have read myself earlier
in life. I always wished some one had done a book about a
boy in a prairie town in the Midwest.

Q.: Mr. Sandburg, can I ask you a question, sir?

S.: Well this is the time. I'm not running for anything, so I'm not scared.

Q.: You are now seventy-five. Would you like to
try for one hundred?

S.: That's a sixty-four-dollar question. Yes, I'd
like to try for one hundred. That's clever. I didn't get it
at first. I had to roll it over. 'You're now seventy-five--
would you like to try for one hundred?' Well, I don't know.
They kind of dodder, in the nineties.

Q.: Here's a fellow who's eighty-two. He doesn't
look doddery.

S.:   Well, he's about the age of Barney Baruch and
Barney says, 'I'm old, but I'm not senile yet. '

Q.:   Think of how old you'd have been if you hadn't
smoked cigars.

S.:   That's a fair question.   That's hygienic.

Q.:   Do you ever smoke cigars?

S.:   Once in a while.   I cut 'em in three or four
pieces and reduce the nicotine intake.

Question (by a pink-cheeked young reporter):   That
gives me great faith, because I'm a great cigar smoker.

S.:   Oh, you mean with all that billion dollar (cigarette) advertising, they haven't got you yet?   Every cigarette
claims it's milder than every other cigarette.

Q.:   Mr. Sandburg, as a biographer of Lincoln, what
do you think of politics nowadays?

S.:   It's about the same old thing.   It hasn't changed
much--just about the same average of integrity, the same
average of double crossing.

Q.:   We haven't gotten any worse?

S.:   Lincoln, in his campaign in 1860--he didn't say
a word for publication, didn't make a speech.   He said,
'I've said enough.   If you want to know where I stand, go
read my speeches. '   He was in quite a different spot from
that of Eisenhower.

Q.:   No one writes as good speeches now as he did?

S.:   Well, that's debatable.

Q.:   Well, I suppose you've read some of Adlai
Stevenson's speeches.

S.:   I read all of them.   And I read all of Ike's.   I
wouldn't hesitate in saying that Stevenson is more of a master of prose than Ike.

Q.:   Do you think that any of Stevenson's speeches
compare favorably with those of Abraham Lincoln?

S.:   Yes, parts of them will be in future anthologies
of American eloquence.

Q.:   Did Abe Lincoln have much help in writing his
speeches--as much, let's say, as Stevenson did?

S.:   Well, if you read my book, you will find that
one time he wrote a speech that had in it the sentence,
'Broken eggs can never be mended.' And there were some
rhetoricians that cut that out. It was 'lacking in dignity,'
they said. But he fooled them by putting it into another
speech later.

Q.:   Looking back, sir, over seventy-five years,
what could you say has happened to us, good or bad, that
has impressed you most?

S.:   Well, I'll say that the thing that I keep rolling
over in my mind a little more often than anything else, cul-
turally speaking, is the new media that's come across the
last thirty or forty years. The movies, radio, and now
television.

Q.:   You say that as if you don't exactly shout and
rave about television.

S.:   Well, I mean all three of these 'media.' (I've
been around the advertising world. Down in the advertising
department they'll talk to you about media.) The main evil
about these is that they go to many people who don't know
they are time wasters, that while they do deliver a good
many things that are priceless, the habit of sitting there
hours and hours and taking whatever they give you. You
then become an addict, which in other terms is a dope.
Too many people, and particularly young people, have not
learned to be selective about movies, radio, television.

Q.:   Were young people selective about Cap Collier
(a mythical hero of the nineties), Mr. Sandburg?

S.:   He's been reading my books, the son of a gun.
No, but I know the danger. I've had experience. And
Nick Carter--oh, I've read some of the comics that are
around now, a dozen or two, just to find out what some
people are trying to do to the youth of the country. I met
a college boy a while ago. We got to talking, and I found
that he had heard three hundred Jack Benny shows. Comes

Sunday night and he's got to have that dope. (Makes a gesture like shooting a needle in his arm.)

Q.: What do you think of the effect of the comics on the young people?

S.: Well, I've got grandchildren, but so far they've been limited in their use of them. Those who read them by the dozen every week are in a bad way.

Q.: Are you thinking now of the ones in newspapers or the comic books?

S.: The comic books. I think 'Pogo,' for the young or the old who understand it, it's health to them.

Q.: In other words you go Pogo.

S.: I go Pogo.

Q.: Mr. Sandburg, what would you say about this atomic age these days?

Voice: He wants to know if you're in favor of it.

S.: It's like the weather. You better accept it. It's here.

Q.: What do you think of the books that are being written today?

S.: There were eleven thousand last year--eleven thousand published last year--and I read only fifteen or twenty of them. How can I tell you about them? I would refer you to Fanny Butcher, Van Allen Bradley, or brother (Herman) Kogan.

Q.: What have you been reading lately, Mr. Sandburg?

S.: Well, I read Jim Randall's Midstream, the second book in a series he's doing on Lincoln during the Civil War. Now I'd have to stop and think. I reread Ernest Elmo Calkins' book, They Broke the Prairie, which is about the best book ever done about an Illinois prairie town ... a hundred years, from 1837 to 1937. I read and would highly recommend Thomas Hornsby Ferrill's New and

Selected Poems. He's one of the poets who isn't included
in the anthologies, but he has far more on the ball so far
as I'm concerned than most people that are included. He's
terrifically and beautifully American.

Q.: Mr. Sandburg, do you think your description of
Chicago in the poem, "The Hog Butcher," still stands?
Would you add or take anything away from it as it is?

S.: That's like something a man did long ago, and
nothing can be done about it.

Q.: You mean to say you regret it?

S.: I wrote that when I was with System magazine
up in a cubicle in the Kestner building. I'm not sorry about
it, but I'm amazed at the way it gets reprinted.

Q.: If you had in mind a revised version, would the
things that you said in those days about the city still apply
now? Would there be things that you would add to it?

S. (in a deep resonant voice): Yes, because in a
certain way it stands up before New York, Paris, London,
and Rome and Berlin and Moscow and says, 'You say we
ain't got culture. All right, you can have it, but we're
livin' and we're eatin' regular. And we know a little about
democracy. '

Q.: We haven't gained any culture since then. Are
we still the hog butcher?

S.: It's still very good bacon we have with the eggs
of a morning.

Q.: Mr. Sandburg, you've written a lot about the
American man, his hopes and ambitions. Have your own
ambitions been realized on your seventy-fifth birthday?

S.: Well, I wrote Fanny Butcher in a letter a few
years ago that I'm amazed that I'm ambulant and in my right
mind. There are times that I wonder that I'm ambulant
and in my right mind after what I have been through. When
that book, Complete Poems, was published two years ago,
there was a new section of pieces that had never been
gathered into a book before and some that had never been
printed before. You'll find part of the answer there.

Q.: Mr. Sandburg, do you think that <u>Always the Young Strangers</u> is your last book?

S.: Well if I live I'll do some kind of a sequel to it. Lord knows what it will be like. I'm still groping.

Q.: Does this new book represent your final thoughts, the accumulation of all that you've learned in the years that you've been writing?

S.: You mean <u>Always the Young Strangers</u>? No, that covers that one period.

Q.: I mean the reflections that are in it. Would you say that it was based on your experience, et cetera?

S.: Well, where the Republican and Democratic parties appear in the book and I have a viewpoint about them--it's about the same now.

Q.: Do you think that parades have improved over the years? Would you say that the Grant funeral procession was the greatest parade you've ever seen, or do you think that now we have greater and better parades that mean more to the boy standing on his father's shoulder and the crowd beside him?

S.: I doubt that any crowd or any parade that I've seen since then has ever been the equal of that. Gosh, he's read the book!

Q. (to Mrs. Sandburg): Mrs. Sandburg, does he talk his books before he writes them?

Mrs. Sandburg: Well, he certainly has talked this last book long before he wrote it, not only to our families but I'm sure to all of his friends.

S.: About half the book I would bring down to the dinner table and read to my grandchildren, and they would say, 'more, more.'

Q.: Mr. Sandburg, we all have our Sandburg favorites, but what is yours? What do you like best of all you've written?

S.: I try to think of some mother that has one boy

who was six feet six, and another one that came only to
five feet six, and she was as proud of one as of the other--
along with three or four daughters.   One who was beautiful
but dumb and one that was very intelligent but not much on
looks, and said she was proud of all of them.

Q.:   Now that you are seventy-five, sir, what do you
think of the celebration in Chicago in your honor, and also
the one in Sweden?

S.:   Well, I was thinking that when something like
that would be put to me here or when I should stand up before that dinner party tomorrow night, I would use a quote
that has come to me since I wrote the book, or I would have
put it in the book.   It was quite a saying among us kids--
'You ought to crawl into a hole and pull the hole in after
you.'   On arriving I'm surprised at the warmth of the greeting and the faces and something happens to me, and I feel
easier than I thought I would.

Q.:   Outside of the publication of the book, sir, and
the dinner perhaps, what would be the nicest birthday present
you'll have for your seventy-fifth birthday?

S.:   I don't have the slightest notion what will happen
there tomorrow night.

Q. (by a newsreel photographer with a Brooklyn accent):   Mr. Sandburg, for the newsreels here, would you
say something in connection with your seventy-fifth birthday
for national consumption.

S.:   You want me to think of something right off--
apt and smart for the newsreels.   Well, I never thought
that if I should reach three quarters of a century that there
would be set up before me a newsreel camera where I
would be required to talk to the millions of people to whom
the newsreel goes.   I could say that I'll give each and
every one of the millions that see the newsreel--I'll give
them an old Scotch toast, 'May the road to hell grow green
waiting for you.'

Q.:   Mr. Sandburg, on your views on television,
would you appear on a show tomorrow and give a couple of
those views for four or five minutes?

S.:   Well, if it's sometime after I get up.

Q.: Well, it's on WGN and I'd like to have you as
a guest on this show.   We'll talk for a few moments.

S.: Where's Catherine McCarthy? She knows my
schedule.

Q.: How's the farm? (at Flat Rock, North Carolina)

S.: Oh, we've got about forty acres of pasture that
will stand us in stead if runaway inflation comes.

Q. (to Mrs. Sandburg): How many goats do you
have?

Mrs. Sandburg: Oh, about eighty now including kids,
and a few beef cattle.

Q.: Can Carl still milk a goat?

Mrs. Sandburg: Oh yes, he's a very good milker.

S.: Next thing he'll ask me is what do you do with
all the milk.

Q.: Mr. Sandburg, you've written so eloquently of
the prairies.   How does it happen you're down there in the
Smokies?

S.: Well, we wanted pasture for the goats.   The
missus wanted to go where the winters were not so long nor
so cold.   We have a few days of zero weather down there,
but somehow you don't have to pile on the wool the way you
do here.   And the 'Tar Heel' state is a good one--a little
more liberal than some northern states.   In 1790 the population of North Carolina was ninety percent Quaker. There's
still that residue there.

Q.: Do you have any trouble fitting yourself in with
those Southerners down there after living all your life in
the North?

S.: Well, they let me make a political speech for
my candidate at the courthouse in Hendersonville.   North
Carolina only half seceded from the Union. She made
trouble through the whole war for Jeff Davis.   You go read
the book (Abraham Lincoln, the Prairie Years, and the War
Years).

Q. (to Mrs. Sandburg): Mrs. Sandburg, which is your favorite book of all?

Mrs. Sandburg: I would really have to say The Collected Poems.

Q.: In reading the new book, it seemed to me that the idea for Lincoln must have touched you as a boy--the idea of writing about Lincoln, and yet you never talked about it when you were younger. What started it?

S.: Well, a curiosity came over me about why he seemed to be a kind of sainted figure to the Republican party orators. But there was not one book among the juveniles--(as a boy) I read biographies of Napoleon, Julius Caesar, George Washington, but not one about Lincoln.

Q.: Have you been to New York lately, sir?

S.: Yes, I was in New York in connection with the closing of the book.

Q.: What is your impression of that great metropolis?

S.: She's got culture.

Q.: Do you have anybody now whom you would call one of your favorite authors?

S.: Thomas Hornsby Ferrill, Robert Frost, and every ten years I reread Rolvaag's Giants in the Earth.

Q.: You talked about the questions that upset you then--that you wondered about. Are there any questions that you wonder about now?

S.: Some of those still bother me. Well, of course, I get to wondering, out of a lot of history that I have read, out of having lived in the past, before I was born, having lived in it with documents, letters, and having seventy-five years in the present, I wonder what the whirligig is going to be like across the future. I'm more and more impressed by how, in the past before I was born, history was made out of so many unpredictable events. Things that happen that most of the learned men had no awareness of, and that's the case now. Across the next ten years there will

be sudden unpredictable events that will change the course
of history.   And I do a lot of speculating about what possible
events might be coming.

Q.: Mr. Sandburg, do you ever expect to do a book
on Chicago newspaper days or Chicago newspaper people?

S.: I hope so, but I don't know how it would shape
up.   I know there will be portraits I hope to do sometime--
sketches of old and dear friends that were a great help to
me and to others--men like Henry Justin Smith, Lloyd
Lewis, even Clifford Raymond over there in the Tribune.
I wrote an article on him one time in praise of him that was
printed in Reedy's Mirror, and I've got clippings of things
that he wrote that I find I can still reread.   He did an
editorial in 1914 as the first World War started--an editorial
titled 'The Twilight of the Kings.'   It was a keen piece of
prose writing and a prophecy put in the right words.   It
would be quite a list of newspaper fellas that I'd have to
cover.   I doubt whether I could do Bob Casey in one long
paragraph.

Q.: If you could write one more book, what would
that book be about?

S.: That's nearly as keen as the question that Tol-
stoy asked some peasant in Russia who was plowing: 'What
would you do if this were your last day on earth?'   He said
that if he knew it was judgment day, he'd go on plowing.

Q.: Would you say that you had more confidence or
less confidence and more pessimism about the future?

S.: Well, there's a possibility the cold war we'll
win.   There's also the possibility that we would win the hot
war if it should come.   In either of these possibilities, I
believe the human family is going to move out into brighter
eras than it has ever seen.

Q.: You're not afraid of any of the A-bombs or H-
bombs wiping everything off the earth and starting all over
again?

S.: Well, as Santayana said one time out of long
observation: 'There is a hard core to the people everywhere
that operates when they have survived revolution and war.'
It's doubtful whether the H-bomb or A-bomb would be more

devastating to the big countries involved than the Thirty
Years' War was to the people of Germany, and they certainly made some awful comebacks.

Q. :   And you don't think that right now the world is
in worse shape than it's ever been in your seventy-five
years?

S. :   Time may say ... the unpredictable event to
come may say that this is the worst era mankind has ever
known.

Q. :   Does this period worry you more than anything
else?   Are you more concerned about the future of the
people than at any other time of your life?

S. :   No, I've seen the human mind at play in so
many directions, and I've seen American youth in epic actions.   You can go back across the Iliads of the past and
the performances of our boys in this last war will bear fair
comparison for valor, daring, endurance, wit in emergen-
cies, with any brave, keen men of past generations.   Sometimes when you read Ernie Pyle, you think that American
youth is better in war than in peace.   I'm writing a book
here--talking off the hook.   (To a reporter with a notebook.)   You're right in taking this down.   I've seen full reporters ... there was a New York Times man with the book
review.   He said he had a photographic memory.   It came
through that he had me smoking a cigarette instead of a
cigar.

Q. :   Mr. Sandburg, do you expect to be in Washington for General Eisenhower's inauguration?

S. :   No, I'm going to get it by TV.

Q. :   Mr. Sandburg, do you think that reporters today
are as good interrogators as they were in your newspaper
days?

S. :   Yes, I think so.   I think they're a little better,
though I meet in them occasionally that fustular (i. e. , fus-
tian) photographic memory.   The United Press boy over in
some town in Ohio, I forget now where, he quoted me as
saying that I knew that Abraham Lincoln, if he were living,
would be for the United Nations.   But I said no such thing
at all.   I said he had an instinct for solidarity, he had an

instinct for unity. He made a decision and brought on a war in order to have unity in his country, and the derivation might be made from that. That he would like unity among the nations of the earth even if it might cost a war.

Q.: Mr. Sandburg, could an ugly man like Lincoln become president in this day of television, and with a bad voice on radio?

S.: Oh, he'd be a prize for TV ... Lord, Lord! Study the ninety photographs of him. He had grace in motion, he was a natural athlete. He was a champion wrestler, and his face had a mobility that Raymond Massey hasn't got.

Q.: Didn't he have a high squeaking voice?

S.: He had a voice that when there was a crowd of twenty thousand listened to him out of doors with a cold north-west wind blowing on the Knox College campus, he reached the end of that crowd. He had a voice with keen carrying power, a voice somewhat like Will Rogers'. TV would be after him.

Q.: What about our writers today, Mr. Sandburg? How are they affected by the times? Why have we really no great peaks of literature today. All this mass mediocrity ... is it because of unstableness?

S.: Not one great novel about politics, not one great novel about newspapers, the one-party press.

Q.: Do you agree with that concept, sir, about the one-party press?

S.: I know the Cowles' in Minneapolis. They do much better in Look magazine. And I know Mr. Gannett in Rochester. Don't press for names.

Q.: No, but I mean do you believe the charge that we have a one-party press is a legitimate one?

S.: Well, I don't take it as a charge. I take it as a fact.

Q.: Do you think that maybe the press is even worse than TV?

S.:   Well, I would take Doug Edwards or Ed Murrow as against what you get for something like eighty-five percent of the newspapers of this country.

Q.:   How about Mr. Kaltenborn?

S.:   He's a friend of mine.

Q.:   Mr. Sandburg, would you say that there has been a new woman evolved in the past years since suffrage?

S.:   Well, I'd rather say I think there is one evolving.

Q.:   What is the principal change that has taken place in woman's adjustment since suffrage to make you say you think there is one evolving?

S.:   Well, the new refrigerators and washing machines.   I don't know.   The new labor-saving devices have had perhaps as much of a role as the suffrage, though there is something ghastly I've seen in more than one city in the United States ... a big hotel room with three hundred or four hundred women playing bridge on a beautiful spring or summer day.

Q.:   Then you would say that one of her biggest adjustments is to more leisure time?

S.:   Yes, and what to do with the leisure.

Q. (to Mrs. Sandburg):   What do you think about that, Mrs. Sandburg?

Mrs. Sandburg: I don't play bridge.

Q.:   Even if you did, you wouldn't play in a big room with three hundred or four hundred people?

Mrs. Sandburg: No, I wouldn't play anyway.   I have too many other interesting things to do in this world.

Q.:   Mr. Sandburg, you said that you thought that we would enter a bright new era even if it were the cold war or the hot war.   What do you think is going to bring us through?

S.:   Well, there was a time when the masses of

people had to struggle hard with the earth in order that they should have food and clothes. For the masses there wasn't much time to think things over. But with what has happened across the last hundred and twenty-five years, across what the historians call the industrial revolution, you could say in the present hour in this country, that all war production could be eased off, and there would be no straps, there would be no suppression of the new devices through patent controls. You would have a universal five-hour work day and five-day week. The engineers are all agreed on that. It's possible that those hurdles and obstacles would be overcome.

Q.: How about Russia?

S.: Yes, the Politburo is something tough to look at. I look at the face of Malenkov and read what has come from him occasionally. I hate to think of his following Stalin. It'll be from bad to worse.

Q.: Do you think that an agreement between the great nations not to use A-bombs or H-bombs against large cities would be kept even if it was a treaty, in the case of war?

S.: I wouldn't accept any promise from Russia.

Q.: How do you think we will beat them?

S.: You want me to tell you how the war is going to be fought? What little I know from scientists and Air Force men, I'm not going to divulge here.

Q.: Mr. Sandburg, when you were reporting in Chicago, do you recall that somebody was always investigating somebody ... the police investigating the aldermen, the aldermen investigating the mayor, etc.?

S.: It got so we would spell it 'another investigation.'

Q.: Do you think that all the things we have to make life easier now have increased man's ability to enjoy life more than your father did?

S.: You're going into something now that needs a novel like the Lincoln or <u>Remembrance Rock</u>. You're going

into the matter of the use of leisure and quality and quantity
of entertainment. You're going into this terrific matter of
the new media--they operate against creative solitude. Too
many people are afraid to be alone. They got to have something going in the media.

      Fanny Butcher: Thank you, Mr. President! (Ap-
plause.)

A Norwegian Meets a Swede*

[Mrs. Edward Liemohn's husband was a member of
the Artist Series Committee at Wartburg College, Waverly,
Iowa. Each member of the committee was asked to provide hospitality for one of the performers. Mrs. Liemohn
chose to be hostess for Sandburg on his visit to Wartburg
in October, 1955:]

      As a person of Norwegian ancestry, I thought it
would be interesting to entertain a man of Swedish ancestry,
and so I chose Carl Sandburg as our house guest.

      He missed a plane and did not arrive as early as we
had anticipated, but came instead the afternoon of his performance. Dr. Alfred Swensen brought him over to our
house. He was surrounded by people wanting to tape his
performance, and he was indignant and felt that, "People
want everything for nothing." I was almost sorry he was
going to stay, as I didn't think he was pleasant. Dr. Swensen told me to ask him what he wanted to eat, and then I
met the real Sandburg. He asked if he could rest while I
prepared the meal.

      He rested about an hour, and I had his dinner ready.
He asked me to sit by him and sing! I was amazed and
said, "I'm not a soloist!" "I don't care. Sing some songs
you learned as a child. I collect folk songs." So "I sang
for his supper." He told me stories about his childhood,
and he sang. He said, "Tonight we will sing when we come
back." I told him he would be at the home of the president
and all the English teachers would be there and we would
scarcely have time to sing. He said, "I never go to bed
before 2 a.m. We will have plenty time."

---

*Letter from Mrs. Edwin Liemohn, Northfield, Minn., May
21, 1970. By permission.

There was a cloudburst that evening, just as we were leaving for the auditorium. The man who came to pick us up was stalled. We arrived a little late and found that the place was almost surrounded by water. Mr. Sandburg didn't have rubbers. One of the students gave him some boots, but in order to get them on he had to remove his shoes. I carried his shoes as we went in. He was not in the least bit excited, borrowed a guitar, and started rather late.

After the performance, an important individual asked him for an autograph for his son. Sandburg gave no autographs. The man stated his position, and Sandburg said, "That must be a nice job!"

We were at the president's house when two of his friends from Cornell College in Iowa said they wanted to take him to Cornell that evening.

I noticed he treated people coolly if they tried to impress him, but we had wonderful rapport when we treated him as a friend.

He told me he was sorry he couldn't spend the evening singing. I said, "You slept here, so I can put up a sign: 'Sandburg slept here!'"

Before he left I said, "I want six autographs!" I didn't know about the incident at the college. He said, "You are special. You will get them." He wrote special greetings to my daughter, son, sister, and the rest. I had promised him some cold cream and rubbed some on his hand. He asked me to rub some on his face. I gave him the jar, and he said, "I'll bless every room before I leave!"

When I opened the door of my closet, I found his shirt. I thought he might need it on his trip, so I did not mail it right away. He called me one evening from Chicago and talked in Swedish to tell me about his shirt. I told him I planned to cut it up and sell it in little squares. He laughed. I said, "Shall I mail it to your home?" He said, "Yes, but you don't know where I live." I told him, "That is what I do know. I know a lot about you personally." He had enjoyed the Norwegian songs, so I said, "Shall I let you borrow my song book?" He said, "Would you trust me?" I told him he could have it for two years.

I received a letter from him after he received the

book and the shirt; unfortunately the letter has been lost.
I wrote to him after the two years and said I needed my
book, and it was returned.

[After receiving the first letter, the author queried
Mrs. Liemohn on what she meant by "meeting the real
Sandburg." She replied on May 29, 1970:]

I am not too sure just what I meant by the statement.
I am inclined to get carried away when enthusiastic.   I
think what I had in mind was that he found that I was interested in his personal welfare.   He asked me what I planned
to give him.   He asked for a menu.   My refrigerator was
well-stocked, as I had planned to have him for several meals.
I offered him pork chops, baked potatoes, and all the trimmings.   (He does mention pork chops in his autobiography.)
He told me I gave him more than he ordered.

He asked me about my parents, when they came from
Norway and how they earned their living.   I told him my
father was a minister, and I was brought up in a Lutheran
parsonage.   My mother sang Norwegian folk songs.

He said, "My life was different.   My father didn't
believe I should spend so much time reading.   I didn't get
to tell my father I appreciated him.   My mother lived to
see that I turned out all right, and I could tell her I appreciated all that she had done for me.   Be sure to thank your
mother when you have the opportunity."

My son brushed his suit.   My son, as I may have
told you, was overwhelmed by his personality.   He told my
son he must never be ashamed of humble tasks, and he told
how he worked in a barber shop.   I told him our son was a
janitor in a bank while attending school.

He told me many of the stories that I read later on.
He said his mother read the Swedish Bible every day.   He
and I disagreed on doctrine, but we were friendly.

I visited Waverly [Iowa] for three or four days, and
I mentioned Carl Sandburg to a friend, who said I should
mention that Sandburg said, "Now they are starting with TV.
We haven't even perfected radio."

Evading the Sponsoring Ladies in Houston*

Carl Sandburg came to Houston when I was somewhere
between the ages of three and five.   I rather suspect I was
around five, because I believe we had just had the house
partially remodeled, and I know that the year that that was
done [around 1953-54] I was in nursery school, so I believe
I was about five; I could have been younger.   My actual
memory of him is fragmentary because of the very young
age that I was at the time he was here.   But he made a
very indelible impression on me, although he only stayed
here one night.   The only thing I can remember is that he
took my brother and myself on his knee and recited poetry.
I think what he recited was a poem called "The Three Marvelous Pretzels," but that may be an erroneous recollection
because at that time we had a 78 [r.p.m.] recording of him
reading that and it could be that I simply heard that as a
child and thought that's what he said.   But he did take my
brother and myself on his knee or in his lap, and he recited some sort of verse to us; he may also have sung; because I remember that he had his guitar with him.   I don't
know if he got it out and played it for us.   I think it's
quite likely.

My mother often talked about Sandburg's visit in
retrospect, and I'll tell you what she said about it.   Mr.
Sandburg had been brought down here on some sort of lecture, lecture-concert, or straight lecture-tour by a Wom-
en's Club, one of the Houston's Women's civics clubs, the
Junior League, or the Womens' Poetry Club, or the Houston
Poetry Club, or the Houston Study League or some such
rather dour group who had brought him here to, I am sure,
give instant enlightenment on the subject of poetry.   Well,
when Mr. Sandburg accepted this invitation, there was an
announcement in the paper that he was to come.   My father
wrote him in North Carolina and said that he had heard he
was coming to Houston, and would he like to stay here.
Mr. Sandburg had been friends with my father's father, Mr.
John A. Lomax; my father is John A. Lomax, Jr.   Anyway,
he wrote to Carl and asked him to stay with us during his
visit down here, and he wrote back and said that he would
enjoy staying with us.   Well, that was fine until he showed
up.   My father was to pick him up at the train station, and

*Transcribed tape recording made by Joseph F. Lomax,
Houston, Texas, Dec. 7, 1973.   By permission.

he had been very evasive with the women's club brigade
who wanted to meet him and take him to receptions, parties,
book-singing parties, and more or less squire him around
town. This was a very good opportunity to flaunt their cultural finesse or something or other to their colleagues and
so forth. Carl didn't particularly kowtow to these more or
less dowager-type dilettantes, if you could even call them
dilettantes. So he was very evasive about his arrival, and
my father was actually the only person who knew when he
was coming in; I believe he came in on the train. My
father left work early in the afternoon and went to pick him
up, and then took him on a drive around Houston so he could
see the city a little bit before he came back to the house to
get ready for his program. Well, we only had one car in
those days, and my mother had not gotten the chance to go
to the grocery store before my father had left that morning
to go to work, so she was very low on groceries. She
said that the only edible things that she had was about a
half loaf of bread, hard bread, and some cheese and a few
apples. She was beside herself because my father had not
told her that he would be driving him around; she expected
them to come right back. Well, in the mean time, the
grande dame, or should I say the grande dames of Houston's
society were calling the house frantically, wanting to know
where he was, when he was going to arrive, what he was
doing, would he go to so-and-so's party, would he be available after his lecture to attend some function or another,
and of course my mother didn't really know and could not
speak for him. The president of the club, who had brought
him here, was very put out with my mother because she
thought that the show had been stolen from her; I'm sure
she had planned to be his personal escort and squire him
about and so forth, and he really wanted no part of that.
So anyway, Carl and my father rolled up in the driveway
about six o'clock, after the stores had closed. The grocery
stores in those days closed around six; there really were no
other stores to go to. So she just asked him if he was
hungry when he came in, and he said, "Well, a little bit,"
and she said, "Well, what would you like?" "Well, I'd
kind of like to have some hard bread, a few slices of cheese,
and an apple." So that's exactly what she had, and she often
laughed about that coincidence in later years. After his lecture, she said that there was a reception given by the
Swedish Consulate.

Before the reception, the concert ended, and Mrs.
Phelps, who was the president of the club, wheeled her

gigantic black Cadillac limousine out to take Mr. Sandburg
to the reception and he just said, "Oh no, I'll just go on
with John Lomax." My father was driving a ratty, beat-up
'52 Bel-Air Chevrolet. She was very hacked. They got to
the reception, and my mother had to leave early because
she had left my brother and myself at the house with a baby-
sitter. Carl and my father stayed on until the wee wee
hours of the morning, and they both came home about four
o'clock, roaring drunk, and in very good spirits. Carl, of
course, could sleep the next day; my father had to turn
around and get up at 6:30 or 7 and go on to work as usual.
So Carl went ahead and slept on into the afternoon and told
my mother not to accept any phone calls, not to disturb
him. The phone was ringing off the wall constantly. She
had to answer it and fend off all these people who were very
discourteous to her for not allowing them to come over to
interview him, talk to him, take him to lunch and all that.
She really got caught in the middle. It didn't really bother
her because she was not a part of this set of people, anyway. It's just that it was aggravating to have all these
people accusing her of being officious, when actually she
was just trying to follow the wishes of Carl Sandburg.

I did leave out one thing that I should have mentioned
earlier. I do remember that he held my brother and myself
on his knee and I remember exactly which room in the house
it was because my brother and I still live in that house.
And I remember at that age looking closely at his hair. It
was so shockingly white and coarse. He was very gentle and
very smooth talking, deliberate in his speaking. Whatever
it was that he said to us, whatever verse it was, I remember it seemed to flow from very deep inside him. I remember looking at the lines in his face, and looking as a
child would look, not in the sense of this is Carl Sandburg's
face, because at that age he was just another man, someone
who had come to live with us, like a sudden and unexpected
grandfather. But I remember looking in his face and noticing how much expression there was in the lines of his face,
and then this bob of white white hair. I've seen alot of
photographs of him, but they don't give the same effect as
seeing it in person. I suppose as a child, the whiteness of
his hair was stunning to me because I had never seen a
man, or a person for that matter, with hair that was that
straight and coarse and white. It was really what you would
have to call bone white, bleached bone white, very striking,
very striking. Now I wish I had been older when he had
come so that I would have remembered more, and that I

would have been able to have more insight into getting to
know the man somewhat. I have a great respect for his
work, but it's not because he was a friend of the family.
It's just that I think his poetry is so very superb. When I
went to North Africa, I taught English as a foreign language
there. I taught them some of his poems, particularly the
one with the line in it which says, "The past is a bucket of
ashes," and then somewhere an allusion to a sun dropping
into the west and an optimistic looking forward to an ocean
of tomorrows and tomorrows. I recited that poem to them
so many times that I can't believe that I still don't have it
permanently embedded in my memory. I taught them the
vocabulary, and then I made them read it, trying to get
them to read it expressively. I found his poems, at least
the shorter ones, to be excellent teaching aids because his
vocabulary is certainly not abstruse. My students could
understand the ideas well. There are not too many American poets that can be used successfully when you're teaching a foreign language because the word orders are changed
around so much. Words have either peculiar usages to that
poet or definitions that are not really that common. But
Sandburg's poetry was very good for what I was doing.

At the Reisen Hotel*

I saw an article in our paper today about your needing some information about Mr. Carl Sandburg. At first I
wasn't intending to write to you at all, as I'm sure that my
contribution to all the information you might be needing isn't
worth much. But as it says in the paper that you are grateful for any information you might get, here is what I remember of Mr. Sandburg.

At that time (August, 1959) I was a schoolboy of 17
working as a bellboy at the Reisen Hotel in Stockholm during
my summer vacations. I remember having read in the
papers that a very well-known poet--Mr. Sandburg--was
coming to Stockholm. After finding out that he was staying
at our hotel, I got very excited indeed. My happiness was
complete when I got the chance to help him up with the luggage to his room. He looked rather tired and didn't say
much while standing down in the lobby. While walking around

---

*Letter from Lars Looström, Hägervägen, Sweden. By
permission of the author.

in the lobby he moved very slowly. That is what I noticed
about him. All the things he did were in a sort of slow motion. He seemed to be a man who took everything very
calmly--no rush (even when he was thoroughly well-rested).

Talking to him (which I did a lot of times later on
during his stay at the hotel), I noticed another thing, which
I still remember when thinking of him. Even though his
face was rather stiff, his eyes were "living" intensively.
He had a warm, frank and wide-awake look. His eyes
seemed to be smiling all the time.

I liked talking to him very much and he seemed to
like it too. After having run some errands for him he always wanted to talk a little to me before I left his room.

My impression of him after all these years is that
he was a gentle and fine man, a man you could (and would
like to) talk to for hours, a man who could tell you a lot
about LIFE!

Well Sir, I don't know if the impressions of a former
bellboy can help you at all. However, I wish you good luck
with your, I'm sure, very interesting work!

Our Paths Will Cross Again*

It was the night of January 5, 1910, when a comparatively unknown man named Charles Sandburg stood on
the platform of the Presbyterian Church in Homer, Michigan,
to deliver a lecture on Abraham Lincoln.

This was the Golden Age of the Lyceum and Chautau-
qua, and the talent announcement for 1909-10, of the Alliance
Lyceum Bureau, F. Elmer Marshall, Manager, of Jackson,
Michigan, carried the names of such celebrities as Rear Ad-
miral Robley D. Evans, Ernest Thompson Seton, Hamlin
Garland, Hamilton W. Mabie, Helen Keller, John Temple
Graves, together with platform names of lesser reputation.
Among the latter was that of Charles Sandburg, who was to
be known later as Carl Sandburg.

I say lesser reputation, because his first poems,

---

*Manuscript account of F. Elmer Marshall, Plainfield, Ind.
By permission.

published in 1904, had been given little recognition by either
the critics or the public.   His finances were at low ebb,
and he was now trying to gain recognition as a lecturer.

After some correspondence, he seemed happy to sign
a contract with us for a block of his time for six lectures
per week at $10.00 each, plus hotels and transportation.

I had booked Sandburg's appearance with the lecture
course committee at Homer with the understanding that although I had never heard him speak, I would guarantee him
to make good because of good reports from other sources.

Naturally I wanted to judge his work for myself.   So,
my wife, Nina, and I took a train to Homer, and walked to
the hotel, just off the main street.

We found Mr. Sandburg seated in the hotel office.
He rose to greet us, saying, as we shook hands: "Our
paths have crossed at last."

And now, at the church, with the introduction finished,
Charles Sandburg stood before the village audience, which
greeted him with polite applause.   He was by no means a
handsome man, but with rather a commanding figure.   He
had served in the Spanish-American War when he was twenty.
Now, at thirty two, he had a sturdy, earnest face.

I do not recall his exact words, but his message was
delivered in forceful, even tones, and in a style entirely different from his later years.

As his talk progressed, the audience was unrespon-
sive.   There was no applause, and a chill seemed to per-
vade the room.   I kept hoping for a climax.   I pushed my
feet on the floor, and said to myself: "Come on, Sandburg!
Now is the time.   Let yourself go before it is too late, boy.
Stand 'em up!"

Then I relaxed.   There was no climax--it was all
over.   There were a few light hand claps, and with that
the audience slipped quietly away.   Little did they know that
they had been listening to the man who would become, years
later, the greatest Lincoln authority in America.

The lady chairman of the committee, who had been
seated in the pew ahead of us, turned and said accusingly:
"Well, Mr. Marshall, you have HEARD Mr. Sandburg!"

I took a deep breath and replied apologetically: "Yes,
I've heard him, and I'll send another man on a later date
to make good for him."

The lady's face shone upon me, all smiles. "Thank
you. That's fine." Then she continued: "Do you know, I
think I remember this Mr. Sandburg. He came to this town
a year or more ago. He registered at the hotel. Stayed
for about two weeks, and, I was told, he kept in his room
most of the time writing--perhaps it was a book he was
working on."

Her statement reminded me of the man in Springfield,
Illinois, who remarked: "Oh, Abraham Lincoln wasn't such
a great man--I knew him."

As we walked back to the hotel I felt depressed,
thinking about the reaction of the audience, but Sandburg,
on the contrary, seemed to be in good spirits.

He remarked cheerfully. "Well, I think I held that
audience pretty well to-night, didn't you?"

Talent managers were accustomed to speaking frankly, and, in my mood of disappointment, I answered: "On
the contrary, Mr. Sandburg, the people were so disappointed
that I shall have to send them another speaker later to
satisfy the committee."

There was dead silence for a minute, and then Sandburg changed the subject as though I hadn't spoken.

I couldn't understand his reaction.

Arriving at the hotel all was pleasant, and we invited him to spend the weekend with us at our home in
Jackson.

Sandburg's next booking was at Marshall, Michigan,
for a lecture in that Calhoun County seat town. The Lyceum
Course in Marshall had been particularly successful thus
far, and I was anxious that the coming fourth number should
prove a hit.

The never-to-be forgotten weekend of January 7,
1910, preceded the Marshall date. It was Sandburg's memorable visit to our home on Fourth Street, in Jackson,
Michigan.

After dinner, as though by unspoken mutual pref-
erence, we three converged on the kitchen for lengthy conversation. With his pipe in his mouth, and a cup of steam-
ing coffee before him, Sandburg was at his best.

After finishing his first cup of coffee, he remarked,
musingly, "It's a funny thing; I was christened Carl August
Sandburg, but, sometime after I began going to school, I
decided to change my name to Charles. I hardly know why
I did this, but perhaps I felt that Carl was more descrip-
tive of a poor, Swede boy like me, while Charles sounded
classier. Anyway, I made the change."

We began discussing boyhood days, and he and I
found we had many things in common. His father was a
blacksmith's helper in the C. B. & Q. Railroad shops in
Galesburg, Illinois, and my father had his own blacksmith
shop in Albion, Michigan.

We both attended grade schools in the Fourth Ward,
but were hundreds of miles apart.

We wrote our lessons on slates with lead pencils,
and when the slate was filled, we wiped it clean with a wet
sponge or rag, and it was ready for use again. Some boys
spit on their slates and wiped them dry on their coat
sleeves.

When a boy wore new shoes to school we spit on the
shiny leather just for luck.

Our performances in whispering, or writing notes,
in school were similar, punished by being kept after school
and writing a sentence hundreds of times. I can remember
when I filled the blackboard with the sentence: "I waste
precious time in school by whispering."

In both Fourth Ward Schools there was a water pump
near the rear door of the schoolhouse. The pump was
equipped with a tin cup, and when a kid wanted a drink he
held the cup under the spout with one hand and operated the
pump handle with the other. We all drank from the same
rusty, tin cup. We thought nothing of sanitation.

Farther down the school yard, and on each side,
were the two outside accommodations. Around each building
stood a high board fence, and we boys played a ball game

which we called: "Anti-I-Over the Screen." A gang of
boys formed on opposite sides of the building, and one gang
threw the ball over the building, and if some boy on the
opposite side caught the ball, the whole gang ran around
the other side and captured their opponents.

Another favorite game was, "Crack the Whip." About
fifteen or twenty boys would join hands, a big boy for the
leader, and a little boy on the tail end. Then the string of
boys would race across the yard as fast as their legs would
carry them. About half way across the yard the big boys
in the lead would come to a dead stop and reverse the line.
This would cause the small boys on the crack end to lose
their grip, and come stumbling on, while the little fellow
on the end would be hurled through space, and the poor
wretch would come tumbling down with his face in the sand.
Cruel? Not at all, for the little fellow was game and would
try it all over.

Sandburg was reminded of a little boy who was nicknamed, "Ah-ah." One day, when he wanted to leave the
room, he stammered to the teacher, "I have to ah--ah."

Sandburg finished his second cup of coffee.

There was a most embarrassing incident about a
little girl in our school named Neva Sykes. One day, as
a punishment for some little infraction of the rules, she was
told to stand behind a screen in a corner of the room near
the teacher's desk. She was a very nervous type little girl,
and, as time dragged on, before our startled and embarrassed eyes a small stream of water began to trickle from
behind the screen out on to the floor. The teacher sprang
to the rescue and led poor, little Neva, with drooping head,
out to the cloak room. Not even one snicker came from us
kids. The situation was tragic.

We recalled the punishments for chewing gum in
school. The culprit had to stand on the teacher's platform,
with his back to the other pupils, facing a dumb blackboard,
or he might be sent to stand in the cloak room to stare at
the rows of hats and coats.

However, those were mild punishments.

There was a Dutch boy named Otto, who was caught
chewing gum.

"Otto, come here," said the teacher, "Now, take your gum between your thumb and finger. Hold your arm up as high as you can. Stand before the class until I tell you to step down." Otto was a tough little customer and could just about lick any boy in school, but here was a real challenge. Time dragged wearily on. Otto's arm sagged. Teacher, with a good, stout ruler in her hand, gave the boy's arm a resounding whack. This procedure was repeated as the morning wore on. All of us kids watched Otto as tears began to trickle down his tough, freckled cheeks. The teacher finally relented. "All right, Otto, you may return to your seat, but don't ever chew gum in this school again." He didn't and we didn't.

Sandburg remarked: "Many of us boys and girls went in for autograph albums. When they asked me, I wrote:

'When you are old and cannot see
Put on your specs and think of me.'

or, an old rhyme:

'Count that day lost whose low, descending sun
Views from thy hand no worthy action done.'

The first was supposed to be funny and the second serious."

Sandburg grinned, finished his third cup of coffee, and held it out to Nina for a refill.

In boyhood days Monday was wash day. We had mutual memories of how, on summer and vacation Mondays, we carried pails of water from the cistern, enough to fill two tubs. We turned the wringer while mother fed the clothes in. Boresome, tiresome for us, but how do you suppose mother felt, bending over the washboard, scrubbing the dirty clothes with all her strength, now and then beads of perspiration forming on her forehead, and splashing into the hot, soapy water?

Sandburg spoke of his mother and father with love and respect. We both kept the Fifth Commandment through life. I sometimes wonder if that was the reason he was blessed with a long, useful life, and I am blessed with the privilege of carrying on.

Sandburg said that he was sixteen when he rode on

the railroad for the first time, fifty miles on the C. B. &
Q. from Galesburg to Peoria, but at nineteen he decided to
see the world, and I was thrilled by the story of his adventures while traveling as a hobo for a year, riding the bump-
ers, sometimes eating and sleeping in hobo jungles. One
day, while stealing a ride on a freight, he was beaten up
by a "shack," which is slang for a brakeman.

Our guest put his fourth empty coffee cup on the
table with a sigh of satisfaction, and leaning back in his
chair, he said: "Coffee. That was good coffee, Nina."

The Marshall Daily Chronicle of Friday, January 7,
1910, carried the following announcement:

> Charles Sandburg will be the orator next Monday
> night at the Empire Theatre, coming as the fourth
> attraction on the lecture course. He is described
> as a 'thorough and eager student of humanity, a
> college man, a traveller, a New York police re-
> porter, a magazine editor, a writer and a labor
> agitator.' His topics treat of social questions,
> such as America and Socialism, Making a New
> Civilization, and Love, Labor and Play. Which
> one will be selected, the committee cannot state,
> but which-ever one is chosen will be worthy of
> the careful attention of the hearers.

Because of the disappointment with the Lincoln lecture at Homer, I felt that we should not chance a repetition
at Marshall, and the newspaper announcement left us at
liberty to change the subject from a discussion of Lincoln's
life to some other topic.

Knowing that Sandburg had been for a time secretary
to Emil Seidel, the Socialist mayor of Milwaukee, and had
also campaigned for Eugene Debs, in 1908, I felt that Socialism must be dear to his heart, and so I called the
chairman of the lecture course committee, The Reverend A.
A. Geiger, on the telephone, and told him how the Lincoln
lecture had failed to go over at Homer, and suggested that
Mr. Sandburg speak on his subject, "America and Socialism."

Mr. Geiger was a Methodist minister, and Metho-
dists were very conservative in those days; never-the-less
Mr. Geiger said: "Tell Mr. Sandburg to choose his own
subject."

Monday, January 10, 1910, Nina and I sat in the
Empire Theatre, in Marshall, Michigan. We had taken
seats about half way from the stage because I wanted to get
the full reaction of the audience to the lecture.

The theatre was well filled with what appeared to be
a good humored audience. There was no hushed atmosphere
of a church sanctuary, and, as Sandburg's talk progressed,
I relaxed, for I had no reason to push my feet on the floor
and root for a climax.

For an hour and half he held the audience without
resorting to jokes and stories. I was reminded of the
earnestness and sincerity of Eugene Debs, and it seemed to
me that James Whitcomb Riley's eulogy of Debs might well
be applied to Sandburg.

> A man that stands
> And just holds out in his two hands
> As warm a heart as ever beat
> Betwixt here and the Judgement Seat.

Fifteen years passed. Carl Sandburg was booked to
appear in Indianapolis for a program sponsored by the Indiana Historical Society.

In the mean time I had moved, with my wife and
family, to that city, and was teaching at Indiana Central
College. I had lost contact with Carl Sandburg, but was
eager to renew our happy acquaintance, so I called his room
on the telephone at the Claypool Hotel.

His familiar voice asked: "Are you, by any chance,
Elmer Marshall of Jackson, Michigan? Well, I'm glad to
hear your voice. I'm glad to hear your voice. I've often
wondered what had become of you. Now, I haven't a stitch
on me, but I want to see you in a few minutes."

I replied that I wouldn't intrude upon his privacy,
but would see him later at the night's program.

An evening with Carl Sandburg reciting his poems,
playing on his guitar and singing folk songs, was an event to
be long remembered, and yet, I couldn't help remembering
those early days and wondering if there was a message left
unsaid.

The entertainment over, and the audience gone, Carl

shook hands with me, saying: "Our paths have crossed again."

He grinned at Nina. "Coffee, that was good coffee."

Turning again to me: "I always appreciated those dates you booked for me up in Michigan. They came at a time when they were sadly needed--sadly needed."

Our visit over, we clasped hands as Carl said: "Our paths will cross again."

[In addition to what was in the manuscript about Sandburg's appearances in Michigan in 1910, Mr. F. Elmer Marshall told me in an interview on March 23, 1970, there were eight more appearances in the area near Homer and Marshall, but he could not recall the places. He thought one might be Stockbridge. The general area seemed to be founded by Lansing, Kalamazoo, Ann Arbor, and the Indiana line.

He could not find a newspaper account of either of the lectures he witnessed. He did find an advance notice in the Marshall paper and the Homer Index.

He could not remember what Sandburg said in the Lincoln lecture. He was so upset about its "dead level" that he could not remember.

Marshall's wife, who died in 1935, said, "I don't see that Sandburg was a great man."

The Stout Bureau, he recalled well, and believed that it scheduled appearances in Indiana, Ohio, and Illinois.

The Dixie Bureau had headquarters in Columbus, Miss., and a branch in Dallas, Texas.

Sandburg was pleasant but not a flatterer. He had a streak of sentimentality. It was exemplified for Marshall by Sandburg's emphasis on the idea that "our paths have crossed," as already mentioned.

He described his speech as "not sympathetic," saying he was a little formal but not stilted. "He did not attempt to drive home any lesson in his later years," adding reading and guitar playing as opposed to early straight lectures.

Marshall's Alliance Lyceum Bureau listed thirty-seven attractions, including Sandburg. His subjects were given as: "Love, Labor, and Play," "The Poet of Democracy [Whitman]," and "Making a New Civilization."]

"Don't Mind If I Do"*

Yes, I did have a personal experience with Carl Sandburg, and I shall never forget it. It was during the Annual Convention of N. C. T. E. [National Council of Teachers of English] in 1949 at the Statler Hotel in Buffalo. It was rather late at night on the Friday evening of the convention. Carl was to be the luncheon speaker on Saturday. We had had our banquet and it must have been about 11-12 p. m. While I was wandering around the lobby, one of the workers came over to me with Carl Sandburg at his side. It seems that no one was around to receive Carl. The worker had no idea who he was and was merely trying to help the somewhat puzzled poet out.

He came toward me and asked me whether I would know anybody who could take care of Mr. Sandburg. For a moment I did not realize who the gentleman was. But one glance at his wonderful head of white hair and I had no doubts whatever. I noticed that he was wearing a woolen shirt which we in N. Y. C. used to call a "lumberjack." He wore no tie. I told Mr. Sandburg that the chances were that any officers of the Council at this late date would probably be in the bar--the only thing open at that time.

We went into the bar and he was espied at once by William Jovanovich, then a salesman now President of Harcourt, Brace & Co. I believe that Sandburg's novel, Remembrance Rock had been published not long before.

Mr. Jovanovich hailed him with, "Hello, Carl how about a beer?" Carl replied, "Don't mind if I do." And Mr. Jovanovich promised that he would search for someone that would take care of Carl's room and luggage, for I seem to recall that he had not yet registered.

Mr. Sandburg was the least poetic-looking poet you

*Letter from Joseph Mersand, Jamaica, N. Y. By permission of the author.

could imagine. But once seen he could never be forgotten.
While I cannot say that Carl gave me immortal words of
wisdom in our brief conversation, his words "Don't mind if
I do" said much more than one would think.

The Highlight of Thirty Years of Teaching*

[When Jack Norris, science consultant in the La
Habra, California schools, sent permission to use this transcript of a talk he had given to students at Imperial Junior
High School in La Habra, he wrote that the experience it
represented had been "the highlight of a thirty-year teaching
career."]

We went down to Chicago [on February 12, 1958] to
pick him up. We went to the hotel where he was staying.
He has stayed in this hotel every time he has come to Chicago. For the last 45 years, he stays in the same hotel--
not the Conrad Hilton in Chicago which faces Lake Michigan
and is superbly beautiful, not the Conrad Hilton there. He
stays in what is called the Park Dearborn Hotel. It's about
the size of this place right here--only about five stories
high. It's old, it's brown, it's weathered, it's got the soot
of Chicago on it for the last hundred years. But it's a fascinating hotel. It's got a lobby about half the size of this
room.

We walked in the lobby, the three of us, and we all
went up to the clerk at the desk--and at the desk some young
beautiful lady taking our names and taking the message?
No! A little old lady about seventy years old, bent over
with the cutest little voice and the nicest manners. "Yes?"
"We are looking for Carl Sandburg." "Why, Carl's here.
I will call him on the phone"--which she did. And she
said, "If you will go over to the elevator, he'll be down in
a few minutes." So we walked over to the elevator, one
elevator, just one. We watched the number go up to the
fifth floor and stop, and wait, and we knew he was getting
into it. Fifth floor, then it came down four, three, two,
and I was getting more nervous by the minute. The principal started to run away; I grabbed him by the coat collar
and brought him back and we watched as the doors opened.

---

*Transcribed tape recording by Jack Norris, La Habra,
Calif. By permission.

First thing that appeared was the elevator boy. Elevator
boy! That guy was about 80 himself! He was a little bitty
elevator boy, little red cap, little red trousers with a stripe,
and that little tight vest, you know. He stood aside and out
came another man, another old man, but this time a big old
man, with a great, huge coat. Looked like the World War
I coat they wore in the trenches. Big man, big bones, big
wrists. Man alive, if he'd had the vitamins that you kids
have had since birth, he would have been 6' 8'' today. He
was about 6' 2'', I imagine, but bent over. But he was
still big. He towered over me. I'm used to little old men,
but not big old men. But what a wonderful face, what wonderful hair! He didn't comb his hair. He never combed
his hair. In 80 years he's never combed his hair. [An
exaggeration, as explained later.] No, it wasn't down to
here, don't get me wrong, but there was plenty of it and it
was all his. And it was white like snow, and all over his
head. I am sure Mrs. Sandburg gave up telling him to
comb his hair.

Teeth--all his own--80 years old, all his own, and
coming to the dentist in Chicago to get them fixed a little.
A few cavities here and there. So he shook hands with us,
a firm shake, not an old man's shake, but of a man that
likes life, and he likes people and he likes children. Then
he said, "Have you got the car outside?" "Yes, here it
is." We stepped outside and it was the squad car shiny as
you ever saw a squad car in your life. And a police
captain as nervous as he could be because he had
never met a man as famous as this before. And Carl
Sandburg broke into the widest grin when he saw that squad
car. And he asked the captain, "Hey, son, can you turn on
the light?" "Well, I'll try it a little bit. Can't do it too
long or the Chicago cops will pick us up." But we turned
on the light, and he looked up above, reached out the door,
and he looked up, he stood up, saw that light going around.
And the guns there, the guns fascinated him. He wanted to
know about the riot gun in front. And he just enjoyed his
ride back to Wheeling, 30 miles. And I was amazed. He
knew Chicago better than I did. He knew all the little
towns better than I did and he would point out things, "See
that field over there? I slept in that field when I was
twenty-five, when I was a hobo, when I was bumming my
way across the country." And he did. He was a hobo for
a while. At the Plains River there, he said, "I remember
the Plains River when the water was crystal clear before
the factories came in and polluted it, and the fish died and

floated to the top. I used to swim in this Plain River," he
said, "with nuthin' on. But, that was sixty or seventy years
ago, and there warn't nobody around. Maybe just a few Indians." He was kidding, I think, then. I don't know if
there were any Indians around then or not.

We arrived at Wheeling School--the Carl Sandburg
School, to the office so he could take his coat off--he took
it off--an old coat. It must have been 30 years old, and
it was worn around the edges. It had huge pockets. I'll
tell you about those pockets a little later. And then he was
prepared to talk to his first class of kids. Now these kids
were in kindergarten, grades 1, 2, and we gathered them
into a room the size of this right here--this section or that
section but not the whole thing.

And their mothers knew that Carl Sandburg was coming. So every little face was shined up. Every little shoe
was shined. Every little tie was on, but by the time Carl
Sandburg came, some of the ties were this way, some were
down to here. All the girls were pretty as could be. And
he got into the room and he looked at them and he couldn't
say anything.

This man has talked with kings and queens. He's
brushed elbows with the famous people of the world, and
with the infamous people--the bad people of the world. He
has known them all. And for once in his life he couldn't
say anything. He was dumb-struck. He said, "What shall
I say?" And his secretary patted him on the arm and
said, "You'll think of something." And he did. He said
what a poet would say. He said, "You look like a garden
of flowers," and he looked at the little kids. You know,
they did look like a garden of flowers. Some wore pink
dresses and blue dresses. Some little boys in their white
shirts and so forth. They looked like a garden of flowers.

And then to get them to like him (they were looking
up at him like he was a god), to get them warmed up to
him, he said, "How many of you like taxicabs?" Taxicabs!
Man, who doesn't like taxicabs? Every little hand went up.
"How many like red taxicabs?" Red taxicabs! Man, the
hands went up like mad. "How many like yellow taxicabs?"
And the hands went up. See, this is poetry; this is really
poetry. This is how he shows his love for kids. And then
he said, "How many like checkered taxicabs?" Nuthin'
better than checkered taxicabs in the whole world! Every

hand went up. Some little guys got so excited they <u>stood</u>
up! He had them then. They loved him from then on. If
we hadn't watched them, they would have followed him home
to the Park Dearborn Hotel! We would have lost all the
kids like the Pied Piper. They would never have been seen
again. They loved him.

And then he talked about a few poems, too. He
made up a few, actually. And then after the little first and
second graders had bid him good-bye, we went to the third
and fourth grades. And he asked them about TV. That
was 1958. TV wasn't as big as it is now, but it was growing. And he asked them, "How many watch TV for one
hour a day?" A certain number of hands went up. "How
many watch it for two hours?" A few more hands went up.
"How many watch TV for three hours a day?" They went
up and he said, "Oh, my, my." But he didn't say anything
wrong about TV. He said he liked Dragnet and he liked
Gunsmoke. That's all he said. He didn't mention any other
programs. He only said one thing about TV that you might
remember and I try to remember myself--that it can be a
time-stealer. It can steal time away from you.

We had a blind class in our school, and one of the
students had written a poem. Now I don't have this poem.
This poem is with Carl Sandburg and the family at Flat Rock,
North Carolina. It will be at the University of Illinois when
Carl Sandburg dies. It's going to be in the Carl Sandburg
Library. It's strange, it's going to be right in that library.
I hope he doesn't die for a hundred more years, but some-
day I hope that some of you, if you are in Illinois and Carl
Sandburg is dead, and he will be sometime in your lifetime,
that you go to the University of Illinois someday. Go to
the Carl Sandburg Library, and look for that poem from
Wheeling School, by a little blind girl. It will be there.
It'll be hanging up on the wall of the library. And it was
a poem that looked like this. It would be written on paper
like this. This is Braille paper. It's almost like card-
board. Do you see the little raised dots? Now the writing
here is an interpretation for me. I can't read Braille very
well, but I had them transcribe it for me or translate it
into English writing-script. And this was written by a girl
by the name of Kindwin Clepper [sp. ?] who is blind. She
would now be a senior at the U. of Michigan. I know she's
at the U. of Michigan; I don't know if she's a senior or
junior--maybe she's graduated. She's taking up law. She
wrote this poem to myself and my wife at Easter. The

poem that Carl Sandburg has was written by Mary Ann
Brady (maybe O'Brien, not sure).   She came up to Carl
Sandburg, and she handed this poem to him.   It was like
this, on this paper--one sheet, though, instead of three like
this.   She handed it out to him.   He reached down from his
great height and took it, and he said, "Ah, I'll read this."
He put on his spectacles.   Most of the time he doesn't go
around with glasses.   That old man's in good shape.   He
doesn't need glasses.   He puts them on to read, and he
comes out like this.   He started reading, but he couldn't
read!   Why couldn't he read?   He started to cry.   He was
touched--a very sensitive man.   Tears started rolling down
his cheeks.   He said, "Honey, would you read it for me?"
And she read this poem, this poem by a blind child and
that's when he said, "That's going to be a treasured possession of mine, and it's going to be at Flat Rock, North
Carolina, right in our parlor, where people can see it when
they come in."   We finished the third and fourth grades,
then we went to the Junior High and the seventh and eighth
graders met in the gymnasium, about 250 of them (sat in
chairs) and he talked to the pupils, and he read a few
poems to them.   And then some of them wanted autographs.
But he wouldn't sign any autographs, because he was an old
man, he said.   If he started signing autographs he'd never
be able to stop.

        I remember one boy was kind of disappointed.   And
Carl Sandburg knew that he was disappointed.   So he went
over to that boy, and he put his arms around that boy and
hugged him and he said, "Son, don't worry about autographs.
They don't mean much."   He said, "Just that you and I
talked.   That's more important."   And then the kid realized
that he had just had Carl Sandburg grab him and hug him!
Man, that's better than an autograph!   Anybody can own an
autograph.   You can buy 'em with shekels, with money.
But how often do you get to talk to somebody that's important?   How often does somebody important think enough
of you to hug you a little bit and pat you on the head?

        Oh, his coat.   That big huge coat.   He told us about
that coat--that old coat with big pockets.   He takes walks
in the woods in North Carolina.   They live out in the country.   When he leaves in the morning Mrs. Sandburg makes
him sandwiches.   Those big sandwiches that farm people
used to eat long ago made out of good country bread.   With
good ham in it.   And he said, "She makes me big sandwiches, and I put them in my pockets and then an apple and

an orange," and he said, "You know, see those pockets?
You can't even tell I've got sandwiches. These pockets are
big. Then when I get hungry and I'm walking in the woods
and I sit down and start talking with jack-rabbits or the
birds, we start eating sandwiches. Some for me and some
for the animals." I was interested in such a big old coat.
But I realize now that all of his clothing was good, was
serviceable, had been repaired. Buttons had fallen off--
they'd been sewn back. Cuffs were kind of worn, and they'd
been sewn together--patched. But it was a good overcoat
for an old man. He liked it.

You're going to be interested in the fact that he remarked about riding his bike in the country years ago and
didn't have to worry about traffic. He'd ride for miles.
He bought his bike from Sears and Roebuck. Paid $29 for
a brand new bike in those days. He said he could take it
apart and put it together in 15 minutes. He was proud of
that. Here was a guy who had written poetry and is a mil-
lionaire and was proud of the fact that he could take a bike
apart and put it together in 15 minutes. He said, "I think
I could do it today."

You know, Carl Sandburg had been a milkman at one
time, and worked in the circus as a roustabout. He had
come out to California when it was all orchards and beautiful, a long time ago, and he worked near Los Angeles for
awhile. What did he do? He worked in a hamburger joint,
making hamburgers. He was a short-order chef. He had
also been in the Spanish-American War as a dough-boy, a
soldier over there. He had very interesting experiences.
You'll have to read about that yourself.

We took him back to Chicago--to the Park Dearborn
Hotel. He slept all the way back. Then he woke up when
we got to the hotel. We left him at the Coffee Shop there.
We asked him if he'd like coffee and a doughnut. He said,
no, that he thought he'd buy a paper. This man's a mil-
lionaire. He went and bought his paper, and I thought he'd
take out his wallet and maybe pull out a couple of big bills,
you know. No--he reached down in that big overcoat and
he came up with an old granddaddy's purse, those brown
purses with a little clip--beat-up purse. He opened it up
and I looked in. What did he have in there? A lot of
money? No, he had pennies and nickels and dimes. And
he very carefully reached in and took out a nickel and put
it there for the paper. He took his paper and he walked

up to his room and he said goodbye and added, "This has
been one of the greatest days of my life. I'll come back
again someday." He never did. [tape finished]

[Mr. Norris added a few comments which follow:]

[I had used] exaggeration in places to get the children
enthused. Carl Sandburg said that he was very touched by
the little girl who gave him the poem. Sandburg said that
he would always remember the girl's lovely hands and he
was quite pleased at this. He said he would never forget
her beautiful dark eyes and dark hair. She smiled very
beautifully for him.

On the way back in the squad car, which included
the driver, Captain Arnold Drause, Mr. Omiatek, Carl
Sandburg, of course, and myself, Sandburg remarked, in
passing a town, "Those houses are all alike. I wonder if
they all think alike. I wonder if they all read the Chicago
Tribune?" And I said, "My God, I hope not." And he
laughed heartily at my reaction. This, of course, is very
revealing. It is something he might have wondered about
in regard to the many new modern sections.

In regards to naming of schools after famous people,
I made up a list of 50 people, and they chose Carl Sandburg's name for the [new] school at Wheeling. The list is
still being used. There should be a trophy case back there
of sorts that has all of the books he sent to us. He sent
us a box of books.

I am not an autograph hunter, but I did want his
autograph. In searching for a book of his, none seemed to
show up, so my secretary handed me the book, Lincoln and
his Generals, by T. H. Williams. And Carl Sandburg
signed the inside cover, and that book is right here in my
office today, a treasured possession.

Sandburg remarked, "Children can be tiring, but I
loved them all. God bless them." He read to the upper
grades in the gymnasium: Arithmetic, Slip Foot. They
seemed entranced. He (Sandburg) summed it all up at the
hotel: "I had a feeling something wonderful would happen
when I visited Wheeling."

Notes of Conversation*

[When Sandburg was at Indiana University in March, 1942, Professor Russell Noyes, of the Department of English, recorded these notes from his conversation:]

He was gathering material for a gates of Heaven anthology--an oil magnate managed to get by St. Peter but he found Heaven crowded--besides he missed his old cronies-- a rumor spread that a big gusher was struck in Hell--the oil magnate got worried--believed there must be something to it so takes off for the infernal region.

This is the only specific example so far discovered of material he and Professor Frank Dobie of the University of Texas were planning to publish collaboratively.

[Sandburg also professed that] modern sophisticated poets are negativists--they are wearied with life--they are like the jaded Hedonist who throws himself fully dressed on his bed and when he is awakened in the sweet dawn cries out, "Conscious again, God damn it!"

[Noyes recalls that Sandburg] felt relieved when the Lincoln book was done--didn't think he'd make it. The tremendous tedium of the task at times overwhelmed him-- he thought of flood, of fire, of ill health. Finally he experienced a feeling of elation when he took the manuscript in a taxi across Hellgate Bridge to the publishing house. It was the biggest manuscript ever moved into the cultured mecca of America--it was already contracted for far ahead of time.

His eyes were small but deepset and keen--light blue with a smoky, far away haze; his hair straight and silver white, parted a little off center; his face, like his style, rugged and individual; his lips set and protruding; his laugh sharp and bell-like.

Sandburg's conversation was piquantly touched with an irony of understatement--sometimes he would pay no attention to questions or responses, as though his mind was shaping something else--he mocks at the pretenses of the

---

*Letter from Russell Noyes, Indiana University, Bloomington. By permission of the author.

"arty" people--[there was] a toughness and a hard, fierce
intensity about his thought.

On the Indiana University campus [Sandburg re-
marked]: "You're better dressed every time I come....
People go to college or to hear Aida to make sure they
haven't missed anything and find they haven't. ... The
Roosevelt haters are smitten with disease. They have to
relieve themselves about once a day by opening an ulcer
and letting the pus run out. "

He laughed at the bust of Paul McNutt in the Union
Building--thought he was a "stuffed shirt"--thought the bust
was well done from the chin down, especially the medals--
told the story of the Roman senator who would rather have
people ask why there was no bust of him than why there was.

Performing with Laryngitis*

It was a cold, clear, winter evening, January 25,
1934, when I met Mr. Sandburg at the train station. He
was wearing a big, floppy, felt hat and his throat was en-
gulfed with a huge muffler. To my consternation I discovered that he was speaking in a hoarse whisper. He had
contracted laryngitis! He avowed, however, that a good
rest and a good meal would probably put him in shape.

I drove him by the Bates College campus (Lewiston,
Me.) which was glistening in the bright moonlight, and he
remarked what a jewel of a picture that was. For the night
of the lecture the chapel was filled. (We had sold tickets
to defray the cost of bringing Mr. Sandburg there. I do
not recall the cost of the tickets nor the amount of honor-
arium which we had agreed to pay Mr. Sandburg.) I had
expected that President Gray would introduce Mr. Sandburg,
but he was away at the time. I had next contacted the
Chairman of the English Department, but he was unavailable,
also. Thus the suggestion was made that I, as president of
the organization sponsoring the lecture, should chair the
meeting. Naturally I was very pleased to do this, but I
wondered whether or not Mr. Sandburg would feel let down
to be introduced by a mere student!

*Letter from Albert L. Oliver, Philadelphia, Pa., Aug. 10,
1970. By permission of the author.

I made the apologies for Mr. Sandburg because his
sore throat was still bothering him, and then I retired to a
corner of the stage when he took over.   Speaking in a
hoarse whisper Mr. Sandburg made some introductory remarks, read some of his poems, and finally brought forth
his trusty guitar(?) to accompany himself on a few numbers.
Oh yes, I noted that before going on the stage Mr. Sandburg
carefully disarranged his hair.

For those who could hear Mr. Sandburg, the presen-
tation was well received.   However, the Bates Chapel at
that time did not have the modern amplifying system; so
many people in the rear of the chapel were disappointed because they could hear him only now and then.   After the
lecture we retired to one of the nearby dormitory dining
rooms where a reception was held.   I recall that one student pushed forward for his autograph and presented an anthology containing the writings of many authors.   Mr. Sandburg brusquely turned away and said that he refused to sign
anthologies.   Also, there was one individual--I do not recall whether he was a student or a member of the faculty--
who had come from Mr. Sandburg's area and professed to
know something of the people in that area.   I had then
made special arrangements to have him talk with Mr. Sandburg.   I soon noted Mr. Sandburg turned away from that
man and ignored him thereafter.   Later on he told me that
he could not tolerate a conversation further with that individual since he was a "phony."

Sandburg on the Telephone*

The tape recordings by Leo Orso of Sandburg's
voice were so numerous it took more than a thousand pages
to prepare a typescript.

On Sunday, September 20, 1959, Orso apologetically
called Sandburg and recorded the conversation.   After Sandburg jovially reassured him, Orso mentioned three tapes he
had just sent to Sandburg and asked permission to record
the current conversation.

Sandburg: "Why, I wouldn't have the slightest objec-

---

*Based on a transcript of tape recordings made by Leo Orso;
supplied by the Wayne State University Library.

tion. I would say, you do whatever you want with my out-
pouring. "

Then Orso revealed an "absolutely fabulous idea" to
promote the sale of the one-volume edition of Sandburg's
life of Lincoln. The idea was to give a recording of Sandburg's speech to the Joint Session of Congress (on February
12, 1959) with the book. Mentioning he had already prepared copies for Representative Fred Schwengel of Iowa and
Justice William O. Douglas, he wanted to know if Sandburg
had copyrighted the speech. Sandburg replied that since it
had been published immediately in the newspaper, it had
gone into the public domain.

After a loose-knit cataloging of various recordings
made and anticipated, including comments as to which ones
he preferred, Sandburg said he would go in on any kind of
arrangement Orso might develop. Noting that he wanted to
be certain that Caedmon Records would not object, Orso
talked enthusiastically of plans for publicity and sales,
quoting a recent remark of Justice Douglas that "we will
never achieve real friendship and understanding" ... until
Sandburg's Lincoln biography would be produced in India
for a few cents a copy. Sandburg said he had not seen the
remark, which Orso told him was in Think Magazine.

Orso's plans for the promotions involved getting organizations to buy a copy of the Joint Session proceedings
for each classroom in each community, as a public service.
People would not be able to buy the record but would be
able to make donations so as to provide distribution
of "Sandburg's Lincoln biography to send to libraries
overseas and give to students and so forth...." When Orso
assured Sandburg that groups he had mentioned the matter
to were eager to get started, Sandburg showed no skepticism
but said rather the enthusiast-promoter could tell Caedmon
that "you have the go-ahead from me on it completely...."

When Orso asked if Sandburg would send a note of
his approval, Sandburg wanted to know if he were talking
about "the Asheville speech, " not previously mentioned in
the conversation. When Orso said that it was the Joint
Session speech, Sandburg readily acquiesced.

Promising to give him all the details of the arrangements when he got them made, Orso mentioned commercials
Sandburg had done for American Airlines, at which point

Sandburg interpolated, "There are fifteen of them...."
After talking about getting copies of the commercials, which
Orso did not want to do against Sandburg's volition, he was
assured: "... I would say you just go ahead with that."

Then Orso asked Sandburg how long he thought he
would be at Flat Rock. The reply was until October 5 or
6, when he would go to New York and possibly Washington.
Then he said he was going to Portland, Maine, in an unidentified connection with Norman Corwin. He was going to
stay in New York with some "old, old friends." He mentioned a commitment to attend the dedication of Carl Sandburg High School in Mundelein, Illinois, near Chicago, on
October 14. Two days later he had to see an unidentified
dentist.

When Orso told him he would be working to get all
the arrangements made, Sandburg advised: "You work hard.
You've got a capacity for hard work."

Noting Orso had his Flat Rock telephone number, he
gave his New York number as Gramercy 7-8717 so that Orso
could contact him there. After more effusion from Orso on
his promotional plans, Sandburg said he had told a librarian
in Chicago, who thought Sandburg's Joint Session speech
would last as long as those of Lincoln, to go ahead and
print it.

Orso said the identification of Sandburg with Lincoln
was so great people did not know when one ended and the
other started. Sandburg replied: "I am willing to be taken
as a disciple of Lincoln. I'm not a double."

After more promotional effusion by Orso, Sandburg
amused himself by saying, "Yes, they ought to do that for
the writer of the foreword to Harry Golden's Only in America.

As the conversation entered its final stages, Orso
mentioned the privilege it was to know Sandburg and that he
had "flipped" over him during the Democratic Convention of
1936 or 1940 and had continued to do so. Then Sandburg
asked that two copies of the Joint Session address be sent
to his New York friend, Dr. William Braye, in Apartment
AE, Village Apartments, explaining this was an old Chicago
friend. Orso considered it a privilege.

Sandburg ventured the suggestion that he would like

to send a memento to Orso, who quickly disclaimed any
idea of obligation. Sandburg said that, in the word of an
English proverb, he was "beholden" and that the Brayes and
his "other friend" would appreciate getting the recordings.

Orso said in closing, "I certainly have enjoyed talking to you, and I am going ahead on this public relations
idea, because I think it's a fabulous opportunity to help to
wake up America a little bit. " Sandburg: "Well, you know
your ground and you have been around and I'll be seein' ya. "
Orso: "Thank you so much. Bye-bye. " Sandburg: "God
love you. "

Guiding Carl Sandburg*

Ailese Parten was a senior at Mary Hardin Baylor
College at Belton, Texas, when Sandburg appeared there in
the spring of 1925. She was president of Theta Sigma Phi,
sponsoring organization, under the English Department, and
its head, Dr. W. H. Vann.

Miss Parten was invited to go with Dr. Vann to get
him at Temple, ten miles away. The train, due at 11:30,
was ten minutes late. When it and Sandburg did arrive,
Sandburg was in a discussion with the Pullman porter because of missing pajamas and cuff links.

Attempting to get him to a luncheon in Belton by noon,
they finally got him into their car. He immediately said,
"How far is it to a jewelry store?" They tried to explain
they would prefer he wait till after the luncheon, at which
30 people were waiting. He insisted on the deliberate purchase of a pair of cuff links.

A home economics class was putting on the luncheon
as a demonstration meal. Both teacher and students were
quite upset at having to hold up the meal. He seemed to
have no conception of the disruption his lateness had caused.

After the meal was started, he got to talking to the
waitresses, ignoring the faculty and other guests.

He displayed an inquisitiveness which appeared to be

---

*Based on an interview with Ailese Parten, Riverside, Calif.,
February, 1970.

generally characteristic.   He wanted to know what was in
each dish and how it was prepared.

Just as the meal was ending, he asked Dr. Vann,
"Who is going to show me the campus?"   Dr. Vann assigned
an unwilling Ailese to the project.   Sandburg, who was staying at the campus guest home, wanted to go at four o'clock,
taking time to rest first.

Ailese got a friend, a student from Constantinople,
to go with her to conduct Sandburg on what was expected to
be a short tour of the campus, for which they had allowed
about 30 minutes, knowing he had a dinner to attend with
the English faculty at six and his lecture to present at 8.

As the campus tour began, he displayed interest
in all forms of plant life, being especially curious about
the mesquite trees.

At the edge of the campus, Sandburg noticed a road
and asked where it went.   He was told it went to town, a
mile and a half away.   "All right," he decided, "we'll go
to town."

The girls, in high heels, were totally unprepared
for this turn of events.   In addition to inadequate footwear,
there was also inadequate time.   Also, girls were not
allowed to leave campus without permission.   But Sandburg
was on his way, being oblivious to any problems.   The girls
were trotting to keep up with his long strides.

He said, "I want to see the tree into which Sam
Bass shot his initials."

"That is not in Belton," Ailese replied.

They bickered about this point as they went along,
Ailese being certain the tree was in Round Rock, fifty miles
away.

As they arrived at the town square, the girls asked,
"Mr. Sandburg, what do you want in town?"

His reply, that he wanted a pair of pajamas and a
box of cigars, shocked the girls, who did not expect to have
men's pajamas mentioned to them.   (On that campus, girls
who played men's parts in plays wore skirts.)

Attempting to avoid as much embarrassment as possible and yet comply with the request of the "odd man with lock of hair always falling into his face," she took him to "The Haberdashery," where there were at least no women.

In the center of the store was a pier glass. Piled against it was a stack of sombreros, elaborately embroidered and painted. He made a beeline for them and modeled each of the several dozen hats.

It was after five o'clock by then. The girls mentioned to him that they needed to return to the campus, but he ignored these remarks, continuing to try on the hats. Additionally, the store closed at six.

The store owner asked what Sandburg wanted. Miss Parten, being embarrassed at the idea of mentioning pajamas, said, "Mr. Sandburg, he wants to know what you want." He replied, "Well, go pick me out a pair of pajamas!"

Faced with the necessity of action, she inquired, "What color, Mr. Sandburg?"

"Blue!"

The cost of the pajamas was five dollars, which was paid as he went on trying on the sombreros.

In this interim, Miss Parten decided to ask her companion to go to the drugstore and ask Mr. Pyle, the local historian, where Sam Bass shot his initials into a tree. The expert was just four or five stores away.

Six o'clock was by then right on them. It seemed unlikely they could get back to campus on time. The time problem related to the dinner with the faculty was pointed out.

He replied, "Oh, I'm not going to the dinner."

At this point he became interested in the architecture of the covered walk in front of the stores surrounding the town square. They made a tour of it, Sandburg commenting on all the variations which had been built into it.

The objective of the guides had now changed to trying to get Sandburg back to campus by eight o'clock so he could give his lecture.

"What is that over there?" he inquired.

"The Philip Nolan Creek," he was informed.

"Well, we'll go look at that," he decided.

The creek ran under a bridge on the road between Dallas and Austin. It had a walkway and a place for pedestrians to stand to enjoy the view. This he did, exclaiming and gesticulating, as passing traffic slowed down to observe him.

They finally got him off the bridge and to the corner where they had bought the pajamas. There he bought a box of cigars and started back to the campus with them under his arm.

"This is the way we came?" he queried. Finding it was, he insisted that they go back another, more winding route. All this time, the high heels the girls were wearing had become an increasing problem. The road was not only winding but also was unpaved and had no sidewalk. They tried to head him back to campus over rocks and in painful shoes.

They came to a house with a clump of trees in front of it.

"What are those trees?"

"I don't know."

"Go in and ask them."

The woman in the house told her, and she dutifully reported.

When they finally arrived where the meal was in progress, it was after seven. The regimen at the college generally called for missing a meal if one were not on time. Generally one did not ask to be fed at an unusual time.

As an attempt was being formulated to meet this problem for themselves and their guest, the girls heard Sandburg say, "Just send me tea and toast to my room."

Miss Parten decided, "That's Mr. Vann's business. He got me into this!"

She explained to the English faculty that he just would not return in time for the dinner and that he wanted tea and toast sent to his room. She concluded her report to Dr. Vann by saying, "And you can tell the dietician to feed me and Lala."

Her annoyance and frustration were not quite too great to keep her from his performance. However, she did not see him the next day.

* * *

In 1935, Miss Parten was teaching at National Park Seminary in Washington, D. C. She was often invited to the home of her friend, Ruby Black Little, in Alexandria, Va.

Journalists and celebrities often visited the home of Herbert Little, who was with United Press. But on this particular weekend, it was to be quiet. She went on Friday afternoon and did encounter an evening of family talk with no visitors.

The prospect for Saturday evening was a small dinner, including Congressman Maury Maverick and his wife. This prospect was maintained until Herb came in about six that evening and said, "Well, I ran into Carl." ... "You didn't ask him to come out, did you?" his wife immediately asked.... "He just said he was coming out." By this time the guest had asked, "Carl who?" On being told, she exclaimed, "Oh, no!" the memories of ten years before flooding back. Ruby Little's reaction was the same: "He'll bring his guitar and will bring everybody with him."

Before dinner was over, he arrived with his guitar. Ailese had explained her previous encounter. Maury Maverick told Sandburg the young lady had met him before. He recalled the missing pajamas and cuff links, stating the Pullman Company had found and returned the pajamas but that the cuff links had not reappeared. He still thought Bass had shot his initials into the tree in Belton.

The group went into the living room. Within a short time thirty or thirty-five people had arrived at his invitation.

One had a zither and half-a-dozen had guitars. All were
playing and trading folk songs. Two reporters were just
back from the International Ladies Garment Workers Union
convention, where they had learned The Internationale and
taught it to the group. There was a profession of all kinds
of songs.

About twelve Maury Maverick slipped out, much later
than he had intended to. At two Sandburg was still going
strong. At three everyone else had left but Sandburg was
still there and did then make his departure.

The Respect of Sympathetic Listening*

A man who has spent years of his life reading and
writing about Lincoln sees his country through compassion-
ate, kindly eyes that crinkle at the corners. That man,
Carl Sandburg, talked about America, told some tall tales
and sang some folk songs playing a Santa Barbara guitar.

He left a capacity crowd at the Santa Barbara High
School last night feeling it had been part of his travels
about the land gathering folklore, peering into the depths of
Lincoln's soul, cheering workmen, scorning "cultural" gad-
gets such as radio, television and movies, viewing politi-
cians and rejoicing in an America that laughed and worked,
experimented on the Marshall Plan, that produced men like
Lincoln, Jefferson, Robert E. Lee and Roger Williams
(born in England) and read good books.

Carl Sandburg is of medium height. His snow white
hair, parted in the middle, slipped down in horns to the
corner of his smiling eyes. He wore the bronze button of
the Spanish-American War veteran in the lapel of his dinner
jacket. And, figuratively, he brought along a well stuffed
carpet bag to the podium and dipped into it often for Americana or politicana, or for just sweet, heart-warming things,
including some of his own poems.

He picked up one item and hurled it out. It was

*Litti Paulding, "Sandburg's Poems, Tall Tales and Songs
Give Warm, Vigorous Picture of America," Santa Barbara
News-Press, Nov. 15, 1957. Reprinted by permission of
the publisher.

about a certain wing of the Republican Party that stayed too
close to tradition. There were some brickbats, too, for
modern poetry. And one for Henry James, of whom Owen
Wister said he might just as well have written on white
paper with white ink. He resented it that shelves of books
were written about this man now who could not see anything
good in America. "Why didn't they write shelves of new
books about Mark Twain and Walt Whitman, or William
James, Henry's brother?" he asked.

When lampooning radio, television and movies, he
said he thought the Edgar Bergen shows had something about
Mark Twain in them.

The great men learned through great books and knew
the value of time--time to meditate, the poet said, and
loneliness to grow a worthy personality. He quoted Pascal,
too, on loneliness.

Out of this mythical bag he took an unpublished poem,
entitled at the present "Ever the Prophets are a Dime a
Dozen." It spoke of change, of one age not foreseeing the
next, the Stone Age, the Pharaohs, the Romans, the Dark
Ages, the global age. "Even Gutenburg and Caxton did not
foresee the truck delivering the newspapers," he said.

Commentators are in the dime-a-dozen-prophets
class, and the one affirmative voice he singled out for
praise, as a newspaperman and statesman, was Edward R.
Murrow. Most of them just speak words--democracy, re-
public, liberal, radical, free enterprise, capitalism and on
and on, he said.

Reading thousands of letters and newspapers for his
books on Lincoln, he found many men who wrote much, who
did not see the history in the making before their eyes. Included among them were Charles Sumner of Massachusetts
and Jeff Davis of Virginia. The time of Lincoln of the War
Years was much like our own time.

Remembrance Rock, one of the late Sandburg books,
good for reading and re-reading at any time, but especially
at this season, is a story of America.

There were many other pieces from the "carpetbag."
Perhaps the poet chose some of his lighter pieces because
he thought he was speaking to a high school crowd, since

his appearance was scheduled for a high school.   There was
plenty of humor, philosophy and wit in these poems--"The
Big Hat, " "The Abracadabra Boys" and "Boxes and Bags. "
A new one was "Peace Between Wars, " saying: "Who pays
for my freedom and what price?" and asking, "Am I somehow beholden?"

The poet never considered our freedom so much until
Thomas Masaryk of Czechoslovakia in 1919 said that this
country started with three great things--no military caste,
no titled nobility and with religious liberty.   Early in American Colonial history, Roger Williams, who came to this
country in 1630 on the Lyon, knew about freedom, too.   He
differed with John Cotton in the first days of Cambridge,
choosing democracy instead of theocracy, and fled into the
wilderness to live among the Narragansett Indians.   He was
the father of religious liberty in this country.

The last of his poems he read before singing his tall
tales was "The Long Shadow. "   It appeared in the Saturday
Evening Post during the war and was about Lincoln, who
asked that we "disenthrall ourselves" from old ways that
have lost their meaning and that we dream dreams worth
dying for--"Sing low, sing high, sing wide, Earth laughs,
the sun laughs. "

Then he took up his guitar and sang the tall tales.
America's voice, it was, singing a Quaker wooing song from
Ohio, a tune from Hopkinsville, Ky. , and one from the White
Chapel Club of Chicago newspapermen.   The negro spirituals
he sang with a poignancy of one who has warmed his heart
at the living shrine of the Great Emancipator.

Carl Sandburg liked his audience, too.   In Hollywood,
where he spoke a night or so ago, the audience jumped to
its feet as one person when he came on stage.   Here they
applauded and paid him the respect of sympathetic listening.

"I think, " he told this reporter afterwards, "there
must have been many New Englanders in the audience.   I
could see this early American heritage in their faces. "

The program was sponsored by the Woman's Club
and the City Teachers Club.   Roderick Mount, president of
the City Teachers Club, introduced Mrs. Clifford Jones,
president of the Woman's Club, who presented Sandburg.

Carl Sandburg in Galesburg*

I met Carl in Galesburg through my friend Nelle Townsend.

In those days we never wanted just one beau. Both boys and girls wanted as many as they could get. Steady was a bore.

Carl had lots of girlfriends and surely liked girls.

Nelle made the date for me that she had with Carl because she preferred Will Butcher. Neither of us was love at first sight or ever really love. We each liked history and English drama, music and poetry. Our birthdays were the same month, and I think each on January 6th. Carl was a year or so older than I. He liked the way I recited poetry and wrote some for me and also accompanied me.

We had a new piano. Although he preferred strings, he liked this piano.

We had fun at Knox County Fair--Nelle and Will, I and Carl--and we spent our last money on a half bunch of green bananas because they were so cheap and I forget what we really did with them but they were too green to eat.

My hair was a bright gold color and he called me "Sunlight"--or "Goldie."

He had black unruly hair and he never thought much of his appearance. He was interested in being something or doing things like great men. He had an insatiable admiration for Lincoln and said, "Lincoln is poor like me, but look what he did."

Knox College, Lombard College and Brown's Business College made Galesburg an outstanding town.

Carl was more popular with boys than girls.

Through a friend he got a pass on C & B Railroad to come to Peoria.

---

*Manuscript of Mrs. Jessie Bond Pawson, Los Angeles, Calif. By permission.

I used to recite one of Lincoln's favorite poems and
Carl knew it too, and we used it as a pianologue: "Oh,
why should the spirit of mortal be proud?   Like a swift
fleeting meteor, a far flying cloud, ... " Can't remember
the rest of it, not even the author.

When he came to my home he always wanted to go to
our new piano and Dad nicknamed him "Bang Bang, " but
he won Dad over by painting the doors of the barn, and he
being a Democrat was always a personality, but we never
thought of him as a genius although he did have much wit
and wisdom.   He had a certain tenderness although down to
reality.

He liked to play a guitar and sing.   He was tall and
broad-shouldered and had a dark complexion and black unruly
hair (although a Swede, who was generally fair).   Once I
told him "You will never be called a big Swede. " He called
me "Goldie" as my hair was gold color--my only asset in
good looks.

Neither of us liked arithmetic, but history we both
liked, and grammar.   I was better but he liked it his way.

When I knew Carl we were at the age of growing,
learning, changing, and sorting friends, although we were
around 20 years old.   No one thought him a genius.

Carl was brought up in the Swedish Lutheran Church.
His father and my father had in common the fear of want,
and [both felt they] must save for a rainy day.   Ours was
an economic decade.   We had very little jewelry but it had
to be 18 karat gold.   I don't remember any costume jewelry.

Carl always seemed to want to make a name for himself.   He would read everything he could find on history.
He liked American writers.   He wanted to be a writer, but
he did not shun menial work.   He wanted money and needed
it.

There are companionships in our younger days that
make memory sweeter.   [Mrs. Pawson quoted a passage
Abigail Adams had written to her son, to the effect that
struggling with problems forms minds.   Then she concluded:]
Work and little money were character builders for Carl
Sandburg and for his writings.

More on Carl and Jessie*

Mrs. Pawson's maiden name was Jessie Bond. She
was one of my father's seventy-six first cousins, but the
only child of Levi and Sadie Bond. She was born in Her-
mon, Illinois, which is a small town near Galesburg, and
was introduced to Carl Sandburg by a girlfriend. Carl apparently liked Jessie and courted her for some period of
time. She said he always told her they were meant for
each other because they shared the same birthdate--I think
it was January 6th.

Her father was appointed government tax inspector at
the Hiram Walker distillery in Peoria, Illinois. This was
a political appointment which the Democrats gave to him as
he was a loyal Democrat. Grover Cleveland must have
been President at the time. After the family moved to Peoria, Carl would come to Peoria to see her. But she told
me that because he was so tight with the dollar he did not
have money to spend a night in a hotel and would stay in
their house. He used to play the piano for her, and her
father did not particularly take a shine to Carl but referred
to him as "old bang-bang" because he was always banging
on the piano. She said Carl wrote many verses for her but
she threw them away. Apparently he was too awkward and
lacking in social graces for her tastes. She remembers
distinctly that he usually had dirty fingernails. She gave
me a small china plate, which had been one of Carl's gifts
to her, which depicts a scene of Knox College, although
Carl had gone to Lombard.

Lunch Out of an Old Tomato Can†

While I do not have any information on Carl Sandburg
in Iowa, I do have a recollection of his appearance in Sterling, Kansas, in 1931.

I was a young speech instructor (my first year--and
last) at Sterling College, Sterling, Kansas. One of my

---

*Letter from George C. Bond, Los Angeles, Calif., Sept.
28, 1977. By permission.
†Letter from Glenn Pinkham, Goldfield, Iowa, 1970. By
permission.

responsibilities was to head the Lyceum series there. Why
it was my responsibility, I don't know, but it was wished
off on me. The first two programs were dismal flops financially and the "heat" was on. I called a former professor of mine, Lew Sarett of Northwestern University, and
he helped me to secure Carl Sandburg from the Redpath
Agency for five hundred dollars. Whew, was there ever an
explosion when I announced my brash doings. I will not go
into all the details. It was Depression times. I was told
it had to go or else I would go. I had help through friends,
who were members of certain civic organizations in Hutchinson, Kansas, population of about 25,000. We sold around
2,000 tickets at a dollar apiece. Enough of my problems.
I rented a car and met Mr. Sandburg at Hutchinson. He
was dressed as usual--rumpled suit, hair awry and a big
warm smile. What a fine human being. (I might add, I
was dressed in my one and only suit, a shabby looking outfit.) Guess he sized me up in a few seconds and my circumstances. How human he was. On our way to Sterling,
we passed a tiny town of about a hundred or less, called
Nickerson. He asked me to stop by a railroad crossing.
We walked over to the tracks and sat on the rails for about
ten minutes in deep silence. After a bit he said, "Let's
go." Being young and inquisitive, I finally asked him why
we had stopped and he said, "Oh, another old bum and myself shared lunch out of an old tomato can here a few years
ago." Nothing else was said, until we were approaching
Sterling. The town had a huge elevator bulging with thousands of bushels of wheat. Mr. Sandburg became deeply
concerned, and he said, "Look at all the bread that could
be made and thousands of people are going hungry and many
of them around here. Something is radically wrong in this
country."

I need not tell you that Mr. Sandburg wrote much of
his poetry as a protest of some of the evils existing in society in this country.

Of course, the evening was delightful and successful.
Have often thought of that night, one of the brightest in
memory. One of his minor numbers that night made a
lasting impression upon me--"Jazz Fantasia." I know the
power of the spoken word. The "hard jazz" of the 1920's
from Chicago came alive. You could hear the "big band
sounds" of that era, when he delivered it. And another
selection [impressed me]--the story of "Chick Lorimer,"
a girl who worked in a Chicago department store. At that

time, girls were being paid ten cents an hour for sixty
hours a week. Try living on six dollars a week in Chicago,
even in Depression times. Another selection he read was
"Clean Curtains." It represents a woman's effort to maintain clean and respectable living quarters in a poor neighborhood. Her battle against the dust and grime from passing
cars and trucks and soot from coal-burning stoves and factory furnaces slowly broke her spirit. After a time, she
gave up the struggle. The poem reveals, so clearly, the
frustrations and tragedies of that period--because Carl
Sandburg lived it and understood. And finally that powerful
selection "Chicago." Often I have heard it "bellowed" by
others, but Mr. Sandburg's rendition had that city rising
from the Midwest prairie--lusty, brawling, husky but always
magnificent--to the gateway to the West.

That night in his room at the little hotel in Sterling,
he was surrounded by about twenty of us--and yes, he was
passing out "cheroots," long, crooked, wine-flavored cigars.
He loved them. Naturally they were inexpensive. I don't
think the man ever used anything except what the most ordinary of us would. What an evening of philosophy of life.
Since then, I know I love my fellow man a little bit better
and feel more compassion for the ones who have misfortunes
of life. Which leads to this one conclusion. One can be
touched by a great person for only a few minutes and have
his life changed. I can never forget this one experience.

Journal Notes of a Sandburg Appearance*

Was to have eaten lunch with Carl Sandburg today
[April 19, 1932]--along with the rest of the English Department. But the poet sent word along about 11 o'clock that he
was tired and wanted to sleep....

Attended Sandburg's lecture (or recital or reading or
poem or what-you-will) at U. Hall this evening. He had a
full house, very appreciative.

Sandburg undoubtedly has a charm. It is as difficult
to define as the overtones which he describes as poetry.
There is an elusive childlikeness about him that is winning.

After a discussion of the modern free verse movement

---

*From a journal by Robert Price. By permission.

he first read a group of his verses then took up his guitar
and closed the program with a number of American folk
songs which he has collected.

The poems read were: "Losers, " "Broken-Faced
Gargoyles, " "Jazz Fantasia, " "Bricklayer Love, " "Southern
Pacific, " "Buffalo Dust" (which, he says, has musical intentions), "Ossawatomie" (John Brown--this poem got a good
hand), "The Windy City" (several passages, most of the
above were from Smoke and Steel); "Timber Moon, " "We
Have Gone Through Great Moons Together, " "Precious Moments, " (these from Good Morning America).

Sandburg told a couple of his "Rootabaga Stories"--
that of the two skyscrapers who decided to have a child, and
that about Peter Potato-Blossom Wishes.

With his guitar and seated, Sandburg presented the
following songs: One from Brown County, Indiana; "A Hundred Years, " the sailors' windlass song; "Unconstant Love";
a Kentucky song giving advice to young people; "The Quakers'
Wooing, " which he found in Ohio; a Great Lakes boatman's
chanty; a song composed by Louisville-Nashville railroad
laborers; a Negro song from the Brazos River; a cowboy
song from Sante Fe; and an arrangement of Negro spirituals.

What Sandburg read and sang may not be great poetry.
But one came away with a feeling that Sandburg himself with
his shaggy gray hair and pug-nosed, Swedish face and whim-
sical lovableness WAS POETRY.

* * *

[In a later entry, Price records:] Sandburg appeared
on the Otterbein College artist's series on the evening of
December 13, 1948. As usual when he was in the area, he
was the guest of Mrs. L. S. Teeter and her daughter, Mary,
at their spacious home on East Walnut Street, Westerville.

Sandburg's performance was not up to the usual billing
and the large and eagerly expectant audience felt considerably
let down.

His hostess said later that she never had known him to
appear so tired. Remembrance Rock was just off the press,
and all the attendant labors seemed to have been too much
for him.

Sandburg Visits the Johnsons in the White House*

Lynda Johnson Robb recalled the visit Sandburg made
to the White House in the spring of 1964.

Mrs. Robb and her friend, in college at George Washington University, came in from school to see Sandburg.
"We came in like six-year-olds to see the Good Humor [ice
cream] man. "

Physically, Sandburg reminded her of "a big, shaggy
dog. He was a little bit bigger than life. "

Mrs. Robb was not certain what the actual occasion
of inviting Sandburg was, but the emphasis was on Lincoln
in the conversation. There had been a big Lincoln party,
to which performers and others, like the historian Bruce
Catton, had been invited. Probably this invitation was in
the same vein.

When Mrs. Robb went to live in the White House,
she studied its history, to see "what ghosts were walking. "
Regarding Lincoln, she found Lincoln's son, Willie, had
died in the room she occupied.

In talking with Sandburg, as the episode about the
Gettysburg manuscript suggests, the emphasis was placed on
Lincoln. In response, Sandburg seemed to Lynda to be
"irreverent.... He knew Lincoln so well that he couldn't
understand that we didn't. " He made a remark to the effect
that Lincoln had had quite a few illegitimate children. Mrs.
Robb thought he was probably joking but could not say for
certain at the time of the interview. "I couldn't tell whether
he was laughing at me or not. "

The hour the Sandburgs and the Steichens were at the
White House was spent in the Lincoln bedroom on the Tru-
man balcony, and in the rose garden. Mrs. Carpenter,
Mrs. Johnson's secretary, seeing a large painting of Mrs.
Lincoln in the Lincoln bedroom, where Lincoln signed the
Emancipation Proclamation, asked Sandburg about Mrs. Lin-
coln. "Tell us about her. " Finally Sandburg said, "You'll
have to read my book.... "

---

*Based on a telephone conversation with Lynda Johnson Robb,
Arlington, Va. , July 28, 1971.

Steichen and his wife were there.   Steichen made tender remarks about his little sister (Mrs. Sandburg).   There was some talk with Steichen about plants, in which field he is expert.

The group had tea and coffee on the Truman balcony before going to the Rose Garden, where L. B. J. joined them. He kidded and laughed with the President.

Mrs. Robb was taking a literature course at that time.   She got her textbook and received Sandburg's autograph of his poems in her book.   Mrs. Johnson got him to autograph works of his in the White House collection.

Mrs. Robb thought it would be acceptable to write Mrs. Johnson about her recollections.   Address: Attention: Helene Lindow, Federal Office Building, Austin, Texas 78711.

* * *

After she reviewed the foregoing notes, Mrs. Robb wrote (September 9, 1971) that Sandburg repeatedly asked a question that was a favorite joke relating to his brother-in-law, Steichen: Who was the biographer of a famous photographer?   Too, she recalled Sandburg's stipulating six Lincoln bastards.

Before the interview, she had written that Mrs. Johnson had pointed out that the White House had a copy of the Gettysburg Address in Lincoln's "own handwriting."   Lynda recalled the Sandburg rejoinder: "So what?   We all know he could write!"

Though she did not include this remark in her A White House Diary, this remark may have prompted Mrs. Johnson to comment that most of what Sandburg said during the visit was intended to evoke laughter from his audience.

A Tedious, Artificial Mediocrity*

I never had intimate knowledge of Sandburg as [a]

---

*Letter from E. Merrill Root, Kennebunkport, Maine.   By permission.

man, but of course I read his poetry.   I liked "Fog, "
"Chicago, " etc.; but much of it seemed to me tedious, splay,
lacking in condensation and finesse.   He seemed to me a
poetic demagogue, making a kind of sentimental "democracy"
a cult, and lacking in all original insight.   And (as at the
dinner I wrote about) he seemed to me to pose, to play the
role of an oracle, to regard himself as a great Pooh-Bah.
I don't much care for free verse, and he of course wallowed
in it.   He seemed to me a poseur masquerading as a poet.

This of course may be quite wrong.   But that is just
the way he always affected me.   And he also seemed to feel
that Lincoln had been born so that Sandburg might write
about him.   He seemed to me a tedious, artificial mediocrity.

I can't remember about others at the dinner.   Most
who were there were, I believe, awed by his reputation and
took him as fashion told them he was.

Observations of a Sculptor*

[According to Prof. Donald T. Brodine of Saxtone
River, Vermont,] Herbert Rosengren met Sandburg at Cornell College (in Iowa).   When Sandburg was covering the
Democratic convention in Chicago in 1932, they became friends.
One result was that Rosengren went to Sandburg's home in
Harbert to spend a week sculpting his head.   The head was
never finished, perhaps because, Rosengren suggested, it
began to fit too well the nickname Sandburg applied to himself, "Potato Face. "   Rosengren enjoyed hearing Sandburg
read his work in progress and discussing such subjects as
his dislike for Vice President Charles G. Dawes.

[Rosengren wrote the following to Prof. H. C. Lane
at Cornell College on July 15, 1932:]

A few days ago I saw Carl Sandburg at his home in
Michigan.   I began a sculpture of him.   He was hard at
work on his Lincoln book.   We spent a lot of time walking
along the sand at night.   I got some good dope on him.   I
can't repeat it here, but he thinks his most significant contribution is his Rootabaga stories.

_____

*Letters from Herbert Rosengren, Woodcliff Lake, N. J., Oct.
2, 21, and 27, 1969 and Sept. 6 and 8, 1970.   By permission.

You know the Mercury panned him this month, Edgar
Lee Masters did, in his article.   I read it up there.   One
day while I was working on the head of him up in the attic,
and he was sweating over "Lincoln" I said casually, "I saw
the article in the Mercury.   What has been your relation
with Masters...."   He looked up, biting his cigar, and said
softly, "I'm thinking hard on Ben Butler right now."   I
guess even big-shots get their goats taken every once in a
while.   I think I'd only laugh.   Just think what it would
mean to be panned in the Mercury.

[Rosengren also recalled of Sandburg:]   Sandburg was
taken with me right off, I believe, because I had the same
kind of parents and early environment.   I was born in
Kewanee, Illinois, which is only about 25 miles or so from
Galesburg, and Galesburg was one of those mythical places
like Peoria that one would get to see when one became a
man....   Carl's parents were Swedish, as you know.   His
were illiterate, he says in his autobiographical things.   His
father was a blacksmith in a railroad shop, I believe.   My
parents also were Swedish.   My father was a potter in the
Old Country (en krukmakare); he was not illiterate, worked
in the Western Tube Mill until we left Kewanee in 1920.
Anyhow, I was brought up as Carl was in a bi-lingual home,
two words for everything, and some sounded very funny.
We made sport (as Swedes) of "Amerikanarna" and their
strange ways, and sport of Swedes as "Buck-Olees" when
they tried to speak English.   We had a great time--we would
roll on the floor, my brother and I and our cousins, who
also were knowledgeable, at the high absurdity of both languages.

When I first met Carl, I recall telling him one of
those stories, supposedly true, from our neighborhood:

One of the fellows (the guys, we called them) was
nicknamed "Bullhead" Johnson.   We called him Bullhead,
and he didn't mind.   His Old Man was a Swede, of course,
working in the furniture factory, Illinois Cabinet, taking
boards away from a rip saw.   The gang, one evening, gathered in Johnson's yard.   We called out, "Bull--Head!
Come on out...."   No answer.   We hollered and hollered.
Finally the front door swung open, and the Old Man stamped
out onto the porch; he was in his undersleeves (underwear,
with suspenders over them).   He glowered at us, and then
raised his fist and hollered: "De lefver inge bullhead här!"
(There live no bullheads here!)

Carl liked that. He got it right away, that absurd crossing over of the two languages.

Another one of a similar nature, almost surrealistic, and true--I recall the kids would work up weird "sayings," and repeat them from time to time, in funny voices. This was aimed at Old Mrs. Carlson (she had a goiter and a high chicken voice). The saying had to do with how Mrs. Carlson scolded the boys one night for tormenting her chickens. It went like this: "O dom pojka! De feeder mina schickens spunge käk, o de kaller mej 'Hee Haw Maud.'" (Oh them boys! They feed my chickens sponge cake, and they call me 'Hee Haw Maude.'--from Opper's Funny Paper characters, if you are old enough to recall that). Carl laughed-- roared, in fact.

We were discussing the necessity for humor in the make-up, and as [one] of the qualities of a great man. In fact we concluded that every great man views his greatness through his sense of humor. Humor in its broadest sense implies humility and great understanding. Dreiser, to Carl's mind, was without the quality of humor. Eugene O'Neill on the other hand, in spite of his tragedy, had a sense of humor or of the sardonic which gives his work flavor.

In this vein we went on, and I ventured that Carl's style owed much to his humor.

"Well," he said, "life is not funny, but it farts once in a while."

Sandburg's having me do a sculpture of him was not unusual; I had done a very good likeness of my father which he saw. He said, as I've mentioned to you, he wanted to "lie low," a remark that puzzled me (when I suggested the bust be exhibited). Your [Sutton's] explanation sounds reasonable. I didn't know the extent of his WWI activity; it would be like him, though; he had a hostile streak in him, too, a peasant's resentment (and envy) of a "higher" class. In fact, I have an article prepared for Katharsis by a young Englishman student at Iowa City in which he takes off from Rebecca West's spoof satire of H. G. Wells, Galsworthy, etc., in which he (Harold Cooper, pen name Hugh Linley) does a job on E. A. Robinson, Frost, Sandburg and Millay, coming into a room. Sandburg enters and hollers, "Howdy Folks!" ... and has a hole in his sock, etc., etc. You should see this one day, done in 1932. Insofar as pay goes for the sculpture, there was to be none; he was doing me a favor.

One morning Carl was exasperated with his dog, Dan, a water spaniel who had awakened him early in the morning. He led him upstairs to the attic where we work and tied him to a chair leg.

"There, I'll show you to think you're a canary. Don't forget you're just a dog and a spoiled one at that."

Then he gathered the board which contains his notes and sat down for me. He looked up and said, "I don't like this at all." Then there was a pause.

"Do you know all the biographers are dead--Lytton Strachey, Amy Lowell--" etc., etc., and he gave the dates of their deaths. "I know why they can't last. I know why they burn out."

He felt the desire to work before it was too late. That is why he didn't sit still. He drove himself on and on.

The "affected" hair. Yes, Carl with his hair combed back looked like a machinist, nothing Byronesque about him at all. Steichen did that, I believe, and it is a bit absurd, with Carl peeking through that white forelock. Sandburg's face was really very crude, a peasant's mug, "potato face" as he himself said, but it was kind and easy to be with, a workman's face, not an aristocrat's.

Insofar as your question about Sandburg's attitude toward "academics" goes, you can be sure he had a deep resentment toward the superficial and bureaucratic aspects; he identified with the pee-pull who resent any unearned notice or acclaim. But, being a performer himself, this could be explained away in simplified psych-terms (projection no doubt). Scratch a socialist and you'll find an uncrowned monarchist (Sen. Eugene McCarthy--our latest "uncrowned king"--the phrase he used was better--was it "your government in exile"? Anyhow, I thought he revealed his true needs which I had suspected all along, and, being a poet to boot--a good one too--that clinches it). Why should Sandburg be against the "academics"? There was something of Eric Hofer's 14-K malice in Sandburg, too. Curiously, Toppy [Clyde C. Tull, head of English at Cornell; see his reminiscence on page 264], who was academic, too, sided

with him, for one part of Toppy was pure Chautauqua public
relations and far from the ivory tower notion that still per-
meated campuses in the 30's.

How far is Sandburg from Ginsberg, for example--
and would Sandburg take to LSD if he were a young man to-
day--and other things?   Did Sandburg speak for his time,
or for a romantic version of the fading American frontier
dream?   I often wonder.   Was he really a kind of circuit
riding preacher--though I sensed he was not religious; certainly he didn't accept the quaint and vicious dogmas of his
own Swedish people (the Christers), and he used his energy
in his work (his art) primarily and did not squander it.   I
know he took a drink, even got loaded once in a while (when
he came to see us in our cellar rooms during the '32 convention he had been up all night with the boys).   He was
the kind of Swede who can drink and drink and drink and
the only noticeable effect is that his mouth turns down just
a little lower and he has more trouble with his snuff juice
running down the side of his mouth, and his eyes get icier;
that's the sign he is getting close to dropping off to sleep,
or, there is nothing bloodier.   No--I think there was a kind
of majestic, self-assured, kindness in Sandburg, and a pa-
tience, steadiness, reliability that is (or so some like to
think) a second nature of the Swede, especially the peasant-
grown Swede.

Sandburg's Visit to Åsbo, 1959*

On arrival, he first visited the old church of Åsbo.
He was very interested in the old chandeliers and the old
font, and asked many questions of old things in the church.
Afterwards he visited the local museum, a cottage called
"Hybbeln," where he made a thorough study of all the old
things kept there.   Also here he asked a lot of questions of
how people lived in the old days, and how the food and
housing were.   Then followed a small garden party outside
the museum, where coffee and real Swedish cream cake was
served, which he liked very much.   Afterwards he wanted
to be photographed together with a girl dressed in a typical
dress from the landscape of Östergötland.   Photos were
also taken together with his cousins who were also present

---

*Interview with Mrs. May Samuelsson, Hägersten, Sweden,
January, 1970.   By permission.

this afternoon. He seemed to like this visit very much.
My most vivid memory from this occasion is of Carl Sandburg standing beside the old cottage, his white hair shining
in the summer sun and he said "How beautiful, how beautiful. "

Days in Östergötland*

Carl Sandburg: The smoky air of Chicago with soot-
vomiting stacks of factories. A resting giant in whose veins
of stone the pulse beats hot and violent. Further away there
is the prairie with small towns drowsing in the heat, their
names both familiar and strange. Still further away there
is the Caribbean Sea with distant islands which once belonged
to Spain and for which U. S. A. fought a war in 1898. Still
further away, on the other side of the Atlantic there is
Europe: the original continent without which America of
today would have been a different America. And furthest to
the north, almost as far north as one can go, there is Sweden and the plains between Vadstena and Linköping with a
small red-painted farm where his mother was born on a
summer day in 1850, and which she left 23 years later,
never to see again. Carl Sandburg: American, poet, jour-
nalist, soldier, globe-trotter, lute-player and historian,
errand-boy in Galesburg, hotel man in Denver, farmer in
Kansas, 81 years old but spiritually only in his twenties.

All this is in his face. It is a face not like anybody's, full of secrets and closed like the face of an Indian
totem pole. It is heavy and firm and full of secrets even
when it breaks into friendly smiling wrinkles. Carl Sandburg is an American, with an American's openness and need
of contact with people and the surrounding world. But he
is also an artist, and at the bottom of his personality there
is a closed room to which nobody is admitted. He smiles,
but utters kind words to all people crowded around him,
giving him crocheted small table cloths, old letters and
books bound in red cloth-binding with the fantastic ornamen-
tations of the 19th century. But he permits nobody to look
deeper inside him than he is willing [for them] to.

In the two days he has spent in Östergötland he has

*Gunnar Samuelsson, Trans., Norrkopings Tidning-Öster-
götademokraten, Aug. 13, 1959. By permission.

come close to the roots of his life. He of course never
saw Sweden until he became a man of mature age. His
cradle stood in the new country, his parents came from the
old country. He became the American with the Swedish somewhat americanized name. Today he likes to tell that he
spoke Swedish before he learnt to speak English. What were
his thoughts when on this Wednesday he wandered in one of
the most Swedish cities, the Vadstena of the Swedish national saint [Birgitta]. What were his feelings when he saw
the castle of Gustav Vasa? Was he reverent in front of the
Swedish founder of a kingdom from the 16th century, or did
he in him recognize the brutal rulers of today?

Nobody knows. When he strolled over the yellow
plains, yellow of oat and wheat, he might have remembered
another poet, once much honoured, today almost forgotten:
Verner von Heidenstam. Heidenstam's vision was different.
He wrote about the Sweden of the Folkungs and the Karls.
Carl Sandburg writes about the America of engines, about
blood in the slaughter houses. There is an insurmountable
abyss between the minds of these two poets.

However, this cannot be seen on Carl Sandburg. He
utters kind, obliging cordial words about everything and
everybody. But his face is there, fascinating, ambiguous
and completely closed around a non-accessible inner nucleus.
The photographers studied this face--they saw it enlightened
by the daylight from small narrow church windows, they saw
this face smile and be serious again, they saw its mildness
and calm. And they took photos--during the two days Carl
Sandburg visited Östergötland he was the victim of an actual
siege by people running around him with cameras in their
hands. But he didn't expose himself.

In one place the people on his arrival greeted him
with the song of Östergötland. Carl Sandburg took off his
cap and stood to attention like a young cadet from West
Point. He questioned people and jotted down notes in a note
book like the journalists around him. He sat at dinner-
and coffee-tables, talking and laughing. He stood looking
out over the golden yellow plains rolling towards the hori-
zon. His face was constantly changing, like the incessantly
changing shadows of the clouds on the plains.

But he didn't betray himself. He looked at dry
straws of timothy and corn-flowers and declared his joy of
being at home in Östergötland. But at home to him is

America. Gustav Vasa is not his ideal. He pays homage
to Abraham Lincoln, who, no doubt, is better qualified for
the admiration of posterity.

Perhaps, as he was standing there on the plains in
the midst of all the noise and turmoil, he was longing for
America. Nobody knows. Carl Sandburg does not betray
himself.

Folk Song Adventures*

That night he stayed at home with me and we worked
out plans for the next day. As we were retiring he found
that he had left his pajamas in the berth on the train. I
lent him a pair of my pajamas, somewhat short for a fairly
tall man. Next morning, although the weather was obviously
set for an all-day rain, we started out on our fifty-mile
jaunt. As we moved along, we went through numerous
showers so dense that we had difficulty seeing the road.
You may know how I felt with my rather precious cargo.
Near Mt. Vernon we took a bad skid on Route 3 on a section that in those days was paved with brick. My car
turned around a couple of times going down hill and finally
banged into a guard rail, knocked off a board, and ended
up going up hill instead of down. That made us think we
were a couple of damn fools and that we'd better return to
Columbus. Carl thought we ought to go to Mt. Vernon,
county seat, and pay for the damage to the rail. I pointed
out to him that slippery brick pavement was a menace to
the traveler and that the county should pay me for the damage to my fender, not really too bad for the bump we took.
We got back to Columbus for dinner. I took him to a first-
class restaurant called The Barn, out of existence now,
where we had some Maryland fried chicken, the best, he
said, "he ever put under his belt." Then we went around
to the hospital to see wife and daughter. He tweaked her
little toes and said something about "toes as pink as the
petals of fresh flowers." Next morning I put him on a
train for Chicago.

*Letter from Paul L. Schacht, Columbus, Ohio, July 18,
1969. By permission of the author.

* * *

[A student of Prof. Schacht's, Ada J. McKitrick, *
recalls that] during my senior year in high school away back
in 1914 and 1915, I had a very young English teacher, just
graduated from Capital University. He had quite a flair for
dramatics and poetry and the classics. He also taught the
Latin IV class of three girls and I remember as though it
were yesterday when he required us to translate many passages of Virgil into English using the same meter and phras-
ing in which it was written. That was fun and when he read
us a play or two he had written, one called "The Purple
Roses" in particular, we were entranced. Along with his
teaching of classics he was also interested in country music,
maybe more like soul music as we know it now. Knowing
that my father had brought quite a fund of country and hill-
billy songs with him when he came north from the hills of
Ohio as a young man, he asked me to write them out for
him.

Later sometime in 1925 the young man, now Professor
Paul M. Schacht of the English department of his own university, wrote me asking if he could bring to my home an expected visitor, one Carl Sandburg, who was interested in
securing the airs to the lyrics I had given him when he was
teaching in our high school. My husband and I were living
in a small old farm house, rather sparsely furnished, and
we were expecting our first child in a couple of months, so,
since forty-five years ago one did not entertain celebrities
at such a time, I begged off at having my callers.

I heard later from Professor Schacht that Mr. Sandburg visited him in Columbus sometime in July of 1925, I
believe, and was delighted to add the old songs to his
Americana collection. The Schachts had a tiny baby daughter at the time and I remember that they said Sandburg was
delighted with her and said her tiny toes were like the "rosy
petals of a pale pink rose."

*Letter from Ada J. McKitrick, Marysville, Ohio. By
permission.

Enjoyment of Ribaldry*

     When we got together with other Lincoln nuts on oc-
casions mostly in Washington, Carl would ask me to recite
Runt or The Story of the Country Dog, and then he would
tell me to give us the toast to an old man:

> At the close of our existence,
> When we've climbed the golden stairs
> And the chilly winds of autumn
> Rudely toss our silver hairs,
>
> We find our manhood ebbing
> And we're at life's last ditch
> And we find our fruitful peter
> Sleeping soundly at the switch.
>
> Gosh-it almighty! Ain't it awful!
> Don't it make a fellow sick!
> When the painful fact confronts us
> That we got a lifeless dick,
>
> That'll never again bristle
> On a wet and windy day
> When some maiden shows her stocking
> In that bawdy, naughty, funny way.
>
> O, my loyal kingpin!
> How my heart goes out to you.
> And I cannot but remember
> All the stunts you used to do.
>
> How you charmed the maids and maidens
> And the dashing widows, too
> And you had the whole push begging
> For a little piece of you.
>
> Think you now that I'll forget you
> Just because you seem so dead
> And because when I commend you
> You cannot lift your sleepy head?
>
> O, indeed, my valiant comrade!

---

*Contributed by Fred Schwengel, Washington, D. C.   By
permission.

Naught shall rob you of your fame.
Henceforth you shall be my pisser
And I'll love you just the same.

A Soviet Recollection*

I'll feel glad if my letter turns out to be of conse-
quence so far as the memory of a great and noble man is
concerned.   To the best of my knowledge first poems by
Carl Sandburg appeared in Russian translations by I Kashkin
(who sometimes spells his name Kashkeen) in 1927 in the
anthology Pebousyuonnaie uossue cobperieuuow canada (Revo-
lutionary poetry of contemporary West), Mockobcuiu paedoruu
(Moskow--skij rabovij publishers), Moscow.   However, there
is a predecessor of great importance.   Mr. Kamrad of
Moscow, an authority on Mayakovsky, told me that there is
a book by Sandburg Smoke and Steel that Mayakovsky brought
along from the U. S. A. with marginal notes indicating attempts at translation.   This was the only case when Mayakovsky tried his hand at translation.

I met the American poet July 22, 1959, when he
came to Moscow.   In the house of friendship there was an
evening party devoted to Hemingway and all of a sudden in
the praesidium we saw Sandburg and Steichen.   Carl Sandburg made a short speech there.   I took down his words on
the spot and they can be regarded as a safe quotation, as
well as his opinions expressed later.

He said, "I was friendly with the third and best wife
of Hemingway.   He wrote of her twelve lines in the Life
magazine.   That was the best monument a husband ever
erected for his wife."

All of a sudden Sandburg disappeared from the platform.   I slipped out into the corridor and found myself face
to face with the poet.   I told him who and what I was and
he expressed amazement that people in Moscow speak good
English.   That was certainly flattering and no relation to
the truth, for as you can see I do not master the English
language good enough.   I told Sandburg that I admire his
poetry, especially The People, Yes.

---

*Letter from Andrey Sergeev, Moscow, Oct. 18, 1971.
Paraphrased by the author.

"That's especially fine, " he said.   "There I wrote
about you: the tsar had eight million soldiers. ... "

On July 31, there was a big reception at the writer's
Union.   Seeing me there Sandburg asked if I wanted still to
translate The People, Yes.   I replied that I had already
translated some pieces from it.   And I showed him the manuscript.   "That looks like a book, pretty like a book.   You've
got a nice shirt on, it sings!"   (That was a cowboy shirt, a
most usual piece of summer clothes in Russia).

When everybody assembled he said, "First of all, I
want to read your faces.   Good faces!   I like your faces!
So many good faces!   I feel at home. "   After the usual
procedure of introduction Mr. Surkov, who was in charge
of the reception, wanted to invite Russian singers to sing
folk songs for the guest but Sandburg interrupted him twice:
"There is a lad with translations of my poetry.   I want to
listen to the lad. "   Mr. Surkov who then knew nothing of
my existence got confused, so Sandburg invited me to the
platform and made me read his verse in Russian.   It was
a success.   Incidentally, it was my first public reading.
The singers at the reception were famous Kozlovski, a
tenor, whom Sandburg didn't like very much, and a young
bass Polyakov.   "I really love the young singer, " said
Sandburg.   "He lacks Chaliapin's strength but certain notes
remind me of him.   The guitarist was good.   I know Segovia.   I wrote about him.   Your guitarist was good. "   The
guitarist was our very best Ivanon-Kamskoj.   Sandburg himself sang for over an hour American folk songs, cowboys',
students', Nergoi [Negro?], etc. to the guitar that was
miserably out of time [tune?], though he seemed to pay no
attention to the fact.   Steichen was present there as well
as on August 4 in the Foreign Literature monthly.   Noticing
me Sandburg said, "I'm glad you're here.   I wished to see
you before I leave, you are the People-Yes-Man for me, "
and he inscribed my copy of The People, Yes.   In the magazine Sandburg told of his Congressional address on Lincoln,
and his poetic principles, "I use Russian folklore too.
Sometimes I lack folklore.   Then I invent folklore, here's
an example.   There were two skyscrapers in Chicago.
They never moved, but they said if they got a child it
would be free to move wherever it liked.   And the child
came.   It was a jet-plane.   The skyscrapers were fond of
him and very proud too. "   I asked him a question about
Robert Frost.   The reply was: "He is a good poet really
American, he was never connected with the labor.   He is

a Democrat (in my notes stands Republican, evidently a
mistake). When I published The People, Yes, he said, The
People Yes? No! I know what he meant by it. " Here
Sandburg distorts the famous words by Robert Frost.

There are innumerable translations of Sandburg's
poetry into Russian, most of them unpublished. The case
is that many young people are attracted by the seemingly easy
job of translating verse libre and the results are poor. It
is quite a problem to render in Russian a short poetic en-
tity with all the obertonen of poetic word and meaning. The
very best translations so far are those by Kaskin, Ananiash-
vili and Zenkiewiv. Two pieces from The People, Yes were
published in my translation by the Novyj Mir, W12, 1959,
and a series of miniatures from Honey & Salt by the Moskva
Monthly W5, 1964. I have got many more translations from
the two books which will be likely included into a compre-
hensive collection of his poetry which is being contemplated
by Moscow publishers. I cannot tell you for sure when the
book may come out, the main difficulty being abundance of
poor translations. Sandburg is really difficult to translate.
So far as my work is concerned I do my best to preserve
as much as I can and at the same time build a good Russian
poetry. Several times, my translations were broadcast by
Radio Moscow, many times I read them in public, quite
successfully. Good bibliography of recent publications of
Sandburg's poetry in this country you can get from Prof.
Carl Proffer of Indiana University, Bloomington. By the
way, is there a new edition of the Collected Poetry by Carl
Sandburg including "Honey and Salt" and probably some more
poems?

Rare Memento of a Famous Friend*

A slender book of poetry awaits posterity in the vault
of a Kansas City bank. Bearing the taffied, melodramatic
title, "In Reckless Ecstacy, " the poems written by Charles
A. Sandburg are the earliest published efforts of the renowned
American poet, Carl Sandburg, who died last Saturday, at
the age of 89.

The booklet, 40 pages of poetry and prose, is bound

---

*H. Jay Sharp, excerpt from article in the Kansas City Star,
July 26, 1967. By permission of the publisher.

with heavy brown paper and tied with a red ribbon. It belongs to Margaret Benton Humphrey, whose late husband,
Albert, taught expression and public speaking at Westport
high school.

Albert S. Humphrey was a fellow club member and
close personal friend of the then Charles Sandburg in a 7-
member literary society called the Poor Writers club, at
Lombard College in Galesburg, Ill. about 1900. The Sandburg writings were published in 1904 by the Asgard Press,
housed in the basement of the college [actually in the basement of the home of a professor, Philip Green Wright].

At that time, Humphrey was already teaching literature and speech at the school, later merged with Knox College. Sandburg had returned to Galesburg after having left
at the age of 17 for a roustabout life in the West. He had
worked at harvesting, bricklaying, dishwashing and odd jobs
throughout the prairie country.

Blessed with a perceiving eye, he was beginning to
shape in prose and poetry the images of everyday people
and everyday things.

Mrs. Humphrey remembers her husband's tales about
the Sandburg college days. The Sandburgs were poor Scan-
dinavian immigrants. Humphrey's father was a prosperous
doctor, in a family with several generations of history in
Illinois. During the period before the Civil War, the basement of the family home had served as an "underground
station" for runaway slaves escaping to Canada.

Despite their differences in background, the two
young men had an affinity based on their love for "utter-
ance" and for living. Humphrey told his wife of visits at
Carl's home, where he enjoyed the company and cooking of
Carl's tall, rawboned mother. She entertained them with
stories of the old country and stuffed them with "funny food,
but good."

Mrs. Humphrey recalls a prophetic story told by
her husband. One wintry day, the two young men were
walking through the snow-filled woods near the college.
They walked Indian fashion, Humphrey ahead and Sandburg
behind. As Sandburg stepped into the tracks made by
Humphrey's shoes he said: "I am walking in the great
steps of a man." Hearing this, Humphrey ran around be-

hind Sandburg, and proclaimed: "I am walking in the steps
of a great man. "

Their paths were parted by the Spanish American
War, when Sandburg joined the 6th Illinois infantry and spent
eight months in Puerto Rico. Afterwards he became a
newspaper man in Milwaukee, and served as secretary to
the mayor from 1910 to 1912.

After their college association, Albert Humphrey and
Sandburg did not meet again until the early 1920s, when
Sandburg gave a reading at Park College. At Parkville
[Missouri], Margaret Humphrey met Sandburg for the first
time.

A portrait painter by profession, Mrs. Humphrey
painted a portrait in words of Sandburg. She recalled:
"Even though he was still a young man, his head wore a
shock of white hair above a broad, round, pink face from
which bright blue eyes twinkled with the twang of a string
from his guitar, or clouded over as he spoke of death or
dreams or the death of dreams. "

After the recital, she and her husband stood in a
long line waiting to greet Sandburg. He apparently had
sighted them in the audience; for when he came out to the
reception line, his eyes raced across the faces until he
spotted the Humphreys, then with a warm "Halloo" he
swooped down upon Albert, hugging him and pounding his
back. The two men were so happy to see each other again
that Margaret finally tugged on Albert's coat to remind him
of her presence and her desire to meet Sandburg.

In the 1930s Dr. Clarence Decker, as chancellor of
the University of Kansas City, arranged for Sandburg to
appear at Convention Hall. In the crowd were Margaret
Humphrey, now a widow, and her two small children.

Sandburg recited poetry, cast out aphorisms, struck
chords for folk songs. He would suddenly grow very quiet
as if his thoughts were thousands of miles away; then with
a quick, broadening smile he would strike up some tune like
"Turkey in the Straw" which he would explain is the "Classi-
cal American rural tune that steps around like an apple-
faced farm hand, as American as Andrew Jackson, Johnny
Appleseed and corn on the cob. "

To this Mid-West audience, he spoke of our prairie towns and the winds that blow them about.

The dignitaries gathered backstage at Convention Hall afterward had to wait until Sandburg had sought out and kissed Margaret, tossed and caught Robin, and given Albert, the younger, a horsy ride on his knee.

In 1953, Sandburg was awarded the poetry medal of the National Institute of Arts and Letters at a luncheon in New York City. Margaret Humphrey, living in New York with her daughter, and working as a teacher of ballet and art at a girls' school, was present. Sandburg took time away from the social demands made upon him to share with her his memories of his old friend. She told him that she had his first book, "In Reckless Ecstacy." He laughed.

"Keep it safe," he said. "There are only a few copies left. Someday it should be very valuable."

Sandburg at and about Cheyenne School*

The date was January 29, (1929?). My husband, Lloyd Shaw, was an innovator and an inspired school-master, who tied his community and his student-body to the public at large and to each other by the use of every possible device of communication in the field of what would now be called "curriculum enrichment" or something of the sort. Also he did a great deal with what is now called "resource personnel." Along that line--Carl came in. The newspaper clipping says:

> Carl Sandburg's appearance here will be the big event of the year, and is a continuation of the policy of the Cheyenne School officials to bring one major attraction of merit each season. In the last two years the school has secured the services of McMillan, famous explorer, and Tony Sarg's marionettes, and the public has waited anxiously for its announcement of the 1929 production.

I have two pages of pre-appearance clipping, but have

*Letter from Dorothy Stott Shaw, Colorado Springs, Colo., April 9, 1970. By permission of the author.

not yet located a review of what Carl did, except that his
program was advertised as a miscellany. I can recall picking him up at the Rio Grande Railroad station quite early in
the day, and taking him to the YMCA, where he invariably
stayed, he told us, unless it was some very close friend
like Thomas Hornsby Ferrill who was involved. He would
not accept our invitation to dinner either, as he never ate,
he said, before a performance, except for an apple and a
glass of milk in his room at the "Y."

However there were a number of things he wanted us
to do for and with him, my husband and me. 1) He wanted
to go to all the second-hand book stores in town. He was
doing a research on beards. (This was in the midst of the
Lincoln period, of course.) I have always wondered what
happened to that beard research--there are a lot of people
who might like to quote from it today. He did come away
from a couple of places with unlikely-looking books that had
bits that he could use. At one store he browsed into the
files at the back of the establishment and he came out jubi-
lantly declaring that he had found a copy of one of his own
books which he was going to autograph for me. It was a
second-hand copy of the national magazine in which Good
Morning America appeared in its entirety. He had paid 5¢
for it and was perfectly delighted to be giving me this mu-
nificent gift with his name and felicitations scrawled all over
the margin. It was indeed a priceless treasure.

2) He wanted to be taken to the "Garden of the Gods."
We enjoyed doing this immensely. My husband outlined to
him the geology of these great perpendicular sandstone sea
beds and he immediately picked up the wonder of it and was
charmed to think of the sea having been where he was standing, and of palm trees on the shore.

The concert was tremendous, as I recall it. He read
from his own poems, first. Wonderfully. Then he produced his guitar and sang songs that are in the American
Songbag. Finally he read from the Rootabaga Stories and I
think he read most lovingly the story of the six pigeons who
walked home on their little bleeding feet. One hundred
miles, was it? And the one he loved was called Wednesday-
Evening-in-the-Twilight-and-the-Gloaming.

I failed to make clear that our connection with this
was: My husband was the Superintendent of the Cheyenne
Mountain School District for 35 years.

We always maintained a slight contact with Carl Sandburg after that, and I have a sneaking suspicion that he
came to Cheyenne Schools another time some years later.

The Marshall Field Centennial*

This is in reply to your recent query about how Carl
Sandburg came to be on the Marshall Field & Company Centennial program in 1952. There were so many major events
in that Centennial observance that this one doesn't stand out
vividly in my mind. To the best of my recollection this is
what transpired:

Late in the period of World War II, I renewed my
acquaintance with Carl while he was spending some time in
Chicago working over the Lincoln collection of Oliver Barrett,
which resulted in Carl's book Lincoln Collector, published in
1949. Among other things, at that time Fields planned an
institutional series of Christmas ads, with a whole series of
famous people stating their greatest wish for Christmas.
Among them were then General Eisenhower, Albert Einstein,
Robert Hutchins, Bob Hope, Babe Ruth, Lunt and Fontaine--
and a general cross section of well-known people. I met
Carl in Barrett's office and asked him if he would be one
of the series. After hearing the list of others, he said he
would. He sat down at once, and on yellow foolscap wrote
in longhand his Christmas wish. Handing it to me he
said, "Now you won't sell this will you?" Then, for the
first time I realized that I had in my possession (and still
have) a holograph by Sandburg! As became apparent in
Mitgang's book of his letters, he was careful to type most
communications--and frequently when he sent a poem in his
handwriting added to the letter "please send this back--it's
the only copy I have." So I have a fairly scarce item at
this point.

I told Carl that we were making donations for the
people who wrote these Christmas messages and not paying
a fee. The donations went to a charity they specified. His
eyes twinkled and Carl said, "Well, one of my favorite chari-
ties is Carl Sandburg. Can we do some shopping in the
Great Marshall Field & Company?" I said we could, and

---

*Letter from Lawrence B. Sizer, Harbert, Mich., Feb. 18,
1970. By permission.

suggested various sections with expensive merchandise in
them.   "No, " he said, "let's go to the basement: that's
where us common folks belong anyway. "   So we did, and
he picked out some caps, wool shirts, and several sweaters.
I suppose the whole, at retail, would have cost less than
$75.

        As for Carl's participation later in the Field Centen-
nial, in 1952, if memory serves I was then reading galleys
on his autobiographical book then in work, called Always the
Young Strangers.   Fields was one of the largest retail book
outlets in the country and Carl liked to introduce his books
there on publication.   It was the only place I know of where
he would consent to sit for a day or more autographing
copies.   Our plan was to introduce Carl's book as a part
of the Centennial since some of the mid-life chapters dealt
closely with Chicago's earlier days.   During the Field Centennial we could command almost any kind of gathering we
liked because of the store's fame and the enormous publicity
and reaction the Centennial was effecting.   (Wendt and Kogan
wrote a book about Chicago and the store that sold over
60, 000 copies--was translated into German and Spanish and
recently reissued by Rand McNally in paperback.   The book
is called Give the Lady What She Wants.)

        We gathered a sizeable group of writers/publishers,
social leaders, Chicago officials from past and present--
and all the ordinary people who could cram into the Walnut
room, the store's largest restaurant.   The store was opened
in the evening specially for the event--or rather the restaurant was.   We wanted Mrs. Sandburg too, but she didn't
come along.   Carl reminisced, told old tales about the
Chicago Daily News on which he was a reporter for years,
recalled some of his days in Harbert as well, and in Flat
Rock.   He was about 74 years old at the time, but full of
what he called "ginger"--especially having been fortified by
us with what he called "Dutch Courage, " which came in
bottles.   I'm afraid history does not record what he said.
It was hardly a prepared speech, but as he termed it "a
little gossip with old friends and neighbors. "   He did recite portions of his poem "Chicago, " but only in the context
of his remarks.

NEA Sends Sandburg to Scandinavia*

Yes, I did know Mr. Carl Sandburg, when he was asked to do a series of news articles for N. E. A., Newspaper Enterprise Association, a non-profit news syndicate of Cleveland, Ohio, and "the baby" of E. W. Scripps.

Carl was a guest in our home many times and always, a delightful one. The N. E. A. office looked long for a man to cover the Norway and Sweden area for them, under cover, willing to live in the slums, dark hallways, hidden rooms, willing to eat and not eat as the case may be, talk the language of the street, the alley, or the water front, take the cold of the winter, and the heat of summer, as the case may be. Time was 1917, 1918, World War I. All the news was to be mailed how and when he could get it through. It came--in English-Swedish and Norwegian, no one on the desk could read it. All tried, even the copy boys. More fun--however one of the girls I knew read well. "Winefred Clark" saved it all and when Carl came back to the States he was asked to stay in Cleveland and decipher it for printing, I would say about 1918.

He was a tall, rather lanky looking man, of the rugged outdoor type. Our two little girls about three and four at the time, so dearly loved him. In our home at that time we had a big brown velvet chair with rockers. And Carl spent many hours rocking the two little girls, singing to them all the songs of the street, the woods, and the birds, also the Choo Choo trains; I believe he worked in the Railroad yards at the time N. E. A. hired him. Mr. Sandburg was not what you could call a fashion plate. But he wore a heavy dark grey winter coat, a big heavy collar that buttoned well around his neck, and hung loose and baggy down below his knees. When our little girls would see him coming with their daddy from the streetcar to our house for dinner, Elizabeth would yell at the top of her lungs. "He's coming in his 'Gate cot, '"--great coat to you. He also loved my mince meat pies, which he claimed he drank because of the good french brandy I preserved it in. But he was lovely as a guest, fun as a friend. I suppose you have his book The [American] Songbag. Ours is so well used and much enjoyed that it is in many pieces now. But our children still use it. Also Sandburg's Lincoln.

---

*Letter from Mrs. Leon Starmont, Spokane, Wash. By permission.

When he was first asked to consider the assignment
for N. E. A. , he was overcome, and on second thought, he
said no: "My wife is expecting and I should be by her side.
No, I will have to refuse." When Mrs. Sandburg heard of
what he had done she was on the phone and you know long
distance in those days was not used carelessly. Her decision was "Carl will go. I will be all right and waiting
for him when he returns." She grew immensely in the
hearts of the N. E. A. staff that day. Carl went and the
baby was about six months to a year old before he ever saw
it.

Mr. Sandburg was a lover of all living things, always
had a piece of land, and goats were his favorite on the farm,
from a standpoint of fun and production. Many times he was
seen cradling a goat as a mother holds her child.

Sandburg's Song-collecting Tactics*

Indeed you are right about my acquaintance with Carl
Sandburg many years ago. Four or five of the songs in his
Songbag I gave to him in the academic year 1921-22 when I
was a senior at Wesleyan. Professor Wilbert Snow, now
Emeritus Professor and a poet in his own right, who now
lives in Middletown, Connecticut, was a friend of Sandburg's
and brought him to the College to sing and play at an assembly of students. Half a dozen of us at that time made a
hobby of collecting folk songs and singing them to guitar
accompaniments. After Sandburg's recital Bill Snow brought
him down to the Eclectic Society and some of us stayed up
all night swapping songs.

Sandburg was an impressive person. He had thick
hair even then graying. It fell in two heavy locks on either
side of his forehead. His speaking voice was deep and mellow and he sang a fine baritone. Without any forcing he
could sing for a large audience in a college assembly hall.
I envied him his guitar, a large one with a fine deep tone
which suited Sandburg's voice.

Sandburg was, I think, a self-taught guitarist. The
instrument was then much less common than it now is and

---

*Letter from Arthur E. Sutherland, Cambridge, Mass. ,
June 15, 1970. By permission.

the type of accompaniment for songs was comparatively simple. With six or eight chords, a few runs, a guitar clamp
to change keys, and a feeling for songs, he had all the ap-
paratus he needed. Sandburg got the most out of this level
of skill.

He taught himself musical notation in the simplest
possible way. He would draw five lines in pencil on a sheet
of paper and sketch in the notes well enough to remind him
of the tune which he had heard sung. He would scribble in
the words and so add another piece to his repertoire. I
am sure that when he brought out the Songbag he must have
got a technically trained musician to supply the musical notation.

He loved to sing and treasured a good song. Several
years after the great night in Middletown, he gave a recital
in Rochester, New York, and afterward came to my house.
Again we spent a number of hours talking about old songs.
I recollect Sandburg fingering the tunes on a piano to help
him rough out his peculiar notation. I think that was the
evening when I sang for him "Come in from the Foggy,
Foggy Dew, " which begins "When I was a bachelor and lived
all alone I worked the weaver's trade. " I thought that I
recalled verses with the same structure and nearly the
same refrain occurring in one of Thomas Hardy's books.
Sandburg and I spent an hour or so rummaging through whatever Hardy books we could turn up at the time of night.
We never did find the song and my recollection may have
been entirely amiss. I seem to remember that the version
that Hardy quoted had to do with somebody sticking his (or
possibly her) head out of a cottage window and singing "Come
in from the foggy, foggy dew. " Sandburg liked "When I was
a bachelor. " He found very affecting the lines about the
weaver's son--"And every time I look into his eyes he reminds me of the fair young maid. " He then went off on
another tack saying that he had a young daughter and he
wanted no such thing to happen to her. He said he was
going to teach her to kick, bite and scratch in self defense.

The night that we sat up singing at Wesleyan, Sandburg smoked a large curved briar pipe, of the shape then
called a "bull-dog. " He was wearing an old battered tweed
jacket, and the right-hand pocket was full of loose pipe tobacco. He would knock the dottle out of his pipe into the
fireplace and stick his right hand holding the pipe into his
pocket, wad the pipe with his first finger, and pull the

loaded pipe out ready for a match. When you come to think
of it, that is a perfectly efficient procedure unless somebody
in the household objects to the jacket.

Once Professor Snow and I were talking about Sandburg's unconventional verse forms. I think I remember his
telling me that Sandburg spent a long time when he was
young working at conventional verse forms before he cast
them aside.

Meeting Carl Sandburg (by William A. Sutton)

Being in correspondence with Margaret Sandburg in
1963 over the relationship between the life of her father and
Sherwood Anderson was helpful. However, she agreed to
review my chapter on the subject, after giving me a few
pieces of new information, but she did not return the manuscript after I submitted it to her. I decided whatever was
done was voluntary and let it go at that.

One evening in February, 1967, I returned home to
be told that Margaret Sandburg had called; it was something
about some information concerning Sherwood Anderson.

When I returned her call, I found that she had come
across some Anderson-Sandburg letters and had thought of
me. It happened that our family was already scheduled to
take a trip to North Carolina the next month. An invitation
to consult with Margaret and view the Sandburg-Anderson
materials at Connemara, Flat Rock, N. C. , was extended.

At 1:30 p. m. , March 25, the appointed time, I
knocked on the door of the Sandburg mansion. I said to the
pleasant, sprightly lady who came to the door, "Miss Sandburg?" "Yes. " But I soon found, when Margaret Sandburg
appeared, that her mother had misunderstood me. And her
appearance and manner were such that I could believe she
was her daughter, even though her daughter was in her fif-
ties and her mother in her eighties.

Miss Sandburg invited me to bring my wife and my
son into the house, and the four of us proceeded through
several large rooms into Margaret's study, a room next to
her father's study, where he evidently spent most of his
time, reading and watching television and the numerous
birds which came to the feeders outside the large window.

There we stayed and talked about many things, Anderson,
Whitman, Sandburg, until about 3:45. In the meantime, Mrs.
Sandburg had appeared several times, the first time saying
"Dad," whom we could hear in the room next to Margaret's
study, was "not feeling well today." Later Mrs. Sandburg
offered us some orange juice, which we accepted. When
she brought it, she brought a glass for Margaret, who
frowned and said, "Mother, you know I don't like orange
juice!"

Just at 3:45 Mrs. Sandburg came in and told us that
Dad had had a nap and felt better and invited us to go in
and see him, an invitation we accepted with alacrity, going
directly into the room where he was seated, through a door
from Margaret's room. (I had read that Sandburg, at 89,
walked only seldom and then just around the house; thus it
was hard to guess whether he would be visible or would receive any one.)

As we filed into the commodious but crowded room,
we found the poet seated in a comfortable chair, in front of
a large window, next to a table, and about eight feet away
from a television set placed in his immediate line of vision.
As we entered, Mrs. Sandburg turned the set off.

Directly in front of him was a hassock with various
books and papers on it, including his collected poems and
his latest book, Honey and Salt. (As we were about to
leave, he held this book up and said, without explanation,
"The name on the back [the spine which he held toward us]
is Honey and Salt." It seemed he was reminding us of his
acceptance of both the sweet and sour of life.)

He had on a blue plaid shirt, open at the throat, and
blue trousers. He had a red plaid robe over his knees and
slippers on his feet. Very long hair was loosely controlled
by a green eyeshade. He wore rather thick glasses. His
sight and hearing were obviously good, and his handshake
was firm and warm. We learned his neck size was 16, and
his frame was quite large. He remained seated during the
time we were with him.

The poet, in the later stages of a long life, seemed
to have come to terms with whatever infirmities he had to
endure. His mind was still active, though it seemed he had
not the strength for the creative effort which made him famous. He evidently slept while we were consulting with his

daughter. Mrs. Sutton looked back through the doorway
after we had left the room and were chatting for a few moments with his daughters. He appeared to have fallen
asleep.

The daughter we were visiting, Margaret, was devot-
ing her time to working with his voluminous papers and the
queries and problems of researchers. A second daughter,
whom we met briefly, Janet, seemed to be in charge of the
famous herd of Sandburg goats. We did not get to ask her
about them; we did ask Margaret how many there were, and
she said, in a way which indicated that was not her department, that it was hard to tell at any one time.

Connemara Farm, as the poet's home was known,
covers 241 acres of hilly land. The house, approached by
an extremely winding road up a heavily-wooded hill, was
nearly obscured from the road. It was rather a mansion
than a house, the original part having been built for the Secretary of the Treasury for the Confederate States. We saw
only four rather huge rooms on the second floor. Margaret
Sandburg told us the house had been fortified during the
Civil War, a firing port still remaining in the basement.
The threat, she explained, was more from looters coming
down from the hills than from Federal troops.

The rooms we saw were quite obviously "lived in, "
pleasantly cluttered. We were intensely privileged to see
the Sandburgs at home, as they were, a famous family without pretension and with much love and unity among them.
(A third daughter, Helga, who has had her own career as
a writer, is the wife of Dr. George Crile, Jr., and lives
in Cleveland.)

Our glimpse of Carl Sandburg indicated he was still
the beneficiary of devoted and intelligent care which made
it possible for him to pursue his artistic destiny and to re-
tain, at an advanced age, a great deal of simple zest for
living.

The poet, who obviously had more than adequate
money for his family's needs, has always depended on his
wife for management of his economic and material needs,
as illustrated by their move from Harbert, Michigan, to
Flat Rock, North Carolina. The Sandburgs had moved from
the Chicago suburb of Elmhurst to seven acres of land in
Michigan in 1932, in a vicinity where they had been making

summer visits since 1926.   Their new house to which they
moved in 1932 was specially-designed, commodious on a
dune overlooking Lake Michigan.   Then they moved to North
Carolina in 1945.

When I asked Margaret Sandburg why they had moved,
her first comment was, "You would not believe it." It
seems Mrs. Sandburg thought the Michigan climate hard on
her health and wanted to move.   This was agreed to.   Then
reference books, "atlases and encyclopedias" were resorted
to in a systematic attempt to identify the desired "better
climate."

Through this means California and North Carolina
were identified as being equally desirable in climate.   California was eliminated because of earthquakes and floods.
"All we have here is the occasional tail of a hurricane,"
Margaret pointed out.

The general location having been identified, Mrs.
Sandburg, her sister, and Helga Sandburg made a tour of
the area by car, checking on properties for sale, deciding
finally on Connemara.   Mrs. Sandburg had a farm in mind,
but this huge home, with its small lake just down a hill
from a large porch, a massive double set of stairs approaching the porch, enough space to be a permanent buffer against
the adjacent tourist area, and attractive low, rolling hills
and many trees, evidently won her heart.

Not the least of Carl Sandburg's many achievements
was to find a woman of intelligence he could think of as
"my wife and my pal" who recognized and appreciated his
art and provided a base from which he could explore and
exploit it.

Sandburg, as he enjoyed the later years of an extremely interesting and fruitful life, seemed to have shown
mastery of the art of life as well as of language.

Because we did not know until a few minutes before
whether or not we would get to see Margaret's famous
father, he had no knowledge that he was to have visitors or
who they were.   He questioned me about my name and my
occupation and then the school where I taught.   He was intrigued by the name of Ball State and wanted to know why it
was so named.   After he asked where the school was, my
question "Have you been there?" was added to the answer.

His reply, after a pause: "About 30 or 40 years ago
I was there for two weeks." Since Sandburg performed folk
songs over the country for decades, it seemed likely that
he had appeared at Ball State for that purpose. Subsequent
research established that he did appear at Burris School,
in Muncie, on February 15, 1933. But to have been here
for two weeks seemed strange, so I asked what he had done
for two weeks. "I didn't know if I should tell," he slowly
replied, but, being importuned, mentioned his photograph
selling.

His daughter and Mrs. Sandburg immediately produced
Steichen's album of Sandburg pictures, opened to a picture
of him with a Lombard College classmate, his partner in
the sales venture. Margaret Sandburg said her father's
memory of the date was wrong but that he could very well
be right about being in Muncie. Our city's position on a
main railroad line made the likelihood seem greater. A
letter from Sandburg, posted from Marion, Indiana, in 1908
has been found. Marion is just twenty miles from Muncie.

He asked me if I knew what "stereoscopic photographs" were, and I blunderingly replied, yes. I had looked
at stereopticon slides. "Not slides, photographs," he firmly but pleasantly remonstrated, "and not 'stereopticon.'
That is a hell of a word. They were ste-re-o-scopic pho-
to-graphs."

After that I really did remember the double photographs viewed through lenses on a holder. "Were they any
particular make?" He paused and smiled. "There were
never any as good as Underwood and Underwood." The
Sandburg collection at the University of Illinois has his complete set of these pictures.

Sandburg sold these ste-re-o-scopic pho-to-graphs in
an area bounded by Illinois and New Jersey, particularly in
the summers he was at Lombard College, which he left in
1902, but doubtless as late as 1908. Thus there may be,
in attics across a considerable part of the country, pictures
sold by Sandburg in his years as a working salesman.

Our moments in the Sandburg sitting room flew by,
the poet being in a very happy, teasing mood.

Focusing his attention on our 16-year-old son, Bob,
who stands a little more than six feet, he said mock-

seriously, "I predict this boy will surpass his parents. I can tell by his face and his teeth."

Bob was wearing a surfer jacket, blue with six-inch white stripe across the chest. The white had caught the poet's eye. "Look at that jacket! Jee-sus wept! That is a hell of a jacket."

It appeared to Sandburg that the jacket had a white square on each chest. He kidded Bob about these spaces: "You ought to print the Lord's Prayer on one of them. And the Ten Commandments on the other."

Bob pointed out that the white was not in two squares but that the white insert went all the way around, turning to show him. With a twinkle, Sandburg thanked him for the demonstration and told him he certainly would not have realized this fact without his help.

Falling into the poet's bantering mood, I said to him, "You really don't remember me, do you?" No, he did not. "Well, you ought to; you have seen me." (When the writer made this remark, he thought it was true. Though it has been possible to document more than 700 Sandburg appearances, there is no evidence to support this supposed "memory.")

Without pause, he returned, "Oh, yes. I do remember you. You had that same grey suit on. And you had it buttoned in one place, just as it is now."

Then he turned to Bob and said, "Don't let your father buffalo you the way he tried to do to me just now." Assurance was given that he would not and had not.

In addition to comments on Bob's jacket, Sandburg remarked on his "wild" pink shirt and the fact that his hair was "too long." At this point Margaret told her father he was "a good one to talk", his hair, loosely crowned by an eye-shade, being extremely long and unruly, and still rather thick.

So much had been said about the jacket that it appeared he was rather attracted by it. When I asked him if he would like a similar one, he said he would. His wife demurred but he did not join her. So we checked his neck size at 16, and a surfer jacket, complete with pamphlet giving the authentic surfer's special vocabulary, was sent to him.

Within a few weeks, the jacket was returned to us with a polite note from Mrs. Sandburg that he did not need it. Probably she was all too well aware of the factors which caused him to die in his sleep a few months later, on July 22.

This vivid, unanticipated encounter began ten years of research which have resulted in the collection of more than 8,000 episodes and items related to Sandburg, from which the items in this book were selected.

From Interviewer to Collaborator*

Millicent Taylor decided, in 1925, to give up teaching English and try her hand at free-lance writing in Chicago. She soon received a request from the Christian Science Monitor to do an interview with Carl Sandburg.

Though greatly disturbed, because she had never done an interview, she wrote Sandburg at the Daily News for an appointment. When she arrived at the scheduled time, she had to wait for him. Colleagues assured her he was around somewhere.

When he did arrive, she timidly told him she did not know how to proceed. To her relief, she found him sympathetic. He guided her through the task.

"Not long after I interviewed him, he sent a pleasant note. Right after that he asked if I was free to help him with a book. I worked for four or five months on the American Songbag. We never made any financial arrangement whatever. Every once in a while he'd fish in his pocket and give me a few bills and I took them.

"When I started to work with Carl (in 1925), he had this little hole that he called his Ivory Tower. It was a room on the second floor, which was reached by going up the back way from an alley. A photographer had the other

---

*Based on an interview with Millicent Taylor, Lakewood, Ohio, Sept. 4, 1969.

second-floor room.   The address was 63 W. Ontario Street.
He had a bed, table, chairs.   The furniture was makeshift,
the cover dark and dirty.   All the work on the Songbag was
done there.   He would arrive at about eleven in the morning.   We would go across the street and sit on stools and
have hamburgers. ''

The work Miss Taylor did on The Songbag was to
transcribe his rough, unique, unmusical impressions of the
tunes into musical scores, which were the ones used in the
book.   She has samples of both his notes and her own
transcriptions of them.

Evidently during the interview she did of him, he
discovered she played the violin and thought she might be
interested in helping with the folk song project, which she
was.

Sandburg could not read music.   He would give the
tune.   She would make rough annotations.   Then she played
it on the violin till she got it.   Then she wrote the score.
She did all the songs for the Songbag that way.

"We had great fun.   We got along fine. ''

Miss Taylor made him a manuscript book of all the
songs in Songbag.

A President's Appreciation*

August 14, 1945

Dear Carl Sandburg:

I am indeed grateful to you for that set of the six
Lincoln volumes because not in my day will there be produced another study of the great Civil War President which
will supersede them or, I venture to say, even approach
them as the definitive work on this outstanding American.

I appreciate, too, more than I can say, the profound
sentiments which you embody in the inscriptions on the flyleaves of Volume I of The Prairie Years and the first vol-

---

*Letter from President Truman.   By permission.

ume of The War Years. I like to think that my own Kentucky forebears, who were contemporaries of the Lincolns, represent that responsibility, honesty and common sense which have been the glory of citizens of the Bluegrass State and of the Nation through all the generations from our beginnings onward to this day.

When I read The War Years in haunts made holy by memories of Lincoln, I shall often be reminded of the "White House loneliness and laughter" which you mention with such feeling.

From the bottom of my heart I thank you for a gift which I shall always cherish.

Very sincerely yours,

(Sgd) Harry S Truman

The Cornell College Connection*

Many Cornellians were saddened the other day when they read in the newspapers that Carl Sandburg had died. Of course, I was, but I was not shocked nor surprised, for I had known that he had been ill for a long time. His daughter Margaret wrote that he had not written a letter for two years. Assuming that you have read the papers and listened to tributes on radio and television, I am focussing the column on the very special relation between Sandburg and Cornell, characterized in a Des Moines Register article as "The Love Affair of Carl Sandburg and Cornell College."

From that first exciting night in January, 1920, Sandburg felt close to the college. Once he called himself, "a sub rosa Professor of Cornell College." Another time he said, "When anybody asks if I belong to any organization, I say, 'The only organization I belong to is the English Club of Cornell College.'"

The first reason for his interest in, and attachment to, Cornell was the fact that the English Club introduced him as a platform artist to the academic world. Two of

*Clyde C. Tull, in The Alumnus (Cornell College), Summer/ Fall, 1967.

his biographers mention this point in their books, Carl Sandburg (1941), by Karl Detzer, and Carl Sandburg (1961), by
Harry Golden [see his reminiscences on page 152], both
writers describing with some detail the reception by the students at his debut in the Lower Chapel. His brother Mart
some years later told me that Carl said that the $100 fee,
paid by the English Club, "looked as big as the moon!"
He was working for fifty dollars a week on the staff of the
Chicago Daily News.

     After the family received in 1965 a copy of the Des
Moines Register feature article about Sandburg's tie with
Cornell, Mrs. Sandburg sent a handwritten note: "I wish
you could have seen how deeply moved Carl was, recalling
his annual trips to Cornell and the warm affection shown
him in those early struggling years by you, your lovely wife
Jewell--and all there. "

     Margaret asked to read any letters, written by her
father to me, as she was going over his correspondence at
the time, collecting it for Herbert Mitgang who has been
chosen by Carl's publishers to edit it for book publication.
I sent him a sheaf of the most characteristic of Carl's
letters, from which he could select what he could use. He
seemed pleased and promised to send me an early copy of
the book.

     Carl Allen [see his reminiscences on page 75], '22,
a devoted admirer of Sandburg since their first meeting at
Cornell, was also asked for letters and sent them to the
editor. The Cornellian had kept in touch through the years,
entertaining the poet in his California home, visiting him at
Hollywood, and even having a brief talk with him at the
Connemara farm this summer.   Carl (I mean Carl Allen)
has given innumerable lectures and readings from Sandburg's
prose and poetry.

     While Cornellians have been happy over their part in
proving to Sandburg that an academic audience would respond
happily and enthusiastically to his talks, his reading, and
his singing (students in great universities have sat in windows to hear him), they can also be very happy and grateful
for what he has done for Cornell.   First, in a material way,
after his reputation was established and his engagements
were handled by a booking bureau, he told the bureau that
he would make his own arrangements for the dates at Cornell. As a result, the English Club paid for a program

only a fraction of what other institutions paid the bureau.
I gave him all the receipts, which weren't large, because
during the depression we charged the students fifty cents
for admission! One time at the post-program party, hearing that Ruth Messenger, '29, was going to do a bicycle
trip through England, he reached into his pocket for all the
silver I had given him, and handed it to her, saying, "Here,
buy yourself something in England." One year he declared
"a free show," and the English Club threw the program
open to the public, holding it in the Chapel which was
packed, but he and the students who were interested much
preferred the intimacy of the Lower Chapel and all sessions
were held there thereafter.

But the great beneficence of Carl Sandburg was the
impact of his creativity upon the students. He was writing
all those two decades and creativeness is contagious. There
was a flowering of interest and talent upon which I look back
with wonder. Students who had never thought of writing began to experiment. Poets and poetry lost the curse of ef-
feminacy. "Bumper" Cole, ex-truck driver and football
star, came over to South Hall and took a writing course,
"made" the Husk and the book Stories for the Husk. Sandburg was much interested in the magazine. One day when
Jewell, the dogs, and I were ready for a trip, I got the
mail, found an envelope stuffed with verse, glanced at it.
Imitation of Sandburg, I thought, and left it at the house.
When we returned, I examined it and found that it was a
sheaf of unpublished Sandburg poetry, a contribution from
the poet himself. Herb Owens, '28, did a linoleum portrait
of him and we got out a "Carl Sandburg Number."

I wish you could see the shelf of autographed books
in my apartment, written by Cornellians, graduates of the
Husk. Marjorie Holmes, '31, author of nine books, was
so grateful that out of her busy career and goodness of
heart, she re-read twenty volumes of the magazine, reviewed the poems and stories, and wrote a brochure,
"Twenty Years of the Husk," which the English Club published.

During the actual Sandburg years the English Club
published not only the Husk, of which there is a complete
file in the British Museum, but several hardcover books:
The Little Book of Cornell College Verse, co-edited by
David Fuller Ash, '23; The Cornell College Book of Verse;
Prophecies of Hope, co-edited by Clifford Hand, '45; Jewell's

The Constant Moon; Stories from the Husk, designed and co-
edited by Anya Plummer, '40. Students under the tutelage
of the friendly Art Rogers, of the Hillside Press (another
sub rosa professor), set the type for the books which were
bound by the professional Kolariks, of Cedar Rapids. Art
had to do the press work; he became so deeply interested
in the operation that, after he died, his wife Grace gave the
press to the college and another generation is using it. The
English Club also published twenty-four chapbooks, ranging
from 30 to 54 pages, including "The Leaves of the Tree, "
by May Sarton, and "Planets and Angels, " by Eugene Jolas,
internationally known as the editor of the magazine Transi-
tion.

The Sandburg years covered and, I believe, inspired
the winning of the Atlantic Monthly-Little, Brown & Co.
$10,000 novel competition by Winifred Van Etten [see her
reminiscences on page 268], '26, with "I Am the Fox" and
the publication by the Yale Press of "The Deer Come Down,"
by Edward Weismiller, '38; the winning of Mademoiselle's
short-story competition by Naomi Williams, '46, and the
winning of poetry and short-story awards by freshmen Char-
lotte Radsliff, '37, and Lenore Fliege, '38, both in the
Forum Magazine National College and University Competition involving over 700 institutions. Henry Goddard Leach,
editor of the Forum magazine, was so deeply impressed by
the material submitted by Cornell writers that he wrote:
"I almost wonder if both Emily Dickinson and Whittier are
hovering about this happy campus. "

But Sandburg's influence was not limited to talented
individuals. As Mr. Leach wrote, it was a happy campus
even during the long depression. On their own, a group of
students organized an exchange library with a slogan, "Read
a Book a Week. " The Writers Club met Wednesdays at
four; Lois Henderson headed a group of students and faculty
who met Sunday afternoons to "read Poetry for Fun. " The
English Club brought writers to the college, supplementing
the Artists Course, people like Edna St. Vincent Millay,
Zona Gale, Ruth Suckow, Harriet Monroe, Jay Sigmund,
John G. Neihardt, Marjorie Allen Seiffert, Carol Ryrie
Brink, Badger Clark, Seumas MacManus. And the English
Club promoted related activities such as the marionette
theatre directed by Saralou Jordan, '24, and Margaret
Skewis, '24, who later, with her husband, headed a pro-
fessional marionette theatre. It booked the Devereux Play-
ers and Madame Hammer with the Ibsen plays for several

years and I remember vividly a production of Paul Green's
"In Abraham's Bosom, " by a touring company with an open
date and a reduced fee.

The wonder of this activity by the English Club is
that it was always independent. Loyally and appreciatively
supported by the student body and faculty, it was un-sub-
sidized and solvent.

I'm asseverating that this creative and cultural activity on the campus could not have occurred without the
annual visits of Carl Sandburg. Of course, we didn't realize
this influence at the time. It's an analysis after the fact.
His influence was a catalyst that developed an exciting
Renaissance on the Cornell College campus. This I believe
and I have tried to prove it.

I wanted to write a lot of anecdotes about Sandburg
and Cornell but there is no space. Many students, however,
will have memories: Sandburg at Upper Pal picnics, playing
ball or sitting at the base of a tree, relaxed, telling stories;
in the center of a group of students and faculty at a post-
program party at the Old Homestead, perhaps collecting
songs from Mae Hutchinson and Betty Cottingham, '22, for
his American Songbag, recording the tunes in his original
shorthand; alternately playing the guitar, singing and talking
(you wouldn't know that after you left, he and I would play
and talk till three in the morning); his wonderfully impressive reading of the poem, "For you" (at the end of Smoke
and Steel) required as his blessing for the year. Those
were the Years.

Cornell Connection Continued*

I first came to Cornell in the autumn of the year
1920. Carl Sandburg first came in that same year. There
any resemblance ceases between us. I was from a small
town in a part of the state of Iowa which contained nothing
but even smaller small towns. Sioux City, Iowa, and To-
peka, Kansas, where we occasionally visited relatives, were
my idea of great metropolitan centers. They had streetcars.
Sandburg at that time was a fifty-dollar-a-week man on a

*Letter from Winifred M. Van Etten, Mount Vernon, Iowa,
Aug. 23, 1977. By permission.

Chicago newspaper, a seemingly rough, tough man from a
rough, tough city. But within him lived a poet, a spirit
that had been expressing itself for some time in a new kind
of verse.

This new poetry was duly noted by Professor Clyde
Tull of the Cornell College English Department, who, unlike
many teachers in many such small denominational schools
as Cornell, was quick to take note of what was new and to
investigate it. Thus it came about that Cornell [in Mt. Vernon, Iowa] was the first academic institution to invite Sandburg to lecture and to read his poetry. He never forgot that
it was Cornell that had first bestowed upon him recognition
as a poet at a time when most schools and most critics denied that he was a poet at all. He wrote a certain what-
have-we-here kind of thing, yes. But poetry, no. Cornell
gave him, as far as its limited influence extended, an acco-
lade of respectability.

I have never forgotten that first one of his many appearances at Cornell. He spoke from the stage in what we
called the Upper Chapel. It had stained glass windows, a
pipe organ, pews. It lacked nothing but an altar rail to be
completely churchly in appearance. Nothing more incongruous than Carl Sandburg behind the podium on that stage with
his rumpled clothes, his flopping bang of hair, his guitar
can be imagined. Nor can anything more incongruous than
this poet before this audience be imagined. This was 1920,
the year that Smoke and Steel was copyrighted. Before that
there had been Chicago Poems (1916) and Cornhuskers
(1912). Yet few of his audience had ever heard of Sandburg.
To most of them a poet was someone like, perhaps, Longfellow with a long white beard, who wrote poems nice and
noble. Above all he was dead. All poets, like all novelists,
were, as far as we knew, dead. That was the essential
qualification: dead. And here was this odd-looking man,
with the odd look in his eyes, alive and talking about hog-
butchers, painted women luring the farm boys, broken-faced
gargoyles, hoodlums, killers. He could pair hyacinths and
biscuits as equally relevant elements of poetry. Hyacinths
we acknowledged as poetic, of course, but biscuits? No.
Above all, he didn't commit a single rhyme. So how could
his stuff be poetry when everybody knew that anything that
rhymed was poetry and anything that didn't wasn't?

War broke out on the campus. I recall most of one
class hour spent on those biscuits. It is hard to comprehend

our vehemence now, but it was, of course, the era in
which so many little magazines "died to make verse free."
What seems now most incomprehensible of all is the fact
that to so many Sandburg's verse was incomprehensible.
How could a little thing like "Fog" baffle anyone? What
was its purpose, they asked. We had got a little beyond
saying, "What's the moral?" but actually we were still
looking for one.

In subsequent appearances, yearly over a long period,
Sandburg insisted on moving to what we called the "lower
chapel." Much smaller than the large auditorium in which
he had first spoken, it was a bare-bones sort of place used
for extra-large classes, rehearsals of the oratorio society,
pep meetings, and the like. It suited Sandburg much better.
He stood or sat in a narrow space only a few feet away
from the first row of the audience. Gradually a format for
his readings evolved. First he read or recited from previously published poems. Then he told us what he was
working on, and as a special bonus read a little from the
current, yet unpublished opus. Next he took up his guitar
and sang, in a not-very-melodious voice but one that exactly
accorded with the man and his poetry and his appearance,
songs from the Songbag and other new ones he'd picked up
in his travels. I recall that he found one in Mount Vernon
that he'd never had before. This was the part that the audience liked best. Even so, in spite of his popularity at
Cornell, I believe that there always remained for many of
the succeeding generations of students, as for the first, an
element of enigma about him. We had many poets coming
to Cornell during those years, many distinguished novelists
as well. I think only John Cawper Powys retained, like
Sandburg, that element of enigma that teases the memory.

Vachel Lindsay enchanted us. He lured students to
the stage to stamp out the rhythms of the Congo as he
chanted it. Edna Millay was the goddess of the budding
feminists. We could recite her poetry by the ream. We
felt certain we had adopted her philosophy of burning our
candle at both ends, but, alas, it was still lights out at
ten o'clock for girls at Cornell. And we learned to say in
our minds to discarded lovers, yes, I loved you Monday.
So what? This is Tuesday. But again, alas, lovers were
too few to be lightly discarded by anyone.

Those who got to know him best were those who,
after the reading, repaired to the home of Toppy and Jewell

Tull. There Sandburg sank into the huge easy chair by the
fire, the only other human being as far as I know ever allowed to occupy that throne. There he stayed for hours,
often most of the night. The girls had to go home at ten,
but many of the boys, some town people, some faculty members, hung about as long as Sandburg held out. There was
talk, argument, much telling of anecdotes, and every so
often an interlude of more guitar playing. Toppy, himself
a skilled guitarist, would join in. Songs from the Songbag
many students knew by that time, and they, too, would join
in. It was a small room packed with students spilling over
into the adjoining rooms on stools, on benches, on front and
back stairs, on the floor interspersed with the several dogs
kept by the Tulls, with the cats, one of whom derived her
name from Rootabaga Stories. She was Tuesday Evening
Just Between the Twilight and the Gloaming (a Maltese,
naturally), Tuesday, for short, because she arrived at the
Tull menage on a Tuesday. Over this pack the firelight
flickered, fainter and fainter as it reached the outer edges.

For many years this event occurred annually. As
each of his books appeared, Sandburg sent an autographed
copy to Prof. Tull as a gift. When the Depression got so
bad that students simply could not buy a ticket for the reading, he came at least once for nothing. On another occasion a young woman, new in the English department, entered the Tull livingroom after Sandburg had settled into
his chair. He gazed up at her. "But you're beautiful," he
said. (This I recall, of course, because I was so jealous.)
When he learned later that another girl was about to take a
trip to England on the well-known shoestring, he handed out
of his pockets the entire take of the evening, bills, jingling
coins, all, and gave it to her to help with the expenses of
the trip.

He was not always all jokes and geniality. In his
poetry there was always the celebration of life but also the
wry recognition of humanity's foibles and follies and hate-
fulness. And of the grass that eventually covers all. In
his social relations there was this same duality. He did
not suffer fools gladly. At lunch one day a certain gushy
lady managed to snag a seat right beside the celebrity.
Wishing to open conversation, she cooed, "Mr. Sandburg,
what would you do if your little boy said damn?" He looked
at her coldly, "Teach him to say God-damn," he replied
and turned his back, thereby loosening the Bible belt another
notch for the students listening.

By this time Sandburg was in full fame. It would
have been hard to find a freshman who had never heard of
him. Far from being baffled by "Fog," they could take on
"Prufrock" without going pale. And Sandburg himself was
deep into his Lincoln biography, his huge novel, his motion
picture commitments. It became harder and harder to find
a free date in his calendar that would coincide with a free
date in the college calendar or, as the years went on, a
sizable audience among the students. Time had altered both
people and circumstances. First, a year was missed, and
then another. It became silently accepted that Sandburg
would come no more.

It was, in a way, the end of an era. Also, in a way,
it was mission accomplished. There was no need for him
to come again. He had joked with, sung to, annoyed,
thrilled, irritated, and helped open up the minds of several
generations of Cornell students. But their mutual need for
each other no longer existed.

Still, I have always kept a vivid picture of him as
he sang. He had a way of gazing into far-off spaces as he
sang, spaces into which no one else could see. He had,
as he said of Lincoln in the preface to The Prairie Years,
enough lights, shadows, and radiant colors to call for portraits to be made. However, what I always see is that
long gaze, as if, out somewhere, he found the same "in-
visible companionships" he attributed to Lincoln.

Sandburg as a Believer

[From an article in the Boston Transcript (1927?)
by Caroline Elizabeth Vose:]

You may not want to like Carl Sandburg, you may be
prejudiced against him, you may be determined to resist
him, and yet if you hear him he will almost inevitably win
you over and win you over for keeps. He will do this, too,
without appearing to try. His attitude is more or less that
of "Here I am offering you my best, my whole self. But
take me or leave me just as you wish," and ten to one
you'll "take" him because you can't "leave" him, this man
who opens wide new windows through which you may look at
life.

He opened new windows for me as I rode with him

in an electric car at midnight from Orono to Bangor. He
showed me my own state of Maine, grown a trifle common-
place through familiarity, as a glorious land worthy to inspire poetry "in formal verse, in free verse, or in some
mixture, worthy, too, to inspire great art, " and he helped
me see my Maine churches as "beautiful white treasure
chests. "

More than that, he talked to me of his Rootabaga
stories, a favorite subject with him, and he found me an
eager listener. "You remember, " he said, his penetrating-
grey eyes lighting up, "you remember there's a cigarette
some folks would walk a mile for. Well, I'd walk a mile
to see a person who likes my Rootabaga stories. "

"And I'd walk a mile to hear you read one of them, "
I answered.

"Union Station! Union Station!" shouted the conductor.

Mr. Sandburg wrapped his mufflers around his neck,
picked up his battered suitcase and his precious guitar, and
wandered out into the snowy night. As I peered after him
and waved, I thought that what he has written of Nancy
Hanks might well be said of him:

> He believes in God, in the Bible, in mankind, in
> the past and future babies, people, animals,
> flowers, fishes, in foundations and roofs, in time
> and the eternities outside of time; he is a be-
> liever, keeping in silence behind his gray eyes
> more beliefs than he speaks. He knows--so much
> of what he believes in yonder--always yonder.

--Sandburg, Lombard Review, Jan. 13, 1927

Sandburg in Canada*

The following is a memory of Sandburg at Queen's
University, Kingston, Ontario, in December, 1950:

His homespun interest in music, in animals and his

---

*Letter from Mrs. Lois Wheeler, Locust Hill, Ontario, Aug.
19, 1970. By permission of the author.

human interest in a family such as ours was amazing. My
mother was a fragile, intelligent, and beautiful hostess.
Daddy, a Scotch Presbyterian minister turned into a University Principal, with terrific humor, but pretty strict and
often almost gruff.

I am the youngest of five children, all the others at
that time away at college, or following their professions:
law, chartered accountant, dietitian and violinist. My
sister, the violinist, was a pupil of Leopold Auer in New
York.

I drove out to the Kingston "Outer Station" to meet
the latest guest in our T. Model Ford given to the family
on Dad's leaving St. Paul's Church in Montreal in 1917. It
was complete with brass radiator-cover, three pedals--
clutch; brakes; and reverse. The accelerator worked on a
notched steering wheel with one's fore-finger. Side curtains
were flapping and our magnificent mongrel collie was in the
back seat. His name was Tristram, taken from a naughty
book called Tristram & Shandy (our shandy had died!). Dr.
Sandburg loved him at once.

Our guest reminded me of Rachmaninoff--not as tall,
but a lined-tanned face, shaggy hair, a large felt-brimmed
hat. Clothes almost like a hippie, except that everything
matched--charcoal grey. The whole effect was slightly be-
draggled and extraordinarily interesting.

We talked about his train timetable he held in one
hand (his banjo case dangling in the other). This Trans
Canada train passed through the "Outer Station" only twice
in twenty-four hours--at noon and at midnight. He had noticed the Oshawa Station 90 miles to the west, and had
promptly written a poem about it--fascinated by its phonetic
sound. He kept slowly repeating the word (I thought he was
slightly crazy!), and eventually asked me what happened in
that town. It was making G. M. cars instead of McLaughlin
carriages and is now the largest G. M. plant in Canada.
Mr. R. Sam McLaughlin lived to be over 100. (Has
this poem [about Oshawa Station] ever been published?
Cornhuskers is the only volume I have of Dr. Sandburg's
works.)

After dinner, coffee and a cigar in Dad's study (no
liqueurs in our house then!) I was called from my homework
to "play something" in the drawing room.

Like all our family I was pretty musical, played piano and cello, practicing three hours every day. This was no effort because I loved it and Daddy encouraged me to take ten minutes of every practicing hour to play "nonsense." That meant folk songs, reels, jigs--especially by ear in six different keys--sight reading, ragtime, etc. This type of nonsense eventually became my profession and this was how the friendship with Dr. Sandburg really started.

That first evening after my "something serious" he got his banjo out of its weathered case and we fooled around together. He let me accompany him--all by ear of course as he used no music ever. He sang the whole ballad of Casey Jones and was amused by my new parody he had never heard:

> Oh'! Casey Jones one starry night,
> Set up to Heaven on the tail of a kite,
> The kite string broke and Casey fell,
> Instead of going to Heaven, he went to--
> Ta boodle dee up dum, bum, bum.

The next evening he asked me to be on the platform at Grant Hall, and we played intermittently between his homespun lecture--all kinds of things: if my memory is right. He even asked Daddy and Mother if I could go on tour with him, but at that time, I was just an effervescent kid, and I imagine my parents felt I needed more solid education as well as music.

I'm sure he stayed many days on that visit because I distinctly remember going for walks to the tobacco store across the huge park. With Tristram always walking between us, and insisting that was how he must walk.

We all drove down to the Thousand Island resort of Sananogue, where he jotted down some more verse because of its sound--Sa-nan-ogue.

[Dr. Bert C. Diltz, of Toronto, a student at Queen's College in 1920, has recalled [June, 1977] that Sandburg made reference to the Indian names (Toronto, Oshawa, Ottawa) of Canadian communities. He lost credibility when he carelessly included Montreal in the list.]

Salute to a New Octogenarian: The Rootabaga Special*

Carl Sandburg is not exactly an uninhibited house guest, but he does like to make his own plans, decide whom he wants to see, where he wants to go, and to take walks.

His arrival may be announced by an unsigned telegram which reads, "Rootabaga special arrives 8:15 p. m. " If you are not acquainted with the Rootabaga country, you may have a hard time finding out what track the special comes on.

Last March when Carl Sandburg came to town we had some idea of the time of his arrival because he had a speaking engagement to keep. But dinner time came, early evening passed, late evening and time to go to bed, and when we were almost asleep the phone rang. He was at the Columbus airport.

We got up and hurried out to get him. He had come in from Alabama, where he had spoken. He carried his usual luggage, an old-fashioned well-worn traveling bag and a black leather carryall, which go up and down the land with him. And, though Mike Todd has given him a beautiful new carpetbag, the old carryall is capacious enough to hold all the oddments of newspapers, books, manuscripts and food which he may need.

It is easy to prepare meals for him--the pattern leans to simple things and plain cooking, plenty of citrus fruits, green salads, lean beef, eggs and milk, and honey to sweeten the cafe au lait.

When he retires he takes along three oranges and perhaps some cheese and crackers, for he will not appear before 12:30 or 1 o'clock the next day. He makes it clear that he will take care of his room while he is in residence, and that makes you feel good, for you know that he is at home with you and feels free to do as he would at home.

---

*Mary T. Zimmerman, "Meet the Rootabaga Special, " The Columbus Dispatch Magazine (Ohio), Jan. 5, 1958. By permission of the author and publisher.

Around eight or nine in the morning he may get up and eat, do some setting-up exercises and then go back to bed. The real sign that he is about to put in an appearance is the tuning up for the day: the humming and the singing, like sounding an all clear.

You may take him for a drive in the early spring and mention how full the forsythia is this year; his reply may be, "Forsooth, the forsythia." In speaking of the problems of social security he will not say protection "from the cradle to the grave" but "from womb to tomb." And, if you know him well, you will be part of the ride of the "flimmering floom" and know how to "unscrew the inscrutable." These phrases and many others have real meaning when spoken in context, and certainly Carl Sandburg has as much fun as anyone can have with the spoken or written word.

He may tell you that he likes the curtains in the living room, that they "murmur," or announce suddenly that "there are too many dogs in this room." Well, the portraits of the cocker spaniels do look better hung together along the staircase wall!

One evening the conversation may concern an anthology, found on the bookshelves in the bedroom, or young writers of the '30s and '40s, some who have continued to write and some who have not, but the good lines are marked easily by a poet who recognizes a good line when he hears it. Another evening the talk may concern the stories liked best in childhood, and "the boy who liked pancakes" is one Carl Sandburg likes.

For more times than I can recall I have listened to his stories, followed by the hearty laugh and "the way to say it, what?"

Yes, if Carl Sandburg is your guest, the daily time schedule will need a little adjusting. But the mind schedule must sometimes do a quick double-take, for time and variety are boundless areas to be covered.

Once in Columbus I was in a small group who listened most of the night while James Thurber and Carl Sandburg talked together and, as one of the group said, "sat at each other's feet." It was a mutual admiration society of two of the best users of words and destroyers of humbug that I shall ever see together.

Thirty years ago I first heard Carl Sandburg read his poems. It was an unusual experience, for up to that time I had heard only one real live poet, and that was the Englishman, Alfred Noyes. The clipped English speech of Noyes intoning the rhymed, ballad lines was certainly a contrast to the Sandburg voice, verse and ideas. But, the timbre of Carl Sandburg's voice and cadence of his phrases as he read them caused so distinct an elation that even today I can recall with ease that first reaction.

For many years Carl Sandburg went to visit with the English Club at Cornell College in Mount Vernon, Iowa. Every year I went with my father and mother to hear him and grew to know him as a friend.

Then I moved with my family to Columbus, Ohio. A few months after that change in address The Columbus Dispatch carried a notice that Carl Sandburg was to speak in Mount Vernon, Ohio. Amused at the coincidence in the town name, we drove to Mount Vernon one snowy January evening. The slightly nostalgic Hawkeyes, not yet feeling like Buckeyes, were seated in the balcony of the high school auditorium. About halfway through his program he stopped, looked at us, and said, "Old friends from Iowa." After the lecture we brought him back to Columbus to catch a late train.

Since that time, through the '30s and '40s, and now into the '50s, our home has been, as he puts it, "a way station" for him. My grandfather, who was born on the Illinois prairie and lived to be 91 years old, always called Sandburg "Galesburg," and C. S. returned the Illinois gesture by calling him "Swan Creek."

When he was nine years old Grandfather had shaken hands with Abraham Lincoln, and Carl Sandburg had a "feeling" for anyone who had had that privilege. During his visits in Columbus my father and Carl Sandburg walked together. Night after night they enjoyed a companionable silence and paced off many miles. My mother, who was a book seller, loved and admired Carl Sandburg as the creator of many volumes which she found good, the sort of books she liked to see go into many hands. So we were and are a pro-Sandburg family.

This is a birthday salute to this old friend who lives at Connemara Farm, Flat Rock, North Carolina. The white

house sits on top of a hill. It was built by Christopher
Gustavus Memminger, the secretary of state of the Con-
federacy. The North Carolina neighbors are seemingly not
bothered by the paradox of the biographer of Lincoln living
in the house built by a leader of the secession movement.

The land falls away from the house down to large
ponds on either side of the long winding drive. When the
goats are pastured on the hillside one thinks of Switzerland
rather than the southern highlands. The approach, by the
drive, between tall pines brings you to the front porch,
banked with boxwood. And, on a clear day, if you turn to
look as you mount the steps, you can see Mt. Mitchell in
the far distance.

It is a house filled with activity. Mrs. Sandburg
still keeps a small herd of goats to continue her records on
breeding and milk products, for she is an authority on goats
and judges them at the fairs.

It is a house filled with books, magazines, newspapers. Books are piled on tables, chairs, piano and the
floor, always within easy reach. Every room has bookshelves along one or two walls, and the lower level of the
house has shelving arranged as book stacks in a public library. Margaret and Janet, the daughters who live at home,
pursue their own interests, Janet helping with the feeding of
the kids and Margaret doing reading and research on Hindu
religion. Ling Po, the blue point Siamese cat, jumps into
every available lap and pronounces it good or bad in noisy
Siamese cat tones. And Garth, the Doberman, supervises
every activity within the house and grounds.

As a guest at Connemara you are told when meals
will be served. The rest of the time is yours to sit in the
sun on the big flat rock back of the house, to go on the
Memminger walk through the woods, to climb Big Glassy
which rises a quarter of a mile away, or to sit on the
porch and watch the changing light over the top of the pines.

Just before bedtime an expedition is planned, a slow
walk down the drive to the roadway. It is downhill all the
way and uphill all the way back. Garth runs on before,
and the talk is of the recent reading of John Steinbeck's
latest novel, the voice of Archimedes the bullfrog booming
from the pond, the color of the evening sky, old friends,
old places, and the work in progress.

One evening we all sat together on the porch. My
husband played the guitar, sang some songs, passed the
guitar over to Carl Sandburg, who played and sang.   The
songs ranged from "Beautiful Dreamer" to "Make Me No
Gaudy Chapelet, " from the "Bohemian Girl" to "Git Along
Little Dogies. "   And the comment from Carl Sandburg to
Mrs. Sandburg was "Well, Mrs. S. , this is just about the
nicest porch party I ever attended. "

Many people come to Connemara, all kinds of people.
Some come out of curiosity, some are celebrity hunters,
little people, big people, some with demands for favor, some
asking for autographs.   But many come with the simple desire to tell Carl Sandburg that what he has written means
much to them.

One day it may be a man and woman who drive up
in a Cadillac and call out, "Do you keep goats here?" while
they stretch their necks to take a long look at the man on
the front porch.   Another time the distant tramp, tramp, on
the lower drive and the babble of young voices turns out to
be a group of 40 young people out from Asheville who want
to see Mr. Sandburg.   One day a young man who had hitch-
hiked across the United States from Spokane, Washington,
stopped by to ask him to autograph his copy of the one-
volume edition of The Prairie Years.   Whenever they come
or whoever they are, when they greet him we always in-
wardly say, "the people, yes. "

Perhaps those who do not write need to be reminded
that a writer really works at his job.

A poem does not appear in a whole oneness on the
page direct from the brain of the poet.

The biography of a man does not flow in an easy
stream from the pen of the biographer.   Carl Sandburg
"lived" with Lincoln for years, from the first fascination
felt when he talked to those who had seen and known Lincoln,
during the years of reading all available reports, documents, and memoirs concerning Lincoln's life and times,
through the heartbreaking and overwhelming emotional stress
of writing of Mr. Lincoln's death.   These were years of intimate study and a sort of communion with the unseen presence which lives in the monumental six volumes of the biography of the great president.

At home Carl Sandburg does not appear until lunch

is served. This does not mean that he sleeps all night and through the early hours of the day. The hours alone are the gestation hours, the time to mull over the curious facets of life as he has seen it. He is a hoarder of words. He tries them out, turning them over and over in a singing, sighing, or howling sequence--and so a poem grows.

At home and among friends he is the delighted maker of questionable puns.

The daily mail, which is large, takes much of his time. He is fascinated by postmarks and riffles through a collection of letters to choose postmarks and handwriting which interest him most. Though he reads all the letters through, few will be answered, for that takes time and many do not require an answer.

In 1956, I was at Connemara when the first selection of books and manuscripts to go to the University of Illinois library was made. All of the Lincoln material books and letters were sent at that time. It was difficult to decide what books should be sent and what should be kept. Moving along the shelves to make the choice was like moving into the past and at the same time moving into the future--this book recalled a conversation, an incident, that one an idea untouched or a person unrevealed. The books showed the variety of interests of the man who reads the editorials in a dozen newspapers and at the same time enjoys a volume on the ancient Chinese poets.

This is the birthday salute to an old friend who has received many personal honors, dedications, and accolades. He is a giant of the poetic renaissance of the '20s and remains the authentic spokesman for that generation.

He is a poet, a novelist, a storyteller for children, a ballad singer, a biographer, and now, on occasion, a TV performer.

Tomorrow is his 80th birthday, so I join the many who thank him for being what he is--the seeker, the singer, the demander, the lover of America and all things American, whose understanding of the American past makes him look at America's future with the audacity of fearless hope.

And, if you want, Carl Sandburg, you can say, "That's laying on the purple, so?"

INDEX

283